Whatever Happened to the Human Race?

By Francis A. Schaeffer

The God Who Is There
Escape From Reason
He Is There and He Is Not Silent
Death in the City
Pollution and the Death of Man
The Church at the End of the 20th Century
The Mark of the Christian
The Church Before the Watching World
True Spirituality
Basic Bible Studies
Genesis in Space and Time
Everybody Can Know (with *Edith Schaeffer*)
The New Super-Spirituality
Back to Freedom and Dignity
Art and the Bible
No Little People
Two Contents, Two Realities
Joshua and the Flow of Biblical History
No Final Conflict
How Should We Then Live?
Whatever Happened to the Human Race?
  (with *Dr C. Everett Koop*)

By Dr C. Everett Koop

Scientific monographs, textbook chapters, and
papers on the general fields of paediatric surgery,
nutritional research, biomedical ethics.

The Right to Live; The Right to Die
Whatever Happened to the Human Race?
  (with *Francis A. Schaeffer*)

Sometimes Mountains Move (with *Elizabeth Koop*)

Whatever Happened to the Human Race?

Francis A. Schaeffer
C. Everett Koop, MD

Marshall Morgan & Scott
London

Marshall, Morgan & Scott
a Pentos company
1 Bath Street, London EC1V 9LB

First published by Fleming H. Revell in the USA, 1979.
First British (revised) edition Marshall Morgan & Scott, 1980.
Copyright © 1979 and 1980 by Franky Schaeffer V Productions Inc.

ISBN 0 551 00830 X

Jacket design by The Cioni Artworks, Jeff Barnes/Ray Cioni
Book design by Colin Reed
Chapter opening photos by John Welzenbach
Cage sequence photos by Ross Alan
Double page photos by Mustafa Arshad, Spencer Cunningham, Mimi Roth and Edward Wheeler
Photoset by Rowland Phototypesetting Ltd., Bury St Edmunds, Suffolk
Printed and bound in Great Britain by
William Clowes (Beccles) Limited, Beccles and London

To those who were robbed of life, the unborn, the weak, the sick, the old, during the dark ages of madness, selfishness, lust and greed for which the last decades of the twentieth century are remembered.

Preface

This book was first published in America with primarily the American experience in mind. In this British edition the attempt is made to further the perspective by including the relevant British material.

It has been interesting to note however, despite the differences between the two countries in for example their constitutions and their health services, the way the issues and their consequences have presented themselves have been very similar. It is becoming clear in fact that abortion, infanticide and euthanasia are international issues.

In order to maintain the flow of the book some of the more detailed British material has been put in the notes which are an important part of the book. At the same time for this edition, the valuable material on the Bible and also on Darwin has been formed into appendices.

This volume was written, researched, and produced in cooperation with Franky Schaeffer V Productions Inc.

Franky Schaeffer V Productions Inc. is also the producer of the major five-episode film documentary *Whatever Happened to the Human Race?* The film's screenplay and direction is by Franky Schaeffer, and it is produced by Jim Buchfuehrer. Text and narration is by Francis A. Schaeffer and C. Everett Koop, MD. The photographs in the book are taken from the film series.

Information concerning rental or purchase of this film series may be obtained by writing to:

Marshall Morgan & Scott,
1 Bath Street,
London EC1V 9LB.

Acknowledgments

First we would like to thank Franky Schaeffer V Productions Inc., most particularly Franky Schaeffer and Jim Buchfuehrer, who worked with us in taking the ideas expressed in this book through every stage of development. Their company financed and arranged for the research and made many direct contributions to the text.

Franky Schaeffer wrote the screenplay for this book's accompanying film series and directed the episodes. Jim Buchfuehrer produced the series. As a team, together they made this project possible.

Jeff Barnes and Ray Cioni provided the cover design and illustrations for the book. We want to thank them for that and the staff of the Cioni Artworks for all their hard work on the film.

Another team, the general paediatric surgical staff of the Children's Hospital of Philadelphia and their paramedical personnel, made it possible for one of us to devote the necessary time to complete work on the book and film series.

A number of experts in various fields contributed greatly to the research and development necessary for this project. Professor Kenneth A. Kitchen, lecturer in Egyptian and Coptic at the School of Archaeology and Oriental Studies at the University of Liverpool, added much to our knowledge and research for the archaeological data. We had invaluable help from Ranald Macaulay in general research and through his special assistance with chapters 4 and 5. Professor Robert B. Zachary, FRCS, Professor of Paediatric Surgery at Sheffield University, was especially helpful in the preparation of the British edition.

In addition we would thank the following for their contributions: Francis Ackerman, Jerram Barrs, Dr James B. Hurley, Dr Jeremy C. Jackson, Dick Keyes, Udo Middelmann, Oliver O'Donovan, John Sandri, and Dr Joseph Stanton. Their time and efforts are greatly appreciated, as is the editorial work of James W. Sire, Evelyn Sendecke and Ian Cooper.

Francis A. Schaeffer
Dr C. Everett Koop

Contents

1 Abortion and the Human Race   2

cultures judged by the way they treat people – today we face unthinkable evil – caused by the loss of Judaeo-Christian values – replaced by humanism – where man is the measure of all – where law is what the majority wants – where people are machines to be manipulated – the resulting cruelty exemplified in child abuse – and especially abortion – the 1973 Supreme Court Ruling and the 1967 Abortion Act – the growth of the unborn baby – the harsh abortion techniques – the problem of aborted live births -- the harm to aborted mothers – abortion not a Catholic or feminist issue – returning to pagan ideas and opening the door to infanticide

2 The Slaughter of the Innocents   38

the law's silence over infanticide – the traditional high medical view – starvation of severe spina bifida newborns in Britain today – many doctors now condoning such practices – interviews with handicapped people – the dangers and hypocrisy of arguing from hard cases – a positive response from patients and their families facing the challenge of a congenital defect – the high morale in a hospital geared to treating congenital defects and saving lives – the advocates of infanticide and their arguments – even in the church some support abortion and infanticide – cultural and population pressures against children – euthanasia the next logical step

3 Death by Someone's Choice   68

economic pressures on the elderly – the meaning of 'death with dignity' – the right motivation for doctors – defining death – devaluing old age – false compassion in the euthanasia argument – press reports and predictions on euthanasia – warnings from the Holocaust – the complicity of doctors with Nazi programmes – the distortion of language by euphemisms – danger of today's apathy amidst peace and affluence – putting people first and taking a stand – the special responsibility of Christians – the need for caring, practical alternatives to abortion, infanticide and euthanasia

4 The Basis for Human Dignity   96

our treatment of people depends on our world view – today's world view materialistic humanism – it denies God and puts man at the centre – its superior air and yet its despair – how to look for an adequate world view – the need to explain 'the universe and its form' and 'the mannishness of man' –

prejudice against the biblical answer – the humanists' problem finding a trustworthy basis for meaning and morality – humanist answers finally impersonal – futile attempts to relieve this tension in the West and the East – the resulting modern abandonment of reason – the flight into experience – how the Bible's answer is reasonable – how it explains man's dignity made in God's image – also the world's falleness, yet not originally so – the crucial role of Genesis

5 Truth and History

5 Truth and History   132

the Bible's answers rooted in history – open to being checked – the importance the Bible attaches to history – the nature of truth in the Bible partly historical – Moses and Joshua appeal to Israel on what they have seen God do – the account of Abraham emphasises real life events – the significance of Isaac's 'almost sacrifice' – Abraham's faith and obedience not blind – the same historical emphasis in the New Testament – for example Paul at Corinth – the resurrection proclaimed as a fact – the truth of Christianity made to hinge on it – the removal of Thomas's doubts – our response

6 Our Personal Response and Social Action

6 Our Personal Response and Social Action   148

the Bible's view the only barrier to the flood of inhumanness – first steps in the solution – acknowledging the truth and accepting Christ's salvation – living sacrificially under his Lordship – the need for Christians to face the challenge of upholding the value of human life – what will be the judgement of history – Christ the only solution

Notes   163

Appendices

1 *A Comment on Darwin*   180
2 *The Reliability of the Biblical Texts*   182
3 *Archaeological Confirmation in the Old Testament*   184
4 *Religious Liberalism and Historical Truth in the New Testament*   195

Index   200

Index of Photographs   211

Just imagine that these events were to become known to the enemy! And were being exploited by them! In all probability, such propaganda would be ineffective simply because those hearing and reading it would not be prepared to believe it.

The Reichskommisar for the Ostland
to the Reichminister for occupied
Eastern territories – 18 June, 1943

1
The Abortion of the Human Race

Cultures can be judged in many ways, but eventually every nation in every age must be judged by this test: *How did it treat people?* Each generation, each wave of humanity, evaluates its predecessors on this basis. The final measure of mankind's humanity is how humanely people treat one another.

The great dramatic moments of history have left us with monuments and memories of compassion, love, and unselfishness, which punctuate the all too pervasive malevolence that dominates so much human interaction. That there is any respite from evil is due to some courageous people who, on the basis of personal philosophies, have led campaigns against the ill-treatment and misuse of individuals. Each era faces its own unique blend of problems. Our own time is no exception. Those who regard individuals as expendable raw material—to be moulded, exploited, and then discarded—do battle on many fronts with those who see each person as unique and special, worthwhile, and irreplaceable.

The reason we are writing this book is that we feel strongly that we stand today on the edge of a great abyss. At this crucial moment choices are being made and thrust on us that will for many years to come affect the way people are treated. We want to try to help tip the scales on the side of those who believe that individuals are unique and special and have great dignity.

Yad Vashem is the monument in Jerusalem to the six million Jews and others who were killed in the Nazi Holocaust.[1] It is one of the many memorials that are scattered over the world in tribute to those who have perished in upheavals of rampant evil—evil that swirls in on people when they no longer have a basis for regarding one another as wonderful creatures worthy of special care. Yad Vashem is a fitting place to begin, for it reminds us of what, unhappily, is possible in human behaviour. Those who were murdered were people just like all of us. More important to realise, is that those who murdered them were also people just like all of us. We seem to be in danger of forgetting our seemingly unlimited capacities for evil, once boundaries to certain behaviour are removed.

There are choices to be made in every age. And who we are depends on the choices we make. What will our choices be? What boundaries will we uphold to make it possible for people to say with certainty that moral atrocities are truly evil? Which side will we be on?

The Thinkable and the Unthinkable

There is a 'thinkable' and an 'unthinkable' in every era. One era is quite certain intellectually and emotionally about what is acceptable. Yet another era decides that these 'certainties' are unacceptable and puts another set of values into practice. On a humanistic base, people drift along from generation to generation, and the morally unthinkable becomes the thinkable as the years move on. By 'humanistic base' we mean the fundamental idea that men and women can begin from themselves and derive the standards by which to judge all matters. There are for such people no fixed standards of behaviour, no standards that cannot be eroded or replaced by what seems necessary, expedient, or even fashionable.

Perhaps the most striking and unusual feature of our moment of history is the speed with which eras change. Looking back in history, we notice that cultures such as the Indus River civilisation (the Harappa culture) lasted about a thousand years. Today the passing of eras is so greatly speeded up that the 1960s stand in sharp contrast to the 1970s. The young people of the seventies do not understand their older

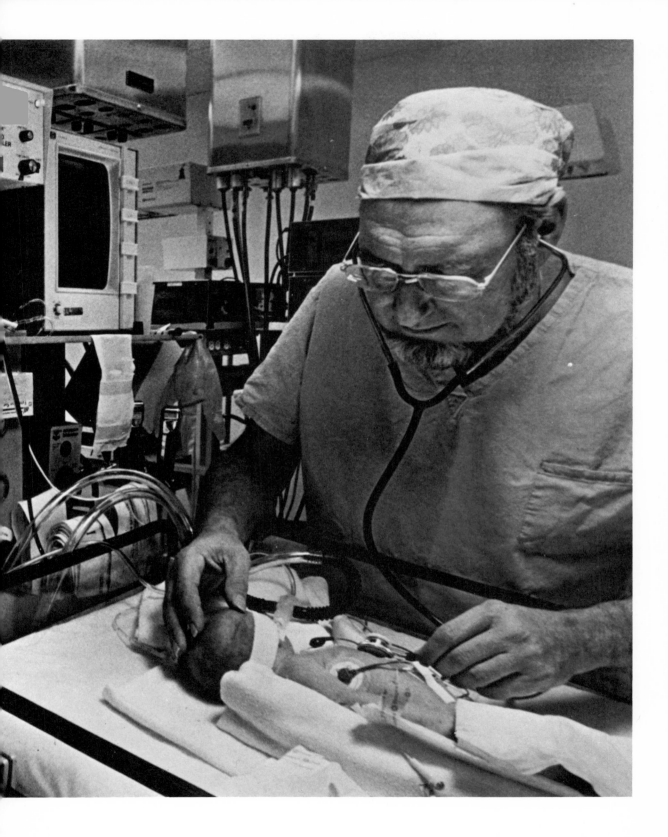

the West. This has had many results, not the least of which is to change people's view of themselves and their attitudes toward other human beings. Here is how the change came about. Having rejected God, humanistic scientists began to teach that only what can be mathematically measured is real and that all reality is like a machine. Man is only one part of the larger cosmic machine. Man is more complicated than the machines people make, but is still a machine, nevertheless.

As an example, in 1968 Dr Edmund R. Leach, Provost of Kings College, Cambridge, wrote in *The Times:*

> Today when the molecular biologists are rapidly unravelling the genetic chemistry of all living things—while the radio astronomers are deciphering the programme of an evolving cosmos—all the marvels of creation are seen to be mechanisms rather than mysteries. Since even the human brain is nothing more than an immensely complicated computer, it is no longer necessary to invoke metaphysics to explain how it works. In the resulting mechanistic universe all that remains of the divine will is the moral consciousness of man himself.

How unsatisfactory this evaluation is can be seen in the fact that a decade later every point Edmund Leach made is still in question.

Nonetheless, even though the years pass and men like Leach do not prove their points, the idea of a purely mechanistic universe with people as only complicated machines infiltrates the thinking of many. By constant repetition, the idea that man is nothing more than a machine has captured the popular mind. This idea keeps being presented year after year in schools and in the media, however unfounded and unproven the hypothesis. Gradually, after being generally unquestioned, it is blindly accepted—just as, after many years of teaching that the earth was flat, the notion was believed because of its sheer pervasiveness. Flawed and erroneous teachings about mankind, however, have far more serious effects. After all, they are talking about *us*.

For a while, Western culture—from sheer inertia—continued to live by the old Christian ethics while increasingly embracing the mechanistic, time-plus-chance view of people. People came more and more to hold that the universe is intrinsically and originally impersonal—as a stone is impersonal. Thus, *by chance*, life began on the earth and then, through long, long periods of time, *by chance*, life became more complex, until man with his special brain came into existence. By 'chance' is meant that there was no reason for these things to occur; they just happened that way. No matter how loftily it is phrased, this view drastically reduces our view of self-worth as well as our estimation of the worth of others, for we are viewing ourselves as mere accidents of the universe.

Sociological Law and Personal Cruelty
Recently a generation has arisen that has taken these theories out of the lab and classroom and into the streets. Its members have carried the reduction of the value of human beings into everyday life. Suddenly we find ourselves in a more consistent but uglier world—more consistent because people are taking their low view of man to its natural conclusion, and uglier because humanity is drastically dehumanised.

To illustrate what it means to practise this low view of man, let us consider some present realities that only a few years ago would have been unthinkable—even on the base provided by a memory of the Christian consensus, let alone within the Christian consensus itself. The Christian consensus gave a basis and a framework for our society to have freedoms without those freedoms leading to chaos. There was an emphasis on the value of the individual person—whose moral choices proceed from judgments about man and society on the basis of the existence of the infinite-personal God and his teaching in the Bible.

The Bible teaches that man is made in the image of God and therefore is unique. Remove that teaching, as humanism has done on both sides of the Iron Curtain, and there is no adequate basis for treating people well. Let us now look at some of those related unthinkable realities. The loss of the Christian consensus has led to a long list of inhuman actions and attitudes which may seem unrelated but actually are not. They are the direct result of the loss of the Christian consensus.

First, the whole concept of law has changed. When a Christian consensus existed, it gave a base for law. Instead of this, we now live under arbitrary, or sociological, law. In the United States, Supreme Court Justice Oliver Wendell Holmes took a big step in the change toward sociological law. Holmes said, 'Truth is the majority vote of that nation that could lick all others.' In other words, law is only what most of the people think at that moment of history, and there is no higher law. It follows, of course, that the law can be changed at any moment to reflect what the majority currently thinks.

More accurately, the law becomes what a few people in some branch of the government think will promote the present sociological and economic good. In reality the will and moral judgments of the majority are now influenced by or even overruled by the opinions of a small group

of men and women. This means that vast changes can be made in the whole concept of what should and what should not be done. Values can be altered overnight and at almost unbelievable speed.

Consider the influence of the Supreme Court in the United States. Ralph Winter, reviewing *The Memoirs of Earl Warren*, said in the *Wall Street Journal* of 27 July, 1977, that a large body of academic criticism has argued that the Warren Court was essentially antidemocratic because it paid little heed to traditional legal criteria and procedures and rewrote law according to the personal values of its members. The late Alexander M. Bickel of Yale University caustically summed the matter up by saying, 'In effect, we must now amend the Constitution to make it mean what the Supreme Court says it means.'[4]

Parliament still makes the law in Britain but a great deal can depend upon the determined manipulation of the minority. Most attribute the passing of the 1967 Abortion Act to the lobbying efforts of the Abortion Law Reform Association whose resource and skill in pulling the levers of power, rather than a widespread desire for such drastic change, enabled them to achieve their aims. This was certainly the view of Mr David Steele whose Bill it was.[5]

The shift to *sociological* law can affect everything in life, including who should live and who should die.

Those taking the lead in the changes involving who should live and who should die increasingly rely on litigation (the courts) rather than legislation and the election process. They do this because they can often accomplish through the courts changes they could not achieve by the will of the majority, using the more representative institutions of government.

The Christian consensus held that neither the majority nor an elite is absolute. God gives the standards of value, and His absolutes are binding on both the ordinary person and those in all places of authority.

Second, because the Christian consensus has been put aside, we are faced today with a flood of personal cruelty. As we have noted, the Christian consensus gave great freedoms without leading to chaos— because society in general functioned within the values given in the Bible, especially the unique value of human life. Now that humanism has taken over, the former freedoms run riot, and individuals, acting on what they are taught, increasingly practise their cruelties without restraint. And why shouldn't they? If the modern humanistic view of man is correct and man is only a product of chance in a universe that has no ultimate values, why should an individual refrain from being cruel to another person, if that person seems to be standing in his or her way?

Abusing Genetic Knowledge   Beyond the individual's cruelty to other individuals, why should society not remake humanity into something different if it can do so—even if it results in the loss of those factors which make human life worth living? New genetic knowledge could be used in a helpful way and undoubtedly will bring forth many things which are beneficial, but—once the uniqueness of people as created by God is removed and mankind is viewed as only one of the gene patterns which came forth on the earth by chance—there is no reason not to treat people as things to be experimented on and to remake the whole of humanity according to the decisions of a relatively few individuals. If people are not unique, as made in the image of God, the barrier is gone. Once this barrier is gone there is no reason not to experiment genetically with humanity to make it into what someone thinks to be an improvement socially and economically. The cost here is overwhelming. Should the genetic changes once be made in the individual, these changes will be passed down to his or her children, and they cannot ever be reversed.

Modern humanism has an inherent need to manipulate and tinker with the natural processes, including human nature, because humanism:

1. Rejects the doctrine of Creation.
2. Therefore rejects the idea that there is anything stable or 'given' about human nature.
3. Sees human nature as part of a long, unfolding process of development in which everything is changing.
4. Casts around for some solution to the problem of despair that this determinist-evolutionist vision induces.
5. Can only find a solution in the activity of the human will, which—in opposition to its own system—it hopes can transcend the inexorable flow of nature and act upon nature.
6. Therefore encourages the manipulation of nature, including tinkering with people, as the only way of escaping from nature's bondage. But this manipulation cannot have any certain criteria to guide it because, with God abolished, the only remaining criterion is Nature (which is precisely what humanist man wants to escape from) and Nature is both non-cruel and cruel.

This explains why humanism is fascinated with the manipulation of human nature.

It is not only Christians who are opposed to the forms of genetic engineering which tinker with the structure of humanity. Others such as Theodore Roszak and Jeremy Rifkin of the People's Business Commission in the USA rightly see this genetic engineering as incompatible with democracy. Christians and other such people can raise their voices together against this threat. That does not, however, change the realisation that the democracy such people are trying to save is a product of Reformation Christianity, which insisted on individual choice, and without Reformation Christianity the base for that democracy and its freedom is gone.

In sociological law, with the Christian consensus gone, the courts or some other part of government arbitrarily make the law. In the concept of genetic engineering, with the uniqueness of people as made in the image of God thrown away, mankind itself is in danger of being remade arbitrarily into the image of what some people think mankind ought to be. This will overwhelmingly be the case if such concepts as what has been called 'sociobiology' are widely accepted.

According to these concepts, people do what they do because of the makeup of the genes, and the genes (in some mysterious way) know what is best for keeping the gene pool of the species flourishing. Regardless of what you think your reasons are for unselfishness, say the sociobiologists, in reality you are only doing what your genes know is best to keep your gene configuration alive and flourishing into the future. This happens because evolution has produced organisms that automatically follow a mathematical logic; they calculate the genetic costs or benefits of helping those who bear many of the same genes and act to preserve their own image. Thus, the reason why parents help their children live is that the genes of the parents make them act to preserve the future existence of like genetic forms.[6]

No one tells us how the genes got started doing this. The *how* is not known. And even if the *how* were demonstrated, the *why* would still be in total darkness. Yet with neither the *how* nor the *why* known, everything human is abandoned. Maternal love, friendships, law, and morals are all explained away. Those who hold the sociobiological view believe that conflict both in the family and with outsiders is the essence of life. This serves as a chilling reminder of Hitler's Germany, which was built on the social conclusions logically drawn from the Darwinian concept of the survival of the fittest.

Harvard University zoologist Edward O. Wilson, who wrote *Sociobiology: The New Synthesis*, says on page 562: 'We may find that there is an overestimation of the nature of our deepest yearnings.' He calls for 'ethics to be removed temporarily from the hands of the philosophers and biologised'.[7]

The humanistic philosophers tried to make ethics independent of biblical teaching; the present tragic result is the loss of humanness on every level. Now, Wilson argues, ethics and behaviour patterns should be made independent of these humanistic philosophers and put into the realm of the purely mechanical, where ethics reflect only genes fighting for survival. This makes ethics equal no ethics.

Time magazine said of sociobiology, 'Indeed, few academic theories have spread so fast with so little hard proof.' Why has it spread so fast with no hard proof? That is easy to explain: We have been prepared for it by all the humanistic materialism of past years. A constant barrage of authoritative, though unproven, statements comes from every side, and gradually people accept themselves and others as only machine-like things. If man is only a product of chance in an impersonal universe, and that is all there is, this teaching is a logical extension of that fact.[8]

To summarise: On the one hand, the idea that mankind is only a collection of the genes which make up the DNA patterns has naturally led to the concept of remaking all of humanity with the use of genetic engineering. On the other hand, it has led to the crime and cruelty that now disturb the very people whose teaching produces the crime and cruelty in the first place. Many of these people do not face the conclusion of their own teaching. With nothing higher than human opinion upon which to base judgments and with ethics equalling no ethics, the justification for seeing crime and cruelty as disturbing is destroyed. The very word *crime* and even the word *cruelty* lose meaning. There is no final reason on which to forbid anything— 'If nothing is forbidden, then anything is possible.'

If man is not made in the image of God, nothing then stands in the way of inhumanity. There is no good reason why mankind should be perceived as special. Human life is cheapened. We can see this in many of the major issues being debated in our society today: abortion, infanticide, euthanasia, the increase of child abuse and violence of all kinds, pornography (and its particular kinds of violence as evidenced in sadomasochism), the routine torture of political prisoners in many parts of the world, the crime explosion, and the random violence which surrounds us.

In Communist countries, where materialism and humanistic thinking have been dominant for several generations, a low view of people has been standard for years. This is apparent not only in the early legislation about abortion but also in the thousands of political prisoners who have been systematically oppressed, tortured, and killed as part of the very fabric of Communism. Now, however, as humanism dominates the West, we have a low view of mankind in the West as well. Let us consider some more of the direct and indirect results that this low view of people has brought into our society in the non-Communist world.

Child Abuse   Dr C. Henry Kempe, a paediatrician in the USA at the University of Colorado School of Medicine, first used the term *battered-child syndrome*. The term *child abuse* covers at least three separate entities: physical assault, physical neglect, and emotional abuse and neglect. In the first of these the child is a victim of an act of aggression.[9] These case histories are typical of thousands:

> *Case 1:* Police found a nine-year-old girl in a closet measuring twenty-three by fifty-two inches, where she had been locked for half of her life. She weighed only twenty pounds and stood less than three feet tall. Smeared with filth and scarred from parental beatings, this child had become irrevocably mentally damaged.

> *Case 2:* An eleven-year-old boy was brought to a San Francisco hospital suffering from severe malnutrition. He weighed forty-four pounds, had a body temperature of eighty-four degrees, and was in coma. The suspicious marks on his wrists and ankles were related to his mother's and her boyfriend's immobilisation of the boy for hours on end by means of handcuffs, chains, and locks.

The second variety of child abuse, physical neglect, is probably many times more frequent than either the medical profession or the police can document. The third form, emotional abuse, is not only difficult to define but more difficult to detect and prove—after which comes the very difficult task of rehabilitative therapy.

So far it is children who have suffered the most from dehumanisation. Nothing could illustrate better the dehumanisation and exploitation of children than child pornography. Why hasn't public outcry in the USA demanded that films depicting child pornography be withdrawn? Because the producers know that they will not be box-office failures. Dehumanisation of both adults and children is taking quantum leaps. The unthinkable rapidly becomes not only thinkable but even welcome as entertainment—and being accepted as entertainment, it becomes powerful propaganda for affecting personal and social practice, further dehumanising young and old alike. In this respect, we are encouraged by the prompt action of Cyril Townsend's Private Member's Bill against child pornography. This became law in 1978 and has helped to curb at least the worst of this exploitation in Britain.

However, to grasp the enormity of the child abuse problem, consider that in 1972 there were in the USA 60,000 child-abuse incidents which were brought to official attention. Just four years later, in 1976, the number that received official attention passed the half-million mark. *Reported* cases of child abuse probably represent only about half of what really occurs. Nothing in the British situation, moreover, can give cause for comfort where the problem is increasing on the same scale. The First Report of the Select Committee on 'Violence in the Family' produced by Parliament in April, 1977, paints a bleak picture of the ever rising number of cases of cruelty to children. Child abuse is no longer a question of isolated incidents but part of a pattern of gathering violence in the home. It is the fifth most frequent cause of death among children.

In *U.S. News and World Report* (3 May, 1976) it was reported that Dr Irwin Hedlener, investigating child abuse at Jackson Memorial Hospital in Miami, said: 'If child abuse were polio, the whole country would be up in arms looking for a solution.'

An especially alarming form of dehumanisation in the USA is the apparent increase of incest. Dr Harry Giarretto, director of the pioneering Child Sexual Abuse Treatment Centre in San Jose, California, says that incest is an epidemic in America.[10] Dr Amanat, who heads the Sexual Abuse Committee in Saint Louis, believes that 40,000 of the 1,000,000 victims of sexual abuse a year are victims of incest. Some say that incest is the most frequent unrecorded crime and much more common than general child abuse or child neglect.[11] Fortunately, there is no evidence that incest is a problem in Britain yet. However, the attempted activities of the Paedophile Information Exchange who want to change the laws governing sexual consent must give cause for a similar sort of concern.

We believe that the increased use of children in sex films has been responsible for much of the sexual abuse of children. When absolute sexual standards are replaced by relativistic ones, and this is coupled with the generally low view of people that modern humanists have been teaching, society is not left with many barriers against the sexual abuse

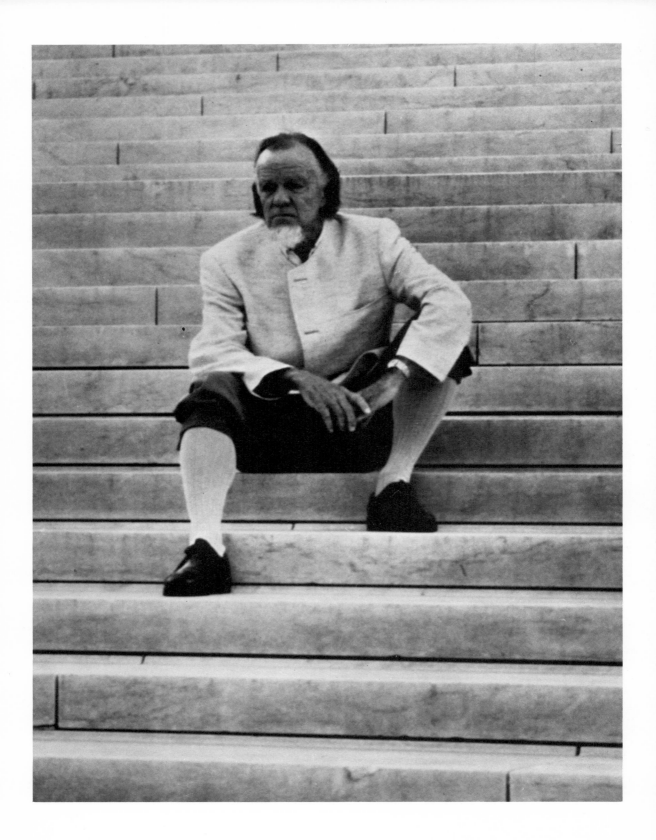

of children. After you remove the psychological and moral barriers imposed by a high and sacred view of human life, child abuse of all kinds becomes very easy, given the stresses of child rearing, especially child rearing in the anti-family climate of today.[12] The Supreme Court ruling in the United States that legalised abortion and the Abortion Act in Britain, involved an arbitrariness of decision regarding who is or is not a 'person' that has broken down barriers. There has been a drastic rise of crimes against children since abortion-on-demand became legal in both countries. We are convinced that this increase is caused in part by the liberalisation of abortion laws and the resultant drastic lowering of the value placed on human life in general and on children's lives in particular.[13]

The forces of humanism have scoffed at Christian morality and ethics as well as at the Christian view of man. These theories of so-called liberation from the biblical absolutes are bearing their fruit. But humanists, far from re-examining the basis of their position now that the situation is souring, stubbornly propose (on the same old base) remedial action to the problems that humanist philosophy itself has created. This action is even more dehumanising in its results, as we shall see later in this book.

Abortion   Of all the subjects relating to the erosion of the sanctity of human life, abortion is the keystone. It is the first and crucial issue that has been overwhelming in changing attitudes toward the value of life in general. The Supreme Court of the United States on 22 January, 1973, in deciding *Roe* v. *Wade* and *Doe* v. *Bolton* declared that a new personal right or liberty existed in the Constitution—the right of a woman to procure an abortion at any time. The right of privacy was given a completely new interpretation.[14]

The Supreme Court went far beyond its own judicial function and invalidated the regulation of abortion in every state in the union. Professor John T. Noonan, Jr, professor of law at the University of California (Berkeley) said:

> *Roe* v. *Wade* and *Doe* v. *Bolton* may stand as the most radical decisions ever issued by the Supreme Court.[15]

Certainly the decision of the Court went far beyond the expectation of the wildest dreams of the pro-abortion elite in the United States. Noonan summarised the situation this way: 'By virtue of its opinions, human life has less protection in the United States today than at any time since the inception of the country. By virtue of its opinions, human life has less protection in the United States than in any country of the Western world.'[16]

Archibald Cox of Watergate-prosecution fame said in his book *The Role of the Supreme Court in American Government:* 'The decisions plainly . . . sweep away established law supported by the moral themes dominant in American life for more than a century in favour of what the Court takes to be the wiser view of a question under active public debate. . . . My criticism of [the decision] is that the Court failed to establish the legitimacy of [its] decision . . . to lift the ruling above the level of political judgment.'[17]

The Court had the opportunity to pull back from its position in a series of decisions in the summer of 1976, but instead confirmed its position and declared that a physician need not provide the same care for a living product of an abortion that would be required for a living baby delivered in a situation where the intent was to have a baby.[18]

In Britain the different legislative traditions and processes have meant differences. For example, no one has the right, as in the USA, to an abortion. Essentially the 1967 Abortion Act only no longer made abortion an offence as long as certain criteria were fulfilled. However, these criteria, especially the one to do with the mental health of the mother, have proved so loose that in practice there has been the same radical change in the law as in the United States. 'Abortion on demand' is now a fact of life in Britain.[19]

Following these changes in the law in both countries it became clear that society was schizophrenic. It became common practice for paediatricians to provide the maximum of resuscitative and supportive care in new born intensive-care nurseries where premature infants were under their care—while obstetricians in the same medical centres were routinely destroying enormous numbers of unborn babies who were normal and frequently of larger size. Again, minors who could not legally purchase liquor and cigarettes could have an abortion-on-demand and without parental consent or knowledge.[20]

In our day, quite rightly, there has been great protest because people in the past viewed the black slave as a non-person. Now, by an arbitrary absolute brought into the humanist flow, the law in similar fashion declares millions of unborn babies of every colour of skin to be non-persons. 'Abortion on demand' has been brought in by law, and with the erosion of society's belief in the sanctity of human life there has followed the killing of more than a million unborn babies a year in the USA and well over 100,000 a year in Britain.[21]

We should say here that those who favour abortion argue that child abuse will decrease if abortion is practised. It is supposed to be kinder to the unborn child to abort it than to allow it to be born and possibly suffer mistreatment. Those who fought for liberalised abortion policies have had their way. Since 1970 it is conservatively estimated in the United States that there are probably over six million fewer children while in Britain starting from 1967 there are about one and a half million fewer. Since these children were 'unwanted' and supposedly would have been prime targets for child abuse, it would seem reasonable to look for a sharp drop in child abuse in this same period. But in fact, since the legalisation of abortion on demand, child abuse has grown remarkably in both countries, and it is not due to just more efficient reporting.

This is because nationwide abortion-on-demand has what might be called an 'educational impact'. The West German Federal Constitutional Court (West Germany's Supreme Court) in its February 1975 decision banning abortion-on-demand during the first twelve weeks of pregnancy stated this: 'We cannot ignore the educational impact of abortion on the respect for life.' The German court reasoned that if abortion were made legal for any and every reason during the first trimester, it would prove difficult to persuade people that second- and third-trimester fetuses deserve protection simply because they are a few weeks older. The court apparently feared that what would happen to older fetuses could also happen to children after birth.[22] As Harold O. J. Brown observes, parents, perhaps unconsciously, could reason, 'I didn't have to have him. I could have killed him before he was born. So if I want to knock him around now that he is born, isn't that my right?'[23]

Is it not logical, after all, that if one can legally kill a child a few months before birth, one should not feel too bad about roughing him up a little bit (without killing him) after he is born? Parents who are apprehended for child abuse must feel that the system is somewhat unfair in that they can be arrested for beating their child, whereas people who kill their infant before birth (at an 'earlier age') go scot-free—in fact, have society's approval.

There is further evidence that society is schizophrenic on these matters. Consider our concern to provide special facilities for the handicapped in public places: toilets that can be used by someone in a wheelchair, ramps instead of steps going into public buildings, lifts on public conveyances to get a handicapped individual onto a bus or train.

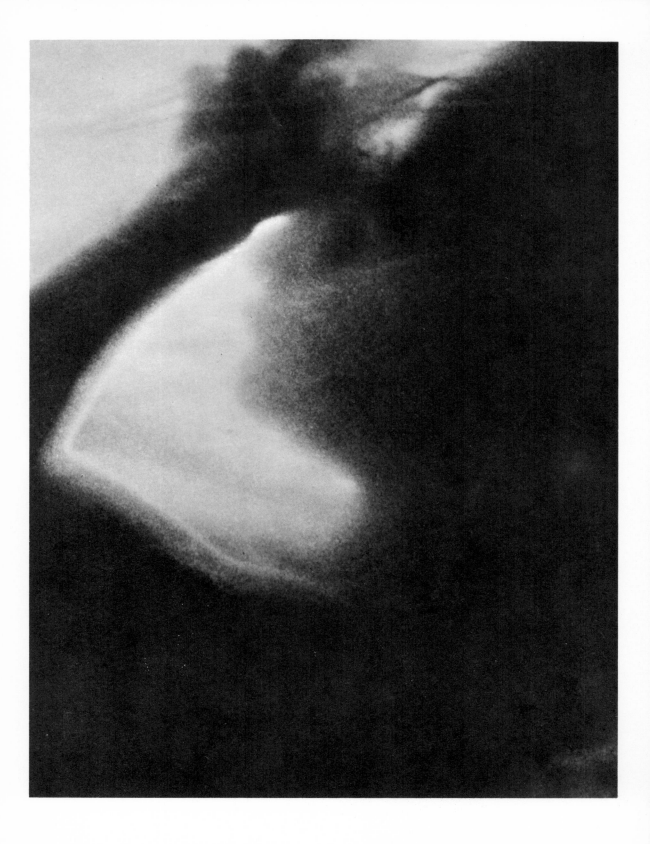

Yet, while having proved that we do have compassion for the handicapped as well as the resources to care for them, at the same time we have a growing tendency to destroy the newborn baby who might have been one of those handicapped individuals.

A much more serious example of this schizophrenic mentality is that we will transport a newborn baby, who is premature and has a congenital defect incompatible with life, to a hospital a considerable distance away—so that a sophisticated team of doctors and nurses can correct that defect and plan for the rehabilitation of the youngster. Meanwhile, in a number of other hospitals nearby, medical personnel are destroying perfectly normal infants in the womb.

The Growth of Human Life

Our reasons against abortion are logical as well as moral. It is impossible for anyone to say when a developing fetus becomes viable, that is, has the ability to exist on its own. Smaller and smaller premature infants are being saved each year. There was a day when a 1000-gram premature infant had no chance, now 50 per cent of those under 1000 grams are being saved. Theoretically, there once was a point beyond which technology could not be expected to go in salvaging premature infants—but with further technological advances, who knows what the limits may be. The eventual possibilities are staggering.

The logical approach is to go back to the sperm and the egg. A sperm has twenty-three chromosomes; even though it is alive and can fertilise an egg, it can never make another sperm. An egg also has twenty-three chromosomes, and it can never make another egg. Thus, we have sperm that cannot reproduce and eggs that cannot reproduce unless they get together. Once the union of a sperm and an egg occurs and the twenty-three chromosomes of each are brought together into one cell that has forty-six chromosomes, that one cell has all the DNA (the whole genetic code) that will, if not interrupted, make a human being.[24]

Our question to a pro-abortion doctor who would not kill a *newborn* baby is this: 'Would you then kill this infant a minute before he was born, or a minute before that, or a minute before that, or a minute before that?' At what point in time can one consider life to be worthless and the next minute precious and worth saving?

Having already mentioned the union of sperm and egg to give forty-six chromosomes, let us briefly review the development of a baby. At twenty-one days, the first irregular beats occur in the developing heart, long before the mother is sure she is pregnant. Forty-five days after conception, electroencephalographic waves can be picked up from the baby's developing brain.

By the ninth and tenth weeks, the thyroid and the adrenal glands are functioning. The baby can squint, swallow, and move his tongue. The sex hormones are already present. By twelve or thirteen weeks, he has fingernails; he sucks his thumb and will recoil from pain. His fingerprints, on the hands which have already formed, will never change throughout his lifetime except for size. Legally, it is understood that an individual's fingerprints distinguish him as a separate identity and are the most difficult characteristic to falsify.

In the fourth month the growing baby is eight to ten inches long. The fifth month is a time of lengthening and strengthening. Skin, hair, and nails grow. Sweat glands come into being; oil glands excrete. This is the month in which the mother feels the infant's movements.

In the sixth month the developing baby responds to light and sound. He can sleep and awaken. He gets hiccups and can hear the beat of his mother's heart. Survival outside the womb is now possible. In the seventh month the nervous system becomes much more complex. The infant is about sixteen inches long and weighs about three pounds. The eighth and ninth months see a fattening of the baby.

We do not know how anyone who has seen the remarkable films of the intrauterine development of the human embryo can still maintain that the product of an abortion consists of just some membranes or a part of the woman's body over which she has complete control—or indeed anything other than a human life within the confines of a tiny body. At the very least we must admit that an embryo is not simply an extension of another person's body; it is something separate and uniquely irreplaceable. Another good reason we should not view the unborn baby as an extension of the woman's body is that it did not originate only from the woman. The baby would not exist without the man's seed.

We are convinced that the reason the Supreme Court decision for abortion on demand never came to grips with the issue of the viability of the human fetus, and why the law in Britain is unable to define it, is that viability (that is, ability to live outside the womb on its own) is really not the important point.

Viable or not, the single-celled fertilised egg will develop into a human being unless some force destroys its life. We should add that biologists take the uniform position that life begins at conception; there is no logical reason why the pro-abortionist should try to arrive at a different definition when he is talking about people, the highest form of all biological creatures. After conception, no additional factor is necessary at a later time. All that makes up the adult is present as the ovum and the sperm are united—the whole genetic code!

Abortion Techniques
There are three commonly used techniques for abortion. The technique used most often to end early pregnancies is called the D & C or *dilation and curettage*. In this procedure, usually carried out before the twelfth or thirteenth week of pregnancy, the uterus is approached through the vagina. The cervix is stretched to permit the insertion of a curette, a tiny hoe-like instrument. The surgeon then scrapes the wall of the uterus, cutting the baby's body to pieces and scraping the placenta from its attachments on the uterine wall. Bleeding is considerable.

An alternative method which is used during the same period of pregnancy is called *suction abortion*. The principle is the same as in the D & C. A powerful suction tube is inserted through the dilated cervix into the uterus. This tears apart the body of the developing baby and the placenta, sucking the pieces into a jar. The smaller parts of the body are recognisable as arms, legs, head, and so on. More than two-thirds of all abortions performed in the United States and Britain apparently are done by this method.

Later in pregnancy, when the D & C or suction abortion might produce too much bleeding in the expectant mother, doctors employ the second most common abortion technique, called the *saline abortion* or 'salting out'. This method is usually carried out after sixteen weeks of pregnancy, when enough amniotic fluid has accumulated in the sac around the baby. A long needle is inserted through the mother's abdomen directly into the sac, and a solution of concentrated salt is injected into the amniotic fluid. The salt solution is absorbed both through the lungs and the gastrointestinal tract, producing changes in the osmotic pressure. The outer layer of skin is burned off by the high concentration of salt. It takes about an hour to kill the baby by this slow method. The mother usually goes into labour about a day later and delivers a dead, shrivelled baby.

If abortion is decided on too late to be accomplished by either a D & C, suction, or saline procedure, physicians resort to a final technique called *hysterotomy*. A hysterotomy is exactly the same as a Caesarean section with one difference—in a Caesarean section the operation is usually performed to save the life of the baby, whereas a hysterotomy is performed to kill the baby. These babies look very much like other babies except that they are small and weigh, for example, about two pounds at the end of a twenty-four-week pregnancy. They are truly alive, but they are allowed to die through neglect or sometimes killed by a direct act.

Hysterotomy gives the fetus the best chance for survival, but at a very high price in morbidity for the mother—fifteen times greater than that of saline infusion, the more commonly used alternative. In 1977 a Boston jury in the USA found Dr Kenneth Edelin guilty of man-slaughter for killing the product of this type of abortion.[25]

That children are often born alive after abortions is fact and not a new phenomenon. A brief in one case before the Supreme Court (*Markle* v. *Abele*) contained a table listing twenty-seven live births after abortions.[26] That was in 1972. In the first year of liberalised abortion laws in New York State, before the Supreme Court decision regarding abortion-on-demand, some of those 'products of abortions' were eventually adopted.

Nothing is more embarrassing to an abortionist than to deliver a live baby. To show that this is so, the following is a quote from a publication of the International Correspondence Society of Obstetrics and Gynae-cologists (November 1974):

> At the time of delivery it has been our policy to wrap the fetus in a towel. The fetus is then moved to another room while our attention is turned to the care of the gravida [the former mother-to-be]. She is examined to determine whether placenta expulsion has occurred and the extent of vaginal bleeding. Once we are sure her condition is stable, the fetus is evaluated. Almost invariably all signs of life have ceased.

What a nice little piece of 'how to' instruction!

It was once thought that live births after abortions would be possible only after hysterotomies. Now it is obvious that babies are born alive after saline abortions as well. Dr William B. Waddill, Jr, an obstetrician in California, was indicted and tried in January 1977 for allegedly strangling to death a baby born alive following a saline abortion.

An interminable trial got out of hand when the issue departed from whether or not Waddill had indeed attempted to strangle a living infant. The trial resulted in a hung jury when the judge introduced for delibera-tion new material concerning a California definition of death, which really had little bearing on this subject. The former mother-to-be of the allegedly strangled infant filed a suit for $17,000,000 on grounds that she was not adequately informed of the possible outcome of the abortion and that she had suffered long-lasting physical and emotional pain as a result of the doctor's actions.[27]

If live babies as a result of saline abortions and hysterotomies cause problems for the abortionist, they are minor compared to the problems that have been introduced by the prostaglandin method of abortion. The use of prostaglandin has multiplied the number of embarrassing situations manyfold. Prostaglandin is a hormone which is mainly used at present to induce abortions. Upjohn manufactures it in the United States, and in September 1977 the Food and Drug Administration approved it for use in hospitals. It is advertised in the pharmacy reports as 'Prostin E. Upjohn abortion inducer'. This warning was carried in the 12 September, 1977, issue of *Weekly Pharmacy Reports*, pointing out the approved Prostin labelling notes that suppository form, unlike saline injection form, 'does not appear to directly effect the integrity of the feto-placental unit and therefore, there exists a possibility that a live-born fetus may occur, particularly as gestational age approaches the end of the second trimester.' So likely is a live birth after a prostaglandin abortion that a medical representative of Upjohn advises using Prostin E. 'only in hospitals with certain intensive care facilities'.[28]

In the USA although technically the product of a legal abortion, each fetus expelled alive because of prostaglandin that lives for several hours, later has to be pronounced dead by a physician, must receive both a birth and death certificate, and is sent to a funeral director for burial or cremation. In Britain certificates are also technically required though unless the coroner or parents require them, this rarely happens.

Live Births After Abortions   In the USA physicians have been reluctant to reveal the number of second-trimester abortions (during the second three-month period of pregnancy) that result in live births. Of 607 such abortions done at Mount Sinai Hospital in Hartford, Connecticut, 45 resulted in live births, including one set of twins. All of these 45 babies were taken to the neonatal nursery for active resuscitation. Physicians there decided how long to continue resuscitation, according to the infant's weight, neurological maturity, and general condition. None of the babies survived more than thirteen hours, despite attempts to save them. These infants were born following an intra-amniotic injection of prostaglandin, and we would expect that the suppository form would produce more, not fewer, of these embarrassing situations for abortionists.

It could be said in passing that there were other complications in addition to the live births in the second-trimester abortions at Mount Sinai. Excessive blood loss occurred in 19.4 per cent of the women; 41 per cent had incomplete abortions, in which case the placenta had to be removed manually. The Mount Sinai series was reported by Dr Wing K. Lee at an Atlanta meeting in the USA in 1977.[29]

Other presentations at that same clinical congress reported that hypertonic saline injections for mid-trimester abortions beyond twenty weeks produce a higher rate of other complications. In spite of that, at least the Nassau County Medical Centre in East Meadow, New York, decided to return to that form of treatment rather than have the embarrassment of live births. Dr Joel Robins of the Stony Brook branch of the State University of New York compared 700 prostaglandin with 170 saline abortions. He found it was not such a bad idea to switch back to saline, because the rates of complication were similar and there were seven live births with prostaglandin and none with saline.[30]

It remained for a Johns Hopkins University team at the congress to introduce an economic factor. They added hyperosmoler urea to augment the prostaglandin. The combined technique was reported to have a lower failure rate and a lower cost. Since the urea dilates the cervix, the Hopkins group found that it is easier to remove fetal parts than with a D & C and that the process carries a lower coagulation risk than saline.[31]

The live birth problem after abortion is not so evident in Britain. This, however, is because of under-reporting which arises out of obvious embarrassment and also since its legality is dubious. As a result, the pressure is to make sure, as in the USA, that the fetus is dead on delivery. For example, the *Daily Mail*, 2 May, 1979, reported that Professor Peter Huntingford, professor of obstetrics and gynaecology at London University, was adding 'poison' to prostaglandin. It also reported him as saying, 'If one has agreed to carry out an abortion for a woman, one's object is that the baby is born dead. I think this is in the best interest of everyone.'

However, it is quite clear that despite these sorts of measures many live babies are being born after abortions. In some recent cases such as Whiston in Liverpool, Wanstead in East London, and Barnsley in Yorkshire, where the pregnancies have been late, the babies born have remained alive for some time. According to witnesses these babies have died of deliberate neglect.[32]

Perhaps the problem of live birth in itself is only temporary, however shocking. We would like to assume the role of prophet and say that since the FDA has approved Prostin E. by Upjohn as an abortion inducer, we think they will before long give Upjohn the approval to market a vaginal tampon with prostaglandin on its tip, which will be advertised as an inducer of menstruation. This would then bring to its logical conclusion Justice Blackmun's statement that the right of privacy covers his decision about abortion-on-demand. With such a menses inducer, any woman could use a vaginal tampon containing Prostin E. once a month and never know whether she was having a normal menstrual period or an abortion. Thus, abortion could become a totally private affair. The only good we can see coming out of that terrible situation is that at least it would eliminate the abortionist.

Inasmuch as the live product (i.e., a living baby, although not necessarily able to support itself outside the womb) of a prostaglandin abortion lives for several hours after the abortion — it is clear that there can be considerable consternation and emotional upset on the part of the hospital staff, particularly the nurses and paramedical attendants at the time of 'delivery'.

About a year ago, in the USA the nurses and medical staff at Holywood's Memorial Hospital (Florida) rebelled after several live fetuses were born during second-trimester abortions. Hospital Administrator Sal Mudano commented, 'We've had premature infants that have lived that were less developed than some of these abortions were. Our personnel are not in favour of working in that kind of situation, and the law says we can't force people to participate against their personal or religious beliefs.' And he added, 'It's not that we're preaching, and we don't have a bunch of religious fanatics on our staff. But our nurses are geared to saving lives and this is just the opposite.'[33]

The nursing supervisor at Hollywood Memorial, Joann Kopacka, said, 'The use of prostaglandin was totally unacceptable. Philosophically, it was a very difficult thing to handle for the nurses. The live fetus is not an "it," or a thing, it is a life.'

Mudano said the anti-abortion feeling among the staff at Memorial is so strong that doctors generally take their second-trimester abortion cases elsewhere. 'We're down to six or eight saline solution abortions a month, which is significantly less than when we started doing them,' Mudano said. 'That's the result of our philosophy of discouraging them.'

Nurses' revulsion is also widespread in Britain though it is usually expressed more individually by making use of the conscience clause of the Abortion Act.[34] This clause, however, is under considerable strain especially for senior staff. For example, doctors wanting consultancies who oppose abortion are finding promotion extremely difficult. In many cases the pressures of the system are such that those unwilling to 'do their share' get passed over.

Good organisation and good management can moreover by-pass those who don't co-operate. For example, in the USA a hospital spokesman for the Broward General Hospital at Fort Lauderdale said the lack of problems with the nurses at Broward General was due to good scheduling by Mrs Moore, supervisor of obstetrical nurses. 'She is careful not to put anyone with strong feelings about abortions in that area,' he said. 'We try to arrange the schedules so that those who prefer not to be involved are not, unless it is absolutely necessary.'

A doctor said he has never seen any adverse reactions on the part of the Broward General staff when a live fetus is born. 'When you have a 10-ounce fetus with spontaneous respiration or movement, it is more upsetting to the lay public than to anybody else. The hospital procedure is almost mechanical at this point. It kind of works very smoothly.'[35]

At least smoothly most of the time but it is worth noting the following kind of example. A publication of Nurses Concerned for Life, Inc., USA, considered these facts reported in the *Pittsburgh Press* on 1 November, 1974:

> A 26-year-old woman requested an abortion of her 5-month fetus, claiming that she had been raped. The woman was first turned down by Magee Woman's Hospital because it was thought the pregnancy was too far advanced. The staff physician estimated the gestational age to be about 25 weeks. It was later established that she had not been raped.
>
> The abortion was then performed by Dr Leonard Laufe of West Penn Hospital in Pittsburgh, Pennsylvania, who decided to use the prostaglandin method. Prostaglandin is an abortifacient drug whose primary effect is stimulation of the uterine contractions. Its use frequently leads to a live birth. Nurse Monica Bright testified that the child gasped for breath for at least 15 minutes following the abortion and no attempts were made to help the child in any way. Ms Bright is a circulating nurse in Labour and Delivery. She further testified that she observed a pulse in the upper chest, left neck area. Ms Shirley Foust, R.N., testified she had seen the baby move and that one of the foreign residents, who was observing, baptised the child. The Head Nurse, Carol Totton, testified that the baby was gasping and a pulse was visible. Both the nurse anaesthetist and Ms Totton refused to administer a lethal dose of morphine to the baby despite the fact that 'someone in the room had ordered it'.
>
> The nurse anaesthetist, Nancy Gaskey, testified that the abortion was performed in a room where there were no resuscitative measures available if the child was born alive.

The entire procedure was filmed for educational purposes and the film showed the baby moving. Dr Jules Rivkind, Chairman, Department of OB and Gyn, at Mercy Hospital, testified that this was indeed 'a live birth'.

The original birth records indicate the baby girl weighed 3 lbs 1 ounce and listed the length as 45 centimeters. Dr Laufe later changed the hospital records to read as follows: weight 2 lbs 9 oz, length 29 centimeters. Lois Cleary, a staff nurse, witnessed this change, and testified that in the 3,000 to 4,000 births she had assisted with there had never been such changes made on original records to her knowledge. This change was also verified by an OB technician who was present. Estimated gestational age 29 to 32 weeks.

John Kenny, a young medical student, testified that he had been threatened by Dr Laufe's attorney if he testified in court against Dr Laufe. The young man was told that he would be unable to get an internship in any hospital in Pennsylvania if he testified. He was also told he would be unable to get a licence to practise medicine.

Editor's note [You Be the Judge]— Dr Laufe was acquitted of the charges because he claimed the baby's brain was dead due to damage caused when he clamped the umbilical arteries in utero.[36]

Widespread concern in Britain over late live births during abortions has been a major part of the motivation of Mr John Corrie's Abortion (Amendment) Bill. This is, at the time of writing (1979), before the House of Commons. Currently one clause seeks to prevent abortions in pregnancies later than twenty weeks. This is in a sense an improvement yet we are concerned that the impression given will be that abortion done early enough is all right.

Embryos 'created' in the biologists' laboratories raise special questions because they have the potential for growth and development when planted in the womb. The work of Steptoe and Edwards is particularly relevant here. At Oldham General Hospital in Lancashire in 1978 they enabled a formerly childless couple to have a baby girl, Louise, after fertilisation in the laboratory prior to implantation in the mother's womb. This is gratifying and their achievement is considerable. Yet trials for this sort of research inevitably involve the disposal of live material and this is disturbing. Dr Leon Kass, a University of Chicago biologist, wonders on such research:

> Who decides what are the grounds for discard? What if there is another recipient available who wishes to have the otherwise unwanted embryo? Whose embryos are they? The woman's? The couple's? The geneticist's? The obstetrician's? The Ford Foundation's? Shall we say that discarding laboratory grown embryos is a matter solely between a doctor and his plumber? . . . We have paid some high prices for the technological conquest of nature, but none so high as the intellectual and spiritual costs of

seeing nature as mere material for our manipulation, exploitation and transformation. With the powers for biological engineering now gathering, there will be splendid new opportunities for a similar degradation of our view of man. Indeed, we are already witnessing the erosion of our idea of man as something splendid or divine, as a creature with freedom and dignity. And clearly, if we come to see ourselves as meat, then meat we shall become.[38]

There are many unpleasant spin-offs from the basic ugliness of the abortion scene. One is that fewer babies are available for adoption. More childless couples remain childless. This seems especially ironic when one considers that many abortions are being performed very late in term and that a prospective mother could, with little more physical trauma, wait to deliver a normal child at full term and give it up for adoption. That this is not done more often raises the question as to whether in certain cases the mother-to-be does not have an instinctive attachment to the unborn child. That she anticipates the sorrow the separation will bring—and would rather kill the child than lose it— testifies to the fact that the mother knows subconsciously that she has in her womb something more than the mere glob of protoplasm the abortionist would have her believe she is carrying.

Obviously many more babies are unwanted early in pregnancy than is the case later in pregnancy or after birth. It is the ready availability of abortion-on-demand, when a pregnant woman first has that natural question about how well she can handle a pregnancy, that leads to the tremendous number of abortions. This can be put in personal terms by asking people, 'If abortion-on-demand had been available to your mother when she first heard she was pregnant with you, would you be here today?'

Recently in the USA several local and state abortion regulations have stipulated that some time must elapse between the woman's decision to abort and the actual procedure. The Akron ordinance passed in March 1978 is the prototype for such legislation. Such legislation does not ban abortion (a ban that would be unconstitutional at the present time), but it does impose some controls. The Akron regulation requires that parents of pregnant girls under eighteen be notified before an abortion is performed. The ordinance also requires that a woman receive counselling by a physician about the results of abortion and that at least twenty-four hours must pass before the abortion can be performed. This provision of course gives a woman more time to think through a hasty decision, so that there will be less chance that she will regret it later.[39]

At the moment provision for counselling is also a feature of Mr Corrie's Bill in Britain. Here the intention is less to give time than to make sure that a woman can get the information which might encourage her to seek alternatives to abortion. In this respect it tries to give some substance to the demand for a 'woman's choice'.

Current sexual mores, sexually permissive life-styles, and the breakdown of the family demand abortion. At the same time the availability of abortion contributes to a change in our sexual mores, our permissive life-styles, and general family breakdown—truly a vicious cycle. The changes in the technical aspects of medicine are almost staggering. It is said that about 90 per cent of the current body of medical knowledge has been learned in the last twenty-five years. We can only regret that ethical views of the medical profession, and of society in general, have not kept pace with the technological advances.

That so many unborn children die each year at the hands of abortionists is sufficient reason for the ardour of those who oppose abortion. When one sees the potential of handicapped youngsters realised through surgery, sees the blessing they are to their families, sees how loved and loving they are themselves, it makes it impossible for some to stand by while millions of normal babies are being killed before birth and discriminated against on so large a scale. As individuals who have marvelled at the unique personalities of even the tiniest infants, something basically human in us is revolted by the thought of the wanton slaughter of the unborn.

Three Final Issues   First, why is it that so little pro-abortion advice is fair to the 'whole person' of the pregnant woman? 'Why didn't anyone tell me?' is a fair question from a girl suffering the after-effects of a recommended abortion.[40] 'Why didn't anyone tell me I would feel like a mother with empty arms?' 'Why didn't anyone tell me I risked spoiling the possibility of having a normal pregnancy, because of the damage that might be done to my body by the abortion?' These are not just theoretical questions put forth in an abstract academic debate. Those advising abortion rarely talk about physical dangers, emotional results, and psychological consequences.[41] They seldom tell the woman what is going to happen or what may be involved.[42]

We need to think seriously about the aborted human beings who have been deprived of a chance to live, but we also need to consider with sympathy and compassion the women being turned into 'aborted

mothers'—bereft mothers—bitter in some cases, hard in some cases, exceedingly sorrowful in other cases. It is unfair not to make the options clear. To tell a pregnant woman that a few hours or a day in the hospital or clinic will rid her of all her problems and will send her out the door a free person is to forget the humanness of women who are now mothers. With many of the women who have had abortions, their 'motherliness' is very much present even though the child is gone.

Abortion does not end all the problems; often it just exchanges one set for another. Whether or not one believes in the reality of guilt is *not* the question at this point. One of the facts of being a human being is that in spite of the abnormality of human beings and the cruelty of their actions, there still exist the hopes and fears, the longings and aspirations, that can be bundled together in the word *motherliness*. To stamp out these feelings is to ensure that many women will turn into the kind of hard people they may not want to be. For others, it is a bewildering nightmare to be overwhelmed with longings for the baby to be back in them and to be able to complete that which had begun. To assume that all women will want to abort—and to give flat advice without explaining the very real problems some aborted mothers have—is cruelty in the wrappings of blasé and glib kindness.

Second, abortion is not a 'Roman Catholic issue'. This must be emphasised. Those who favour abortion often try to minimise the arguments of those who oppose it by conveying the idea that only the Roman Catholic Church is against abortion. We must indeed be glad for the Roman Catholics who have spoken out, but we must not allow the position to be minimised as though it is a 'religious' issue. It is not a religious issue, and it has nothing to do with the separation of church and state.[43]

The issue of the humanness of the unborn child is one raised by many people across a vast spectrum of religious backgrounds, and, happily, also by thousands who have no religion at all. In the USA a picture in the *International Herald Tribune* of 25 January, 1978, showed a Washington protest march on the fifth anniversary of the Supreme Court decision that restricted the rights of states to regulate and thereby curtail the spread of abortion. The most outstanding sign being carried read: IF MY MUM DIDN'T CARE—I MIGHT NOT BE HERE—THANKS, MUM! The young girl carrying that sign did not have to be religious to paint and carry it; all she needed was to be glad she was not aborted. And the right of that girl to express her views on life and death to those who represent her in the democratic process and to be heard in the courts depends only on her being a citizen. Abortion is not a religious issue. It is a human issue.

Nor is abortion a feminist issue, any more than slavery was only a slave owners' issue. Abortion has been tacked onto the feminist issue, with the feminist issue being used to carry abortion. But there is no intrinsic relationship between them. The fate of the unborn is a question of the fate of the human race. We are one human family. If the rights of one part of that family are denied, it is of concern to each of us. What is at stake is no less than the essence of what freedom and rights are all about.[44]

Third, when the United States Supreme Court made its ruling about abortion on 22 January, 1973, Mr Justice Blackmun delivered the opinion of the Court. The first section in his opinion was titled 'Ancient Attitudes'. In it he referred back to pre-Christian law. He said, 'Greek and Roman law afforded little protection to the unborn. If abortion was prosecuted in some places, it seems to have been based on a concept of a violation of the father's right to his offspring. Ancient religion did not bar abortion.' Thus, as his first point, Mr Justice Blackmun based his opinion on the practice of pre-Christian Greek and Roman law. Most people who read this did not realise the logical result concerning babies after their birth. Roman law permitted not only abortion but also infanticide. As we think this over, we ask ourselves, 'Now that this door is open, how long will it be before infanticide is socially accepted and perhaps legalised?' This is true not just for America where the legal rationale has been the most explicit but also for Britain and anywhere where abortion becomes established.[45]

2
The Slaughter of the Innocents

Infanticide is not yet legalised in either the USA or Britain, but the law is strangely silent about what amounts to public confessions in reputable scientific journals by medical doctors who admit that they are indeed practising it.[46] Infanticide is the killing of a born child—whether that killing is accomplished by a direct act on the part of someone, or whether ordinary care vital to the child's survival, such as feeding, is refused. It makes little difference whether infanticide is direct or indirect. Either way a child is killed.

The first effort we know of in the United States to educate the medical profession in the art of infanticide was a documentary motion picture titled *Who Shall Survive?* Johns Hopkins Hospital and Medical School produced it in 1972. It shows a newborn infant with Down's syndrome (frequently called mongolism) who was permitted to die by 'inattention'. We suspect that 'starving to death' would be a more accurate way of saying this.

People who have never had the experience of working with children who are being rehabilitated into our society after the correction of a congenital defect often say that infants with such defects should be allowed to die or even 'encouraged' to die, because their lives can obviously be nothing but unhappy and miserable. Yet it is constantly to be observed that disability and unhappiness do not necessarily go together. Some of the most unhappy children have all of their physical and mental faculties, while some of the happiest youngsters have borne burdens which most of us would find very difficult to endure.

The obligation in such circumstances is to find alternatives for the problems such children and their parents face. Morally and logically, we do not consider infanticide an acceptable alternative. With today's technology and creativity, we are merely at the beginning of what we can do to help such youngsters with formal educational and leisure-time activities.

Who knows what constitutes 'happiness' for another person? And what about the rewards and satisfactions that come to those who succeed in rehabilitating other-than-perfect children? Stronger character, compassion, deeper understanding of another's burden, creativity, and deeper family bonds—all these can and do result from the so-called social burden of raising a child with a congenital defect.

The Medical Profession Views Infanticide

Infanticide is being practised right now in the USA and Britain, and the saddest thing about it is that it is being carried on by the very segment of the medical profession which has always stood in the role of advocate for the lives of children. The fully developed view of the medical profession in the West grew out of the Christian consensus, and, as we have seen, stands in sharp contrast to old Roman customs. The traditional view of the medical profession has been well stated by J. Engelburt Dunphy, Robert B. Zachary, and Peter Paul Rickham. Dunphy is one of the great teachers of American surgery in this generation. Zachary is the Professor of Paediatric Surgery at Sheffield University. He has been in the forefront of developing operations for the correction of spina bifida and its complications: orthopaedic defects and hydrocephalus (water on the brain). Rickham is professor of paediatric surgery at the University of Zurich and has been a pioneer in developing surgery and intensive care for the newborn.

Dunphy said in the USA at the annual oration before the Massachusetts Medical Society in 1976:

> We cannot destroy life. We cannot regard the hydrocephalic child as a non-person and accept the responsibility for disposing of it like a sick

animal. If there are those in society who think this step would be good, let them work for a totalitarian form of government where, beginning with the infirm and incompetent and ending with the intellectually dissident, non-persons are disposed of day and night by those in power.

History shows clearly the frighteningly short steps from 'the living will' to 'death control' to 'thought control' and finally to the systematic elimination of all but those selected for slavery or to make up the master race. We physicians must take care that support of an innocent but quite unnecessary 'living will' does not pave the way for us to be the executioners while the decisions for death are made by a panel of 'objective experts' or by big brother himself. The year of 1984 is not far away!

Robert B. Zachary, on 9 July, 1976, in the Forshall Lecture given before the British Association of Paediatric Surgeons, said:

I believe that our patients, no matter how young or small they are, should receive the same consideration and expert help that would be considered normal in an adult. Just because he is small, just because he cannot speak for himself, this is no excuse to regard him as expendable, any more than we would do so on account of race or creed or colour or poverty. Nor do I think we ought to be swayed by an argument that the parents have less to lose because he is small and newborn, and has not yet established a close relationship with them, or indeed because the infant himself does not know what he is losing, by missing out on life.

Zachary concluded his lecture with these comments:

There are some ways in which modern society cares greatly about those who are less well off: the poor, the sick, and the handicapped, but it seems to me that newborn babies are often given less than justice. Our primary concern must be the well-being of the patient—as far as it is in our power to achieve it. In his battle at the beginning of life, it could well be that his main defense will be in the hands of paediatric and neonatal surgeons.[47]

At the hundredth anniversary of Children's Hospital in Sheffield, in an address entitled 'The Swing of the Pendulum', Professor Rickham said:

How many normal newborn infants will live happily ever after, especially in our present time? It may be argued that by not selecting, we artificially increase the number of people with an unhappy future, but can we be sure of this in any given case? After all, doctors deal with single, individual patients and not with statistical possibilities. It has also been pointed out that even a child with a grave physical and mental handicap can experience emotions such as happiness, fright, gratitude and love and that it may be therefore, in fact, a rewarding task to look after him. It has been further argued that, strictly speaking, selection implies a limitation of resources, because with an optimum of resources and care a great deal can be done for these children and their families. In under-developed countries these resources do not exist, but in developed countries, where such enormous sums are spent by governments on purposes which are of very doubtful benefit to humanity at large, the distribution of resources is a debatable subject. Finally, it can be argued that if selection is practised, it may not be necessarily the fittest on whom the greatest effort should be expended.

The late Lord Cohen of Birkenhead, a man whose name is associated with the beginnings of the National Health Service in Britain, had this to say about the possibility of killing children who are mentally defective or epileptic: 'No doctor could subscribe to this view . . . who has seen the love and devotion which bring out all that is best in men when lavished on such a child.'

This moral view is now very much under strain in Britain among doctors in relation to newborns with severe spina bifida. Commenting on some hospital practices, Dr Colin Brewer wrote in the *Guardian*, 4 February, 1976, the following: 'Those who are not thought likely to benefit from surgery in the long run . . . are starved to death. Those selected for death are fed only if they cry. They are, however, sedated, and sedated infants do not cry.'

In case this is regarded as merely a 'newspaper report', Robert B. Zachary has authoritatively confirmed in the *British Medical Journal*, 3 December, 1977 (pp. 1460–62), that these sedation and starvation practices are taking place. The traditional high view that he has upheld is now being challenged. In his article he exposes first the myth that if severe spina bifida babies are not treated they will all die anyway. This, he confirms, is not true, but the myth makes it easier, he indicates, for such patients to be 'pushed', i.e. sedated and starved. He then shows how drugs eight times the normal sedative dose recommended in Nelson's *Paediatrics* are being administered for this purpose and scotches any idea that they are being given to relieve pain. He reasonably asks why such actions which lead to the death of the baby patients are not regarded as illegal. He goes on to say how current attitudes to abortion have enabled the acceptance of such actions.

Towards the end of the article, Professor Zachary indicates how the attitude towards handicapped newborns is the same as the one depicted by a Christian Aid poster in relation to the hungry, which read, 'Ignore the hungry and they will go away' — to their graves. He concludes seeing no reason why other handicapped newborns will not receive similar treatment and asks whether they will stop with newborns. His final remarks are not idle, since already it is clear that babies with only moderately severe spina bifida, who are unlikely to die even when

untreated, are becoming victims of such procedures. So far is current practice from the traditional high view, and moving further all the time.

In 1975 the Sonoma Conference (in California) on Ethical Issues in Neonatal Intensive Care produced a 193-page report entitled 'Ethics of Newborn Intensive Care'. At the conference, seventeen members of a panel of twenty answered yes to this question: 'Would it be right to directly intervene to kill a self-sustaining infant?' (A self-sustaining infant is a child who can live without technical assistance of any kind. That means he can survive with no help other than normal feeding.) One of the marks of our time is that many of the non-physicians on the panel, including bio-ethicists, lawyers, a nurse, a social worker, a sociologist, an anthropologist, and a philosopher, could see no difference at all between not putting a child on a machine and not giving it food. Letting a dying child die and actually killing a living child by starvation were all the same to them. The physicians on the panel said they themselves would hesitate to kill such an infant directly, but would not prevent someone else from doing so. This is total relativism. Values are a purely subjective matter and could change with any circumstance.

A widely read monthly newspaper for paediatricians in the United States called *Paediatric News* posed questions to three physicians concerning the 1975 Sonoma Conference report. *Paediatric News* devoted a large portion of its April 1977 issue to the answers, which are most significant in a discussion of the implications of this problem—the improper answers to which can shape the foundations of the futures for us all.

One of the physicians interviewed was Dr George M. Ryan, Jr, of the Boston Hospital for Women. He said:

> The most difficult question is obviously whether it would ever be right to intervene directly to kill a self-sustaining infant. It is relatively easy to conceive of ceasing to provide unnatural prolongation of meaningless life by technology, but to actively kill an infant that is living without this support is to me repugnant. I think this action is so in conflict with the concept of the physician as a 'healer' that such a decision should not be thrust upon the medical profession. Clearly the physician can testify as to the physical and medical status of the patient and can even predict some of the elements of the general human potential of the individual, but beyond this point, the physician has no special talent or training not available to the rest of society that might provide him with the capability of making infallible decisions. I am not very sanguine about the wisdom of any one group in making such decisions.

We certainly agree with Dr Ryan on how repugnant this situation is. We agree, too, that physicians have no corner on the market in making infallible decisions, even though they certainly have some knowledge that is not available to the average consumer of health care. The point is that no one should be making decisions to kill self-sustaining infants.

Another of the three physicians was asked his opinion about the Sonoma Conference findings. Dr R. T. F. Schmidt of Cincinnati, at that time president-elect of the American College of Obstetrics and Gynaecologists, answered from the point of view of traditional moral and ethical standards. He said, 'The fact that seventeen of twenty expert panellists believe that some severely defective infants should be killed under certain conditions is deeply disturbing. This position is not only deeply disturbing to our traditional concept of the inherent value of human life but is potentially shattering to the foundations of Western civilisation.'

Dr Schmidt was careful to point out that much of the Sonoma Conference represented sound deliberation, but he felt that the issue of infanticide is of such far-reaching importance that it deserves to be singled out. He concluded his remarks by saying:

> Finally, the issue was clouded by questions raised as to what state of perfection or imperfection qualifies a human being as a person. The Supreme Court decision of 1973 has already severely limited this qualification. Under current law, the existence of every future member of our society may be terminated [within the uterus] according to the value judgement of one or, at the most, two private individuals. To extend this contingency of private value judgement to the newborn infant in either ethical standard or in law would be another ominous step backward.

The Decision to Kill

Although the following headline in the USA is unfair to Dr Victor Vaughn, an ethical and reputable paediatrician and lecturer, once chief at St Christopher's Hospital in Philadelphia, the fact that such a headline could appear in a medical newspaper in 1977 should jolt us to the very foundation of our being: M.D.-PARENT DECISION NEEDED TO KILL INFANT. One only has to read the article to see that it is considered unwise for a parent to decide by himself to kill his child, or for a physician to decide by himself to kill the parent's child, but that their consensus makes such a decision legitimate.

Even more shocking was a recent TV programme in Britain put out by Thames Television on its 'Afternoon Plus' series on 5 and 22 January,

1979. There they showed how a Dr Garrow of Wycombe General Hospital, with the consent and support of the parents whom he had advised, had allowed the death of a baby, Louise, who suffered from severe spina bifida. It was admitted quite openly on the programme that the baby had been sedated and had died of starvation and dehydration and Dr Garrow expressed his admiration for the love and courage of the parents in what he felt was a good decision.

Dr John A. Robertson of the University of Wisconsin Law School and Medical School in the USA spoke what seems to us a word of wisdom to bring this discussion down to earth. He said that 'one must decide for whose benefit is the decision to withhold treatment from a child with severe birth defects. Is no life better than one of low quality? The person to ask is an individual who has a disabling birth defect.' Let us emphasise: *The person to ask is an individual who has a disabling birth defect.*

In preparing for the writing of this book, we did just that and something more. Four patients of one of us—born with congenital defects incompatible with life (who had been operated upon on the first day or two of life)—were assembled with four other children who had developed lethal problems in early childhood. They were not coached in any way concerning what answers they were to give to questions. They were told that we were making some documentary movies and were writing a book on the general topic of 'Whatever Happened to the Human Race?' We allowed them to talk with each other for about an hour, in order to feel comfortable before being asked to participate in our plans.

The patients at the time ranged in age from eleven to thirty years. One patient had been born with a number of major congenital defects down the midline of his body, requiring twenty-seven operative procedures for correction. Another was born without an oesophagus, requiring a transplantation of the colon to replace the absent organ. Still another was born with a tumour of the tongue, necessitating almost total amputation of that structure in a series of operations. The final youngster with congenital defects was born with major defects of the oesophagus, the lower bowel, and the bladder.

The other four children all had tumours. One was a benign tumour of the bones of the face, which had required a number of operations for correction and still had not achieved perfection. The other three had cancers of the adrenal gland, of the parotid gland, and of the uterus.

There can be no doubt about how such young people feel about the joy of living, despite the time-consuming and usually painful medical and surgical procedures they have endured to correct birth defects or those discovered in early childhood. Here is a sampling of their comments:

Because the start was a little abnormal, it doesn't mean you're going to finish that way. I'm a normal functioning human being, capable of doing anything anyone else can. . . .

At times it got very hard, but life is certainly worth living. I married a wonderful guy and I'm just so happy. . . .

At the beginning it was a little difficult going back to school after surgery, but then things started looking up, with a little perseverance and support. I am an anaesthetist and I'm happily married. Things are going great for me. . . .

I really think that all my operations and all the things I had wrong with me were worth it, because I really enjoy life and I don't really let the things that are wrong with me bother me. . . .

If anything, I think I've had an added quality to my life—an appreciation of life. I look forward to every single morning. . . .

Most of the problems are what my parents went through with the surgery. I've now been teaching high school for eight years and it's a great joy. . . .

They spend millions of dollars to send men to the moon. I think they can spend any amount necessary to save someone's life. A human life is so important because it's a gift—not something that you can give, so you really don't have the right to take it either. . . .

I really don't consider myself handicapped. Life is just worth living. What else can I say? . . .

One of our special friends is Craig, who was a student at L'Abri in Switzerland. He is a graduate in philosophy from California State University and is now a theological student at Covenant Seminary in the USA. He was born without a left leg and without arms below the elbows. Today, in some hospitals, Craig might have been deliberately allowed to die at birth, on the mistaken assumption that life is not worth living for the seriously handicapped person. When we asked Craig what he thought about those who say that people born with such serious birth defects should be eliminated, this, in part, was his reply:

They don't really see that what they are talking about is murder. I know, when I was born, the first thing my dad said to my mom was that 'this one needs our love more.' An individual with a handicap needs our love and

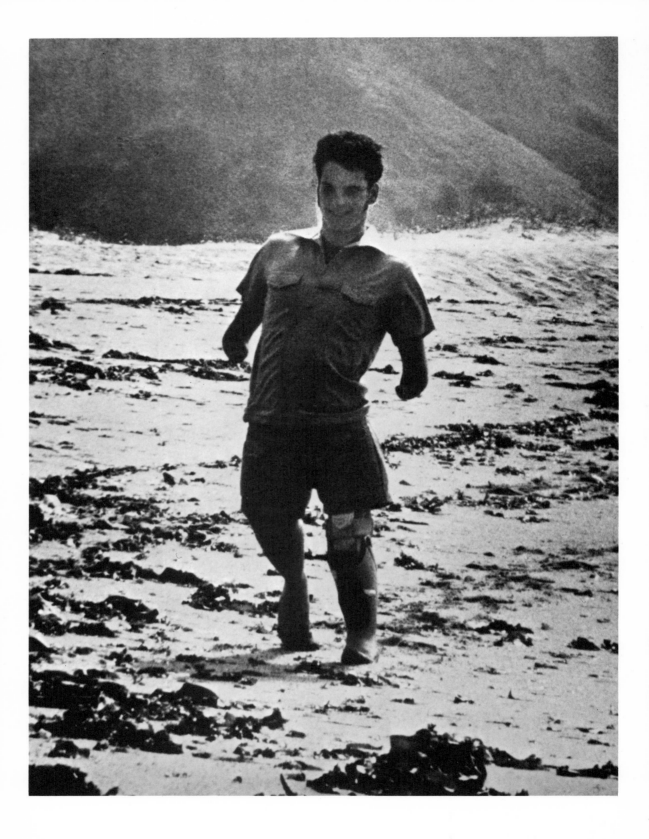

needs us to help him grow into the being that God has made him to be. They are advocating that we destroy these children before they're even given a chance to live and to conquer their handicaps.

I'm very glad to be alive. I live a full, meaningful life. I have many friends and many things that I want to do in life. I think the secret of living with a handicap is realising who you are—that you're a human being, somebody who is very special—looking at the things that you *can* do in spite of your handicap, and maybe even through your handicap.

Our friend and colleague Robert B. Zachary has enjoyed an equally encouraging response in his work in Britain. He tells of how one of his patients, a fourteen-year-old girl with spina bifida was watching a programme about pre-natal screening and abortion for spina bifida. He heard her say afterwards, 'I'm glad they didn't do that to me because I've had fourteen years of love.'

Those who graduated from medical school in the first half of this century probably came out of that experience with the idea that they had been trained to 'alleviate suffering and save lives'. The suffering to be relieved was the *patient's* suffering and the life to be saved was the *patient's* life. This has become distorted in the semantics of the euthanasia movement in the following way. Doctors are to save lives; that is part of their profession. If the life they are trying to save, however, is producing suffering on the part of the family, doctors are to allay that suffering by disposing of their patient. So, in a strange way, it can still be said that doctors are alleviating suffering and saving lives. But the practice of infanticide for the well-being of the family is a far cry from the traditional role of the paediatrician and more lately of the paediatric surgeon.

Abortion, infanticide, and euthanasia are not only questions for women and other relatives directly involved—nor are they the prerogatives of a few people who have thought through the wider ramifications. They are life-and-death issues that concern the whole human race equally and should be addressed as such. Putting pressure on the public and on legislators to accept a lower view of human beings, small groups of people often argue their case by using a few extreme examples to gain sympathy for ideas and practices that later are not limited to extreme cases. These then become the common practice of the day. Abortion, for example, has moved from something once considered unusual and now in many cases is an accepted form of 'birth control'.

Infanticide is following the same pattern. The argument begins with people who have a so-called vegetative existence. There then follows a

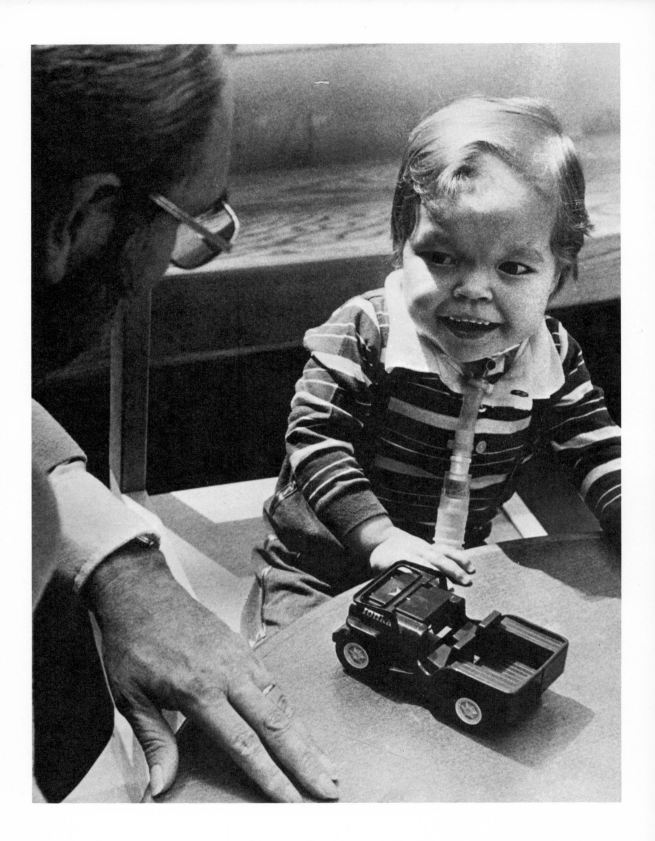

tendency to expand the indications and eliminate almost any child who is unwanted for some reason.

The same movement can be seen with euthanasia. The arguments now being put forward centre on the 'miserable' person in old age — one dying of cancer, for instance. But once the doors are open, there is no reason why the aged, weak, and infirm will not find that as they become economic burdens they will be eliminated under one pretext or another.

At first we hear much talk of compassion for the unwanted. The discussion moves on to 'rights', then to 'my' rights and soon to pure 'economics'. The discussion of life must be brought back to where it belongs — not to emotional, extreme examples, not to selfish questions of rights, not to expedience, and certainly not to economics.[48] The matter should be discussed in terms of right and wrong.

In *How Should We Then Live?* one of us spoke of 'sociological law' — that is, law based only on what the majority of society thinks is in its best interests at a given moment — and 'sociological news', slanted to produce what some person thinks will produce a helpful sociological result. Now arbitrary abortion has opened wide the door at the point of life and death for 'sociological medicine' — not just for the yet unborn but for all human life.

Treating Congenital Defects

The most challenging aspect of children's surgery is the treatment of those congenital defects that are incompatible with life, but nevertheless can be corrected by the proper surgical procedure carried out shortly after birth. We are talking about such defects as those in babies who are born without a connection between the throat and stomach, or with no rectum, perhaps with their abdominal organs out in the umbilical cord or up in the chest cavity, or infants with any one of a great many varieties of intestinal obstruction. Many of those babies are operated on as youngsters and grow into adult life, marry, and have children of their own.

Of course there are problems in raising some of these children, and they may on occasion constitute a burden for the rest of the family. One of us has had thirty-five years' experience in performing thousands of just such operations. No family has ever asked, 'Why did you work so hard to save the life of my child?' No grown child or young adult has ever asked, 'Why did you struggle so hard when you knew the outcome would not be perfect?'[49]

One of us operated at Philadelphia's Children's Hospital in the USA on young Christopher Wall, who was born with *ectopia cordis* (the heart outside the chest), actually performing 15 different procedures over 1,117 days to get his heart repositioned without crowding and to permit his lungs to function adequately. Chris is the first patient who has ever survived after being born with this type of *ectopia cordis*. The case of Chris Wall raises a number of questions asked from time to time: 'Why do you think it's right to spend that much money in caring for one child, when you could take the same amount of money and spread it over the treatment of many children?' Or, as some people asked, 'What kind of life is the child living? He is on a respirator; he has never been home; his parents have almost no relationship with this son who is more emotionally tied to the nurses who have raised him during the past two years.'[50] *Note:* Chris did go home after 1,117 days in the hospital and is off the respirator for as long as 8 hours at a time and will eventually come off the respirator completely. A doctor is responsible to God for the manner in which he works to save a single human life. It is a matter of stewardship. The surgeon is accountable for the way he uses the gifts that God has given him. He is also responsible for the life entrusted to his care. It is a question of moral principle.

But even if we were pragmatists, we would still believe that doctors should work to save the Chris Walls of this world. For when a hospital is geared to save lives at any cost, this attitude affects health care down to the most mundane level.[51] On the other hand, when one set of patients can be eliminated at will, the whole spirit of struggling to save lives is lost, and it is not long before a doctor or nurse will say, 'Why try so hard on anybody? After all, we deliberately fail to treat some patients and we "kill" others.' Even if it were not expressed this blatantly, an erosion would take place, which over a number of years would undermine the care of all patients in any institution that kills any patient placed in its care.

Eventually, abortion must surely have this effect on the field of obstetrics. We do not understand how an obstetrician can destroy a 1000-gram fetus in one uterus and deliver a 1500-gram premature baby from out of another uterus, carrying it to the tender, loving care of the intensive-care nursery down the hall.

Just as child abuse has risen dramatically during the years of legalised abortion, the gradual brutalising of society that is taking place has included doctors and legislators as well as ordinary citizens. If you doubt that we are becoming brutal, consider for a moment that many paediatric surgeons, highly skilled in surgery of the newborn and most knowledgeable about what can be accomplished by rehabilitation, choose not to operate on a given newborn with a given congenital defect. By making the decision of allowing him to die or acquiescing to the parents' wishes not to operate, they allow the baby to die.[52] Think of mothers who express the idea of 'personal rights' by having dragged piecemeal from their wombs the child they have conceived. Think of legislators debating, as if they were talking about the price of coffee, what action they should take to eliminate economic burdens on society by opening the doors to a lack of protection for the weak, the old, the infirm, the young and the unborn — in fact, for all those our society traditionally has protected. Indeed, this protection was once a hallmark of our civilisation. *Whatever happened to the human race?*

Advocates of Infanticide

It frightens us when we see the medical profession acquiesce to, if not lead in, a trend which in our judgment will carry us to destruction. The loss of humanness shown in allowing malformed babies to starve to death is not a thing of the future. It is being put forward as the accepted thing right now in many quarters. All that is left is for it to become totally accepted and eventually, for economic reasons, made mandatory by an increasingly authoritarian government in an increasingly selfish society.

In May 1973, James D. Watson, the Nobel Prize laureate who discovered the double helix of DNA, granted an interview to *Prism* magazine, then a publication of the American Medical Association, *Time* magazine later reported the interview to the general public, quoting Watson as having said, 'If a child were not declared alive until three days after birth, then all parents could be allowed the choice only a few are given under the present system. The doctor could allow the child to die if the parents so choose and save a lot of misery and suffering. I believe this view is the only rational, compassionate attitude to have.'

In January 1978, Francis Crick, also a Nobel laureate, was quoted in the *Pacific News Service* as saying, '. . . no newborn infant should be declared human until it has passed certain tests regarding its genetic endowment and that if it fails these tests it forfeits the right to live.'

Perhaps the paper most outspokenly advocating infanticide was published in the prestigious 167-year-old *New England Journal of Medicine* in the USA. In October 1973, Dr Raymond S. Duff of the department of paediatrics at Yale University School of Medicine and his then colleague Dr A. G. M. Campbell, now Professor of Aberdeen University's Department of Child Health, wrote, 'Moral and Ethical Dilemmas in the Special-Care Nursery.'[53]

Very few parents come of their own volition to a physician and say, 'My baby has a life not worthy to be lived.' Duff and Campbell say that the parents in such a case are not in a condition to give 'informed consent' by themselves. But any physician in the emotional circumstances surrounding the birth of a baby with any kind of a defect can, by innuendo if not advice, prepare the family to make the decision the physician wants them to make. We do not consider this 'informed consent'.

Duff and Campbell acknowledge that the parents' and siblings' rights to relief from 'seemingly pointless, crushing burdens were important considerations' in letting children die. Even Duff and Campbell use the word *seemingly* to modify *pointless*, and we are sure the burden would not be nearly as *crushing* as the guilt many of these parents will eventually feel.[54]

As partial justification for their point of view, Duff and Campbell say that 'although some parents have exhibited doubts that the choices were correct, all appear to be as effective in their lives as they were before this experience. Some claim that their profoundly moving experience has provided a deeper meaning in life, and from this they have become more effective people.' Some of the parents, the two doctors admit, had doubts that their choice to let the child die was correct. If these parents were seeking deeper meaning in life—and if Duff and Campbell were indeed interested in providing deeper meaning in life for the parents of their deformed patients—why not let the family find that deep meaning by providing the love and attention necessary to take care of an infant who has been given to them? We suspect that the deeper meaning would then be deeper still, that their effectiveness would be still more effective, and that they would be examples of courage and determination to others less courageous. Duff and Campbell say, 'It seems appropriate that the profession be held accountable for presenting fully all management options and their expected consequences.' We wonder how commonly physicians are willing to be held accountable for the consequences that may not be apparent in a family until years later?

There have been many times when one of us, having operated on a newborn youngster who has subsequently died, has been inwardly relieved and has expressed honestly to the family that the tragic turn of events was indeed a blessing in disguise. But being able to look on such an occasion in retrospect as a blessing does not, we believe, entitle a doctor to distribute 'shower of blessings' by eliminating the problems that families might have to face in raising a child who is less than perfect—by eliminating the baby.

On the basis of interviews he has given and comments we have read in the press, we believe that Professor Duff is perfectly sincere in believing that he is moving in an ethical and moral direction when he advocates death as one of the options in the treatment of a defective newborn. It should not be thought that we are singling out Duff and Campbell. There are growing numbers of other physicians and surgeons who unfortunately, we believe, are advocating the same course of action. In the USA Anthony Shaw, a paediatric surgeon, has been in the forefront of these discussions from a neonatal surgeon's point of view. He says: 'My ethic holds that all rights are not absolute all the time. As Fletcher points out, '. . . all rights are imperfect and may be set aside if human need requires it.' My ethic further considers quality of life as a value that must be balanced against the belief in the sanctity of life.'[55]

We are moving from the state of mind in which destruction of life is advocated for children who are considered to be socially useless or deemed to have non-meaningful lives to the stance that we should perhaps destroy a child because he is socially disturbing. One wonders if the advocates of such a philosophy would espouse a total blockade and 'starving out' of urban slums as a solution to poverty—considering all the social and economic problems this would solve all at once!

The twentieth century has produced many monsters. One has been the idea of 'built-in obsolescence', not only in material things but also in human matters such as marriage and the responsibilities of parenthood. In interview, Dr Gordon Stirrat, clinical Reader in the Nuffield Department of Obstetrics and Gynaecology at the University of Oxford, remarked that, 'In today's abortion mentality we are beginning to see amongst women a consumer attitude towards their pregnancies—the line is when you order a baby you order a good one and if it's no good, you send it back.' One can picture a parent picking up one baby and, not being quite satisfied with it, trading it in for another one.

Medical science can now make a prenatal diagnosis of the sex of the expected offspring. In spite of the depravity of our society regarding abortion-on-demand, even most abortionists recoil a little from eliminating an unborn child just because it is not the sex the family wants. However, the unthinkable soon becomes thinkable and in the 6

September, 1979, issue of the *New England Journal of Medicine* there is an article reporting this practice in the USA. The author, John Fletcher, PhD, an ethicist of the National Institute of Health in Bethesda, writes how he had changed his mind from believing such abortions to be frivolous and a waste of resources to being a woman's right. After all, he writes, since abortions are given to enable trips abroad it was hypocritical to deny them on grounds of sex choice.[56]

One wonders what the chances are for someone who becomes a burden in a society that practices the concept of the survival of the fittest and has begun this practice by starting to eliminate its children. Most societies, recognising the total dependency of children, have given their young a place of special protection. Since our society has begun by abusing and then killing children, we feel that for us the worst has come first. Where the destruction will end depends only on what a small scientific elite and a generally apathetic public will advocate and tolerate. Any hope of a comprehensive standard for human rights has already been lost.

Meaningful Humanhood

Joseph Fletcher, formerly of Harvard Divinity School and now at the University of Virginia in Charlottesville, talks about 'meaningful humanhood' in an article entitled 'Indicators of Humanhood: A Tentative Profile of Man'.[57] H. Tristam Engelhart, Jr, formerly clinical professor of physiology of medicine at the University of Texas and more recently professor of philosophy and medicine at the Kennedy Institute of Georgetown University in Washington, D.C., writes of 'wrongful life'.[58]

As soon as we let anyone, even a physician, make decisions about our 'meaningful humanhood', about 'wrongful life' or 'rightful life', we have then invited others to make decisions about our worth. In fact Jonathan Glover, Fellow of New College, Oxford, and philosophy tutor, in his popular paperback, *Causing Death and Saving Lives*, uses the criterion of 'a worthwhile life' as being crucial in his advocacy, albeit in limited cases, of infanticide and euthanasia.[59] Yet our worth may be entirely different in the eyes of these men or their followers from what it would have been to anyone in our culture in the past. In fact, it might even be different from the view held by the majority of people today.

If we decide that a child with a chronic cardiopulmonary disease, short-bowel syndrome, or various manifestations of brain damage should be permitted to die (some of Duff and Campbell's examples), what is to prevent us from eliminating an adult with chronic cardio-pulmonary disease—who may be much more of a burden to his family than the child is? Or what about an adult with ulcerative colitis (with symptoms much the same as short-bowel syndrome) and some psychiatric problems as well? Are we to extend the slaughter to all those who in one way or another become a burden or nuisance, or who stop us from enjoying our rights as we perceive them? The word *rights* is meaningless outside the context of some moral framework that extends its protection to the whole human family.

Because a newborn child has the possibility or even the probability of problems in later life, does this give us the right to terminate his or her life now? If it does, then should we also do away with the people reading this book who have chronic shortness of breath, oxygen dependency, paralysis, a sexual handicap, or a psychological problem? The problems in the Duff and Campbell article all have their adult counterparts.

We think many miss the essential message in the Duff and Campbell paper. These authors first brought to public attention death as an option in newborn paediatric care. But it is not always understood that the death they presented as an option *was not the death of infants who could not possibly survive, but rather the death of infants who could live if treated—but whose lives would not be 'normal'*.

The physician's decision—not the infant's defect—becomes the lethal factor. In view of the fact that, to Duff and Campbell, the economic status of the family and the stability of the marriage are mitigating circumstances in deciding on treatment or non-treatment, it is clear that there has been introduced a discrimination just as deplorable as those based on race, creed, colour, or sex. And, as is so often the case, not only is such immoral and discriminatory behaviour propagated, but those who push for it do so with high and lofty pseudo-moral language.

Duff and Campbell offer death as an option in health care, even though they say in one place in their article, 'We recognise great variability and often much uncertainty in prognoses and in family capacities to deal with defective newborn infants. . . . Prognosis was not always exact and a few children with extensive care might live for months and occasionally years. *Some might survive and function satisfactorily'* (italics ours).

When the physician responsible for managing a new born baby with a defect is committed to the thesis that there is some human life not worthy to be lived, and when he considers death as one of the options in treatment, the baby concerned does not have a chance. Obviously, the determining factor is not the baby's physical defect but the physician's decision.

The *Newsweek* (12 November, 1973) report of the Duff and Campbell article quotes Duff as saying, 'The public has got to decide what to do with vegetated individuals who have no human potential.' This was answered by a letter in *Newsweek* two weeks later:

'Life-and-Death Decisions'
   I'll wager my entire root system and as much fertiliser as it would take to fill Yale University that you have never received a letter from a vegetable before this one, but, much as I resent the term, I must confess that I fit the description of a 'vegetable' as defined in the article 'Shall This Child Die?'
   Due to severe brain damage incurred at birth, I am unable to dress myself, toilet myself, or write; my secretary is typing this letter. Many thousands of dollars had to be spent on my rehabilitation and education in order for me to reach my present professional status as a counselling psychologist. My parents were also told, thirty-five years ago, that there was 'little or no hope of achieving meaningful "humanhood"' for their daughter. Have I reached 'humanhood'? Compared with Drs Duff and Campbell, I believe I have surpassed it!
   Instead of changing the law to make it legal to weed out us 'vegetables', let us change the laws so that we may receive quality medical care, education and freedom to live as full and productive lives as our potentials allow.
                                                          Sondra Diamond
                                                          Philadelphia, Pennsylvania

The medical profession has traditionally made its treatment of patients a reflection of our society's concern for those who are ill or helpless. Indeed, it has often acted as an advocate for those who had no one else to stand up for them. Thus it responded, in days gone by, with love and compassion towards the helpless child. Technical skills have increased rapidly and have produced dilemmas that doctors did not face a decade ago. But this does not give them any new expertise in deciding who shall live and who shall die, especially when so many non-medical factors must be taken into account in making the decision. The new gadgetry of medical practice and the growing sophistication of technology do not give a doctor any more right than the rest of us to play God. Many in the medical profession are losing this viewpoint. They are setting the worth of the individual person aside. We would insist that if we cannot cure, we can care; and we do not mean ever to use the words *care* and *kill* as synonyms.

Infanticide and the Church Mauthausen in Austria was a Nazi concentration camp where, between 1938 and 1945, over 110,000 people were brutally killed to help build the Nazi's idea of heaven on earth. There are monuments to the many Jews and non-Jews who died. What happened in Mauthausen shows the lowest possible view of human life. All conventions of war were put aside, as people of all nationalities were tortured and had pseudo-medical experiments performed on them.

To the Nazis the Jews were an unwanted burden on society—parasites who consumed more than they gave. The young, the old, the aged, the weak, and the strong were all eliminated in an attempt to build a perfect race according to Nazi standards. Individuals were no longer perceived as special creatures created in the image of God. Regardless of their nationality or race, people were viewed as pawns to be exploited, and when they no longer fulfilled a function, they were eliminated.

In the USA not so long ago, at the Charleston, South Carolina, slave market, black men, women, and children were sold as cattle. On a balcony they were paraded as so much merchandise before the prospective buyers standing down below. For economic convenience, they had been arbitrarily reclassified by a white society as non-human. The Supreme Court of the United States, in the Dred Scott Decision, upheld this fiction by declaring the black person to be chattel property. Furthermore, it was as chattel that the slaves had been transported from Africa under inhuman conditions. The ships that carried them and those who conducted the trade were mostly British. West African chiefs also helped to organise this human traffic.

These atrocities are not just a record in past history. There is in our own day a low view of human life, not only in the secular world but in certain religious groups as well. The Religious Coalition for Abortion Rights is a case in point. Among what the organisation calls its 'eleven major denominations' are the Unitarian Universal Association, the American Ethical Union, the American Jewish Congress, and the Union of American Hebrew Congregations. This group has attempted to use anti-Catholic thinking as a weapon by declaring that abortion is a

Roman Catholic issue. Its position on abortion is weakened by ignorance—because it seeks the 'legal option of abortion in accordance with sound medical practice'. Actually, this 'sound medical practice' is just the whim of the mother-to-be.

Dean J. Philip Wogaman of Wesley Theological Seminary has espoused the cause of the Religious Coalition for Abortion Rights by ignoring the right of the developing, unborn baby in favour of what he calls 'God's loving intention for existing human beings'. That 'loving intention' for an existing human being turns out to be supporting the mother-to-be in the murder of her unborn child.

'Christians For Free Choice' is the equivalent pro-abortion religious group in Britain. Among their patrons are well-known church figures like Lord Soper and the Right Rev J. A. T. Robinson. In an open letter to Members of Parliament, 3 July, 1979, they encouraged the defence of the 1967 Abortion Act on the grounds that, 'the Act has done much to bring us to a caring and humane society'. Though unconnected with this group, the Bishop of Winchester, as reported in the *Guardian*, 23 June, 1978, devised a prayer to be used after abortion. It read in part, '. . . into your hands we commit the developing life that we have cut short. Look in merciful judgment on the decision we have made and assure us in all our uncertainty that your love for us could never change.' While the report made it clear that the Bishop did not support easy abortion, it is difficult to see how the prayer was supposed to inculcate a reverence for life as the Bishop claimed. At the least, however well intentioned, it could only be confusing. Fortunately the Church of England synod, to whom the prayer had been suggested, saw the gross misunderstanding to which such a prayer was vulnerable and turned it down.

Elsewhere, certain segments of the church are not without an opinion on the subject of infanticide. A task force of the Anglican Church of Canada reached a conclusion in a 1977 report that it could be morally right to terminate the lives of new born infants with severe brain damage. The callousness of the report is evident in its phraseology: 'Our sense and emotions lead us to the grave mistake of treating human-looking shapes as if they were human, although they lack the least vestige of human behaviour and intellect. In fact the only way to treat such defective infants humanely is not to treat them as human.'[61]

The task force was made up of eleven people with backgrounds in medicine, nursing, law, and theology. It is astounding that the professions represented could have produced such a report. It is humanism producing inhumanity. The self-assured language of these individuals and people like them must surely remind us of the words and sentiments expressed by those who in another era were espousing the defending slavery and attempting to prove the non-human status of the black person.

Happily, the general synod of the Anglican Church in Canada did not approve the report, but that such a report came forth from an official group of a major denomination in our day says much about the direction taken by certain segments of the church in regard to infanticide.

That even the church is being used by the proponents of infanticide is particularly alarming. Those who have propagated these ideas or simply not bothered to think them through have had ample warning in history— if they would care to look. Doctors and nurses should be aware of how fallible these decisions are and how disastrous have been simplistic pop-science theories about human worth in the past. Lawyers should be frightened to let down the bars on the killing of any human being, when the decision is made on the basis of the quality of life. And finally, these theologians have obviously forgotten God's view of the worth of every human being as made in the image of God. If these same theologians no longer believe in such a God, they should not use the church as a platform from which to propagate their discriminatory ideas.

In general, liberal theologians and church bodies (those who have tried to mix Christian and humanistic thought) support abortion and thus contribute to the subsequent slide into the loss of humanness. These religious groups have departed from the stand against abortion that the Christian church has taken from its earliest days. The *Didache,* or *The Teaching of the Twelve Apostles,* an early Christian document from the second century (or maybe even the late first century) clearly prohibits abortion. Tertullian, is his *Apologeticus* of AD 197 writes:

> For us murder is once for all forbidden; so even the child in the womb, while yet the mother's blood is still being drawn on to form the human being, it is not lawful for us to destroy. To forbid birth is only quicker murder. It makes no difference whether one take away the life once born or destroy it as it comes to birth. He is a man, who is to be a man; the fruit is always present in the seed.

Those in the church who have not made these questions a burning issue have forgotten the church's centuries-old tradition of social action on behalf of the weak and the unwanted. One remembers William Wilber-force, fighting the slave trade in the British Empire on the basis of his Christian faith, representative of the many down through the ages who have tried to practise what they preach.

What Chance for Humanity?

At a population control conference in Washington, D.C., as reported by writer Norman Podhoretz, one speaker saw 'no reason why any who accepted abortion should balk at infanticide'. Another urged certain medical qualifying tests for all new borns. These would determine their genetic characteristics and, thus, whether their right to life should be forfeited.[62] Of course, at present only a few hold these ideas, but unfortunately they are presenting these ideas again and again. Taken a little more seriously each time, they become just a little more thinkable each time.

Link this view with the abuse of genetic knowledge, the ever-expanding power of the government, and arbitrary law—and, indeed, the prospects for the right of the individual and for humanness are grim. Dr James R. Sorenson, associate professor of socio-medical sciences at Boston University Medical Centre spoke at the symposium 'Prenatal Diagnosis and Its Impact on Society' and said:

> [There is] a developing cultural or social attitude that . . . a couple ought to exercise control over their reproductive fate. While a couple should have as many children as they please (within cultural 'limits'), increasingly our societal view is that they should not have unwanted children. I think that this developing societal attitude can very easily extend to encompass not just control of the number of children but . . . control of their quality as well. In short, I am suggesting that it may become culturally acceptable and perhaps even expected that parents ought to avoid the birth of a defective child, especially when we have a technology that can help avoid such events.

In the light of these reflections we view with particular concern the way in Britain some charities for the handicapped are seeing it as their role to encourage pre-natal screening with the option of abortion. The pressure on parents will become inescapable as will the insecurities of handi-capped children already born.[63]

The matter does not stop with malformed babies, but leads naturally to limiting the number of babies a family may have. In 1971, at the National Conference on Population Education in Washington, D.C., Martha Willing, co-director of Population Dynamics of Seattle, Washington, first proposed tax disincentives for parents who have more than two children. Then the state should proceed 'to penalise deliberate violations of a small family norm and set up controls which prevent such violations'. This was to be done by sterilising any further children of families who exceeded the norm.[64]

Such Malthusian concerns are also widespread in Britain. It seems relatively easy to exploit the popular anxiety of Britain being a small, overcrowded island. In 1973 a National Opinion Poll recorded that over 87 per cent of electors were concerned with overpopulation and 71 per cent thought that the government should take action. In 1977 the *Sunday People* reported on 24 April that Mr Keith Norcross, FRCS, was suggesting that there should be a ration on parenthood with the limitation being maintained by abortion.

Without the Judaeo-Christian base which gives every individual an intrinsic dignity as made in the image of the personal-infinite Creator, each successive horror falls naturally into place. Combine arbitrary law (in which a small group of people may decide what is good for society at that moment of history) with the Supreme Court ruling on arbitrary abortion and the gates are opened for many kinds of killing under the guise of social good. Nan Mizrachi, in 'Eliminating the Medical Hazards of Delayed Abortions', says:

> Arguments that the fetus is only 'human' at a particular stage of gestation violate biological reality. It attempts to over-simplify a complex issue. Whereas the reality that abortion is killing should not, in my view, remove abortion as a socially acceptable surgical procedure, I do think we should face up to the reality of what the decision to abort entails.[65]

In other words, abortion is killing, but it is nevertheless to be practised. But if that kind of killing, why not others?

As much as we would differ with Professor Joseph Fletcher's view of ethics, we can agree that his logic is impeccable when he says in *The Humanist* (July-August 1974): 'To speak of living and dying, therefore. . . encompasses the abortion issue along with the euthanasia issue. They are ethically inseparable.'

Here we come to the next logical step that follows from abandoning the biblical perspective that mankind is unique, in that all men, women, and children are made in the image of God. The wide-open door of abortion on demand leads naturally to infanticide which leads naturally to euthanasia.

3
Death by Someone's Choice

Life is a continuum from conception until natural death. Since life is being destroyed before birth, why not tamper with it on the other end?

Will a society which has assumed the right to kill infants in the womb—because they are unwanted, imperfect, or merely inconvenient—have difficulty in assuming the right to kill other human beings, especially older adults who are judged unwanted, deemed imperfect physically or mentally, or considered a possible social nuisance?

The next candidates for arbitrary reclassification as non-persons are the elderly. This will become increasingly so as the proportion of the old and weak in relation to the young and strong becomes abnormally large, due to the growing anti-family sentiment, the abortion rate, and medicine's contribution to the lengthening of the normal life span. The imbalance will cause many of the young to perceive the old as a cramping nuisance in the hedonistic life-style they claim as their right. As the demand for affluence continues and the economic crunch gets greater, the amount of compassion that the legislature and the courts will have for the old does not seem likely to be significant considering the precedent of the non-protection given to the unborn and newborn.[66]

Euthanasia: 'Death With Dignity'

The word *euthanasia* becomes a respectable part of our vocabulary and consciousness in a subtle way, via the phrase *death with dignity*. This term was first used, as far as we know, in a book published in Germany in 1920 by Karl Binding and Alfred Hoche: *The Release of the Destruction of Life Devoid of Value*.[67] There is no doubt about what the authors meant by the term. They made it the motto of the movement to legalise the killing of a person who had 'the right to the complete relief of an unbearable life'. *But*, we have to ask, *'unbearable' by whose definition?*

Starving to death a newborn infant with a congenital defect is given the name *passive euthanasia*, and somehow or other seems more acceptable in the minds of those who commit such an atrocity than taking an active step to kill the same child.

On occasion, a physician may decide to withhold extraordinary means in the management of a patient. Is there ever justification for this? First of all, one must define the term *extraordinary* as it refers to medical care. Things which are extraordinary today will not be extraordinary next year, and things which were extraordinary last year are ordinary now. There was a day when the administration of oxygen or the use of intravenous fluids was extraordinary—and so it has been with respirators, pacemakers, and heart-lung machines.

One of us has shown that new borns with severe congenital defects (those incompatible with life) upon whom he operates would *ordinarily* never survive—without extraordinary care. Yet, with that extraordinary care, most live and grow and do well without the continuation of any of the extraordinary measures. As a Christian, does this surgeon have any guidelines? For him it comes down to a matter of stewardship. He is answerable to society for the skills he exercises in the care of his patients. Yet, above that, he believes that he is also answerable to God for the skills he has been given, as well as for the care of the patients God has entrusted to him.

To use non-religious terms, the issue is motivation. It is his motivation or intent that a physician must keep uppermost in his mind. He must constantly be aware of the wonderful uniqueness of human life. Of

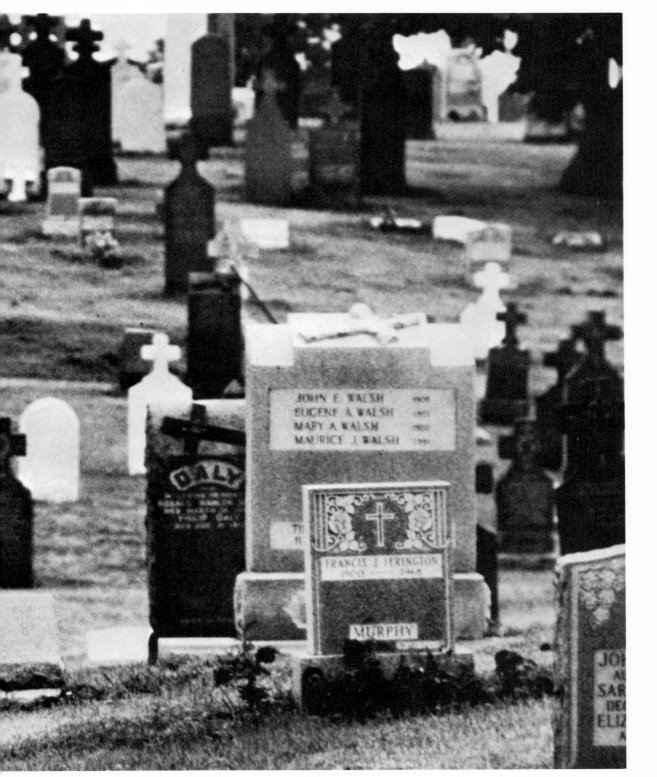

course, at times he faces difficult decisions. Once he believes that the technical gadgetry he is using is merely prolonging the experience of dying, rather than extending life, he can withdraw the extraordinary means and let nature take its course, while keeping the patient as comfortable as possible. This is what physicians have done for years, in the realm of trust between patient and physician or between the patient's family and physician. That is truly 'death with dignity', and no mere manufactured euphemism for euthanasia.

This is not the question being debated today, however. It is not doctors with a biblical view of life who are debating the cases in which death is imminent and inevitable. Rather, it is a whole new breed of medical and paramedical personnel for whom the issues go much further. With these individuals, the intent is to advocate the death of a patient either by directly killing him, or by doing nothing when there could be given help and support that would result in life—even though the circumstances might be difficult. This, ironically, is called 'mercy killing'.

The next step is to destroy human individuals or groups of individuals because they are unwanted, imperfect, or socially embarrassing. Senility, infirmity, retardation, insanity, and incontinence are conditions that come to mind. Obviously, when one comes to that practice, he has gone far beyond even so-called mercy killing. He has entered the same realm as that of Nazi behaviour during World War II. This is essentially what abortionists are doing with unborn babies—because many of these abortionists have no medical concern for whether the unborn babies live. To have those babies is merely inconvenient, uneconomical, or perhaps embarrassing. Carrying this practice to its logical conclusion, we come to death selection and genocide.

Definitions of Death   Some of the problems connected with euthanasia seem most acute with those who seem irreparably injured and are deeply comatose. This is particularly so in the USA where the costs of hospitalisation and the threats of malpractice suits are special pressures. The story of Karen Quinlan is a good case in point. Admitted to hospital after an overdose of drugs and alcohol she never regained consciousness, although she responded to pain, noise and touch. This started legal wrangling by her parents as to whether or not her respirator, which experts said sustained her life, could be disconnected. A lower court declared that would be homicide but a higher court granted permission to disconnect the respirator after which Karen has gone right on living in the same state breathing of her own for three years. We feel that this shows that such matters should be dealt with in the doctor-patient-family context within the strictest medical guidelines and the strictest laws. If this is not done, then given the pressures, a very slippery slope is created.[68]

This was not a case of brain death and is one of very few such instances tried in the United States courts. In general the definition of brain death in the United States is similar to that in Britain, where the Karen Quinlan case would not have arisen, since apart from a free NHS and relative freedom from malpractice suits, her condition did not meet the criteria of 'brain death'. This state involves a situation which can only be followed by irreversible degeneration and only after it has been reached can a respirator be turned off. Merely to be deeply unconscious, like Karen Quinlan, is not enough. The definition of brain death was most recently given in the Memorandum of the Honorary Secretary of the Conference of Medical Royal Colleges and their Faculties in the United Kingdom, 15 January, 1979, and is standard medical practice. Part of the pressure for this strict definition was to allay fears in transplant cases where it was felt that potential donors might not be fully protected. At the moment then, there would appear to be in these cases adequate protection in Britain. Often those involved are young, for example the victims of car accidents. The situation for the old is, however, rather different and the pressures against them are very strong.

Does Anyone Want to Die? The concern about euthanasia and the use of that term in our common vocabulary leads to a degradation of the elderly and, ultimately, to inferior health care for the elderly—as well as encouraging the thought that those who do not want to 'shuffle off' quickly are somehow failing in their contribution to society. Economic considerations then creep in, and old folks are made to feel—in this crazy, schizophrenic society of ours—that they are in some way depriving younger and more deserving people of the medical care that is now being provided them at the same cost. For example, one of the undersecretaries of the United States Department of Health, Education and Welfare suggested in 1977 that the various states that did not enact living-will legislation be penalised by

having withdrawn or curtailed the federal funds that would ordinarily supplement state funds allocated for certain major programmes.[69]

If old people are not yet made to feel that they are depriving the young in Britain, the quality of their lives and the rightness of spending money on them is certainly called into question. In one of its papers, 'Prevention and Health' issued in 1976 by the DHSS it was stated, 'An increasing number of old people inevitably means more cases of disability and more chronic degenerative disease . . . some have questioned the morality of devoting large resources to seeking to extend their lives for what must be relatively short periods of time especially when the quality of such extended life must be open to question.'

Some people not only believe that men and women are only machines, but are acting on the idea that they are only so many digits in one big computer. Feelings that place warmth, love, and compassion— not to mention the beauty and reality of human relationships—above other considerations are often all put aside for the great god of efficiency, especially in the economic realm.

We must be careful not to be misled by the euthanasia forces. They are active as they have never been before. Consider, for example, the following statement under the heading 'The Right To Choose Death' by Professor O. Ruth Russell (*The New York Times*, 14 February, 1972): 'Surely it is time to ask why thousands of dying, incurable and senile persons are being kept alive—sometimes by massive blood transfusions, intravenous feedings, artificial respiration and other heroic measures—who unmistakably want to die.' There are thousands of 'dying, incurable and senile persons' who are alive—not through any extraordinary means, but just plain 'alive'. When Dr Russell says that some 'unmistakably want to die', how does she know that if an appreciable number of these people could be helped to live, they would not be exceedingly grateful for all that had been done to keep them alive? Many of us have heard people say, 'I want to die'—even those without great pain—and find that only a short time later they think completely differently about living.

The advocates of euthanasia for the old are equally strong in Britain and the practical pressures are formidable. In 1967 there was the notorious case at Neasden Hospital as reported in Hugh Trowell's book, *Euthanasia the unfinished debate*. There on a public notice board, was a memorandum headed NTBR. It read: 'The following patients are not to be resuscitated: very elderly, over sixty-five, malignant diseases, chronic chest disease, chronic renal disease.' Fortunately protests led to enquiries and reprimands yet it remains a chilling example. In 1969 there was Lord Raglan's Bill which proposed the use of a 'declaration'. Then in 1976 Baronness Wootton introduced her, 'Incurable Patients Bill' and in 1978 she also proposed the use of 'declarations' (see note 69). Further, in 1976 the Criminal Law Revision Committee in their review of the 'offences against the person' suggested a new offence of 'mercy killing'. This would replace the charge of murder in euthanasia cases and make the offender liable to a period of only two years in prison. One of the criteria suggested was that the killing should be with 'the consent or without the dissent of the deceased'. In virtue of the low sentence, it would appear that the law would almost condone euthanasia as well as open the door to gross abuse — failing to dissent would be costly.

There are put forward so many arguments, using such terms as 'rights' and 'compassion'. These terms are borrowed from a more moral and compassionate age, and their use is purely manipulative and deceptive, because the words can cover the most barbarous ideas with a certain emotional respectability. When these ideas gain acceptance, the results are ugly. The original so-called ideal is soon forgotten and traded in for pragmatic, arbitrary, and economic factors. And the situation becomes more and more brutal and careless of life, people, individuality, and humanness.

When Dr Philip H. Addison was secretary of the Medical Defence Union in London, the British Medical Association Board of Science and Education told the Third World Congress on Medical Law, meeting in Ghent, Belgium, that dying patients seldom ask for euthanasia. Those knowing that they are dying usually welcome any prolongation of life. The report went on to say that the majority of deaths in the present day can be made peaceful, whatever the nature and character of the preceding illness. It has been said that modern medicine can now overcome pain without shortening life. If this is really so, the case for legalising euthanasia is considerably weakened.[71]

Thus we find that the pragmatic arguments for euthanasia are often based on a world view which holds a low opinion of life, rather than being grounded on facts. Even if some token willingness on the part of the prospective euthanasia victim is prescribed as a criterion — in this day of manipulation and the vast potential for the like-minded media to put pressure on people — what real choice will the potential victim have, especially if he or she is ill and in pain?

Another argument for euthanasia is given by Joseph Fletcher, the populariser of 'situational ethics', in his 1973 discussion of death with dignity in the *American Journal of Nursing*:

> It is ridiculous to give ethical approval to the positive ending of sub-human life in utero as we do in therapeutic abortions for reasons of mercy and compassion but refuse to approve of positively ending a subhuman life in extremis. If we are morally obliged to put an end to a pregnancy when an amniocentesis reveals a terribly defective fetus, we are equally obliged to put an end to a patient's hopeless misery when a brain scan reveals that a patient with cancer has advanced brain metastases.[72]

Fletcher declares without discussion that ethical approval has been given to ending the lives of babies out of 'compassion'. Then he puts that very questionable 'ethical approval' in the form of an obligation and says that because we are obliged to do that, we are also morally obliged to put an end to the life of a patient who has cancer with advanced brain metastases. To argue otherwise, he says, is ridiculous.[73]

Thus, once again, the most deplorable sentiments are presented in the guise of some humanitarian gesture. One is reminded of the slave-holders who devoutly espoused the theory that slavery was really for the good of the black man and that in the end he would be thankful for the opportunity to share the white man's culture, even from the distance of the garden shed! The Nazis also argued that their victims were being sacrificed for the high end of the general good of society. We look upon such people as Joseph Fletcher as great meddlers in human lives. They are also meddlers in God's business.

Reports in the Press   With arbitrary abortion already declared legal, the speed with which the other forms of killing are being accepted must take even their advocates by surprise. The medical and scientific professions are not the only culprits. Popular apathy in general and small negatively active groups in particular have contributed much to the demise of the unique worth of humanity. Those in government as well as the press have shut their eyes or simply drifted along, having no firm moral base themselves. But the main culprit is the humanistic consensus, which declares man to be a machine and demotes his unique worth in his own eyes.

Let us examine a few of the discussions of euthanasia in the media. The Associated Press reports: DEBATE RAGES IN ENGLAND 'DEATH PILL FOR AGED'. A British doctor, John Goundry, says that a 'death pill' will be available and perhaps obligatory by the end of the century. He says that doctors should be able to give a 'demise pill' to old people if they ask for it. He also says, 'In the end I can see the state taking over and insisting on euthanasia.'[74]

David Hobman, director of Age Concern in England, has said that the suggestion of a death pill seems to him totally inconsistent with the Hippocratic Oath. This oath has already been changed, as we have seen in some places in the USA, and as there is increasing loss of humanness we can expect to see it changed even more radically.

Swedish public-health physician Ragnar Toss wants to open a suicide clinic for the more than two thousand Swedes who kill themselves each year— 'not to treat them but to help them do it'. Dr Toss, writing in the respected *Swedish Medical Journal* of August 1977, says that this suggestion is related to the choice that women now have about abortions.

So you see, this is not just theory for the future. As people are confronted with the flow of ideas from arbitrary abortion to infanticide to euthanasia, 'death by someone's choice' becomes increasingly thinkable. The case of a woman in Britain is an illustration of the drift to the thinkableness of abortion/infanticide/euthanasia—all part of the natural trend toward the loss of humanness. Yolande McShane urged her mother in a nursing home to take an overdose of sleeping pills that she had brought her. The mother, showing attitudes rooted in Christianity, resisted: 'A dog hasn't got a soul. I'm so afraid of being punished after. It's a mortal sin.' The daughter gave the answer which the erosion of the Christian base and the consequent loss of humanness would naturally produce: 'People are doing it left, right and centre. It's not a sin anymore—it's nothing nowadays.'[75]

Of course, if a human being is *not* made in the image of God, why shouldn't the malformed young and the elderly be put out of the way for the good of society—once society and the courts separate life and personhood? 'Right' or 'wrong' is then only a matter of what the majority thinks at that given moment, or what the courts judge is for the benefit of society at that moment. The next turn of the screw comes quickly, when a noble-sounding phrase like 'the good of society' is replaced by cold, hard economics. Yolande McShane's case is apt in this regard. She was in debt and, had her attempt at euthanasia been successful, would have inherited a considerable sum from her mother's will.

According to a news report, the doctor in England who advocated the 'death pill'—and said that he could see the state's insisting on euthanasia— also built his argument on economics. '[Dr John] Goundry said hundreds of British hospitals have been taken over to house the aged sick and that hotels once serving the rich now house the old. The economics are devastating.'[76]

If you say that this is just the idea of one man, think again. What is the new element in the United States' debate regarding abortion? It is sheer economics. *A Newsweek* article was entitled 'Abortion: Who Pays?' This article dealt with a 20 June, 1977, Supreme Court ruling on abortion funding. With the Christian consensus on abortion thrown out, the argument slides into the issue of which will cost society more—free abortions or caring for the babies who are born. *Newsweek* reports: 'According to U.S. Department of Health, Education and Welfare estimates, the price of a Medicaid abortion in the first trimester is $150, while the first year cost to taxpayers of each unwanted child is $2,200.'[77] This figure, of course, fails to take into consideration the fact that many children who are unwanted in the first months of pregnancy are wanted and loved after they are born, and thus do not become an economic burden on society. In the United States Justice Lewis Powell wrote one of the majority opinions on the 1977 Supreme Court ruling that stated that the individual states may not ban abortions, but that they do not necessarily have to pay for them. Powell also added a footnote: 'Legitimate demographic concerns . . . could constitute a substantial reason for departure from a position of neutrality between abortion and childbirth.' These 'legitimate demographic concerns' mean that the government could give free abortions in one place and deny them in another, in order to increase population in the one location, while holding it down in the other.

Or it could mean that the government could give free abortions to one class of people or one race and deny it to another, in order to change the mix of the population. How could anyone read this footnote by a Supreme Court Justice and not be startled and incensed at the doors it opens for government manipulation and for a further thrust of dehumanisation? Here again, with morals in law gone, we are left with the harsh and ugly linkage of economics and manipulation.

The Holocaust   Does all this still seem an extreme projection? The fork is three-pronged: first, arbitrary sociological law by the courts and legislators; second, the changed attitude of the medical profession; third, the general apathy and selfishness of the population, which in the name of 'rights' grasps at a more and more hedonistic life-style.

Recent history has something to teach us about where we are. We think historians are becoming aware that a great number of the abnormal behaviour patterns of man were concentrated in the Nazi experience. Richard L. Rubenstein, in his book *The Cunning of History: Mass Death and the American Future*, speaks of the Holocaust in this way:

> The destruction process required the cooperation of every sector of German society. The bureaucrats drew the definitions and decrees, the churches gave evidence of Aryan descent, the postal authorities carried the messages of definition, expropriation, denaturalisation and deportation. A place [of execution was] made available to the Gestapo and the SS by the Wehrmacht. To repeat, the operation required and received the participation of every major social and political and religious institution of the German Reich.[78]

The important thing to remember is that the medical profession took a leading part in the planning of abortion and euthanasia. It seems likely that had it not been for the example and active role played by German physicians in the practice of euthanasia, Hitler's progress in the extermination programmes would have been slowed if not stopped. The medical profession went along with Nazism in discouragingly large numbers. More than a few participated in the terror, genocide, extermination programmes, and active and barbaric experimentation on the unfortunate minorities in the Nazi grip.[79]

In 1946 and 1947, Leo Alexander, a Boston psychiatrist, was consultant to the United States Secretary of War and on duty with the office of Chief of Counsel for War Crimes in Nuremberg. In a remarkable paper, 'Medical Science Under Dictatorship', he outlined the problem. His concerns were vital when he first wrote about them in this country in 1949; they are of even greater concern to us today. Here are some of the highlights of Dr Alexander's presentation:

> Irrespective of other ideological trappings, the guiding philosophic principle of recent dictatorships, including that of the Nazis, has been Hegelian in that what has been considered 'rational utility' and corresponding doctrine and planning has replaced moral, ethical and religious values. . . .
>
> Medical science in Nazi Germany collaborated with this Hegelian trend particularly in the following enterprises: the mass extermination of the chronically sick in the interest of saving 'useless' expenses to the community as a whole; the mass extermination of those considered socially disturbing or racially and ideologically unwanted; the individual, inconspicuous extermination of those considered disloyal within the ruling group; and the ruthless use of 'human experimental material' for medico-military research. . . .
>
> It started with the acceptance of the attitude basic in the euthanasia

movement, that there is such a thing as life not worthy to be lived. . . .

[Before Hitler came to power in 1933] a propaganda barrage was directed against the traditional, compassionate, nineteenth-century attitudes towards the chronically ill, and for the adoption of a utilitarian, Hegelian point of view. Sterilisation and euthanasia of persons with chronic mental illnesses was discussed at a meeting of Bavarian psychiatrists in 1931.[80]

Many people, including some in the medical profession, had accepted these principles before Hitler came on the scene.

Alexander says that Hitler exterminated 275,000 people 'in these killing centres'. Then he adds that those so killed were to be only 'the entering wedge for extermination. . . . The methods used and the personnel trained in the killing centres for the chronically sick became the nucleus of much larger centres in the East, where the plan was to kill all Jews and Poles and to cut down the Russian population by 30,000,000.' The first to be killed were the aged, the infirm, the senile and mentally retarded, and defective children. Eventually, as World War II approached, the doomed undesirables included epileptics, World War I amputees, children with badly modelled ears and even bed wetters.

Physicians took part in this planning on matters of life and death to save society's money. Adults were propagandised, one outstanding example being a film called *I Accuse*, which dealt with euthanasia. Commenting on this, Alexander reported:

This film depicts the life history of a woman suffering from multiple sclerosis. In it her husband, a doctor, finally kills her to the accompaniment of soft piano music rendered by a sympathetic colleague in an adjoining room. Acceptance of this ideology was implanted even in the children. A widely-used high school mathematics text, *Mathematics in the Service of Political Education*, Second Edition 1935, Third Edition 1936 . . . includes problems stated in distorted terms of the cost of caring for and rehabilitating the chronically sick and crippled. One of the problems asked, for instance, is how many new housing units could be built and how many marriage-allowance loans could be given to newly-wed couples for the amount of money it cost the state to care for 'the crippled and the insane'.[78]

The second and most widely used edition of this textbook was issued in 1935, soon after Hitler came to power. Alexander continues:

The first direct order for euthanasia was issued by Hitler on 1 September, 1939. . . . All state institutions were required to report on patients who had been ill for five years or more or who were unable to work, by filling out questionnaires giving name, race, marital status, nationality, next of kin, whether regularly visited and by whom, who bore the financial responsibility and so forth. The decision regarding which patients should be killed was made entirely on the basis of this brief information by expert consultants, most of whom were professors of psychiatry in the key universities. These consultants never saw the patients themselves.[82]

There was an organisation specifically for the killing of children, which was known by the euphemistic name of Realm's Committee for Scientific Approach to Severe Illness Due to Heredity and Constitution. Transportation of the patients to killing centres was carried out by The Charitable Transport Company for the Sick. In addition, Alexander notes that The Charitable Foundation for Institutional Care was 'in charge of collecting the cost of the killings from the relatives without, however, informing them what the charges were for; in the death certificates the cause of death was falsified'.

Alexander, under the heading 'The Early Change in Medical Attitudes', gives his warning. It all started with the acceptance of the attitude that there is such a thing as a life not worthy to be lived. That is exactly what is being accepted today in the abortion, infanticide, and euthanasia movements.

Continuing his warning, Alexander adds: 'But it is important to realise that the infinitely small wedged-in lever from which all this entire trend of mind received its impetus was the attitude towards the non-rehabilitable sick.'

This attitude is very much with us today. The 'small wedged-in lever' is opening doors to what would have been inconceivable before.[83] Alexander is quite correct in adding: 'It is therefore this subtle shift in emphasis of the physicians' attitude that one must thoroughly investigate.'

In our present climate, resulting from the humanistic base of society (with its attitude of all things being relative), it is instructive to consider how some of today's university students regard those days of Nazi rule. Dr Richard M. Hunt, associate dean of Harvard University's Graduate School of Arts and Science, says:

> I have taught courses at Harvard for many years. I used to teach these courses from a straight historical perspective. Recently, I tried a new approach and I call the course, 'Moral Dilemma in a Repressive Society: Nazi Germany'. Through case studies of issues and personalities I try to present the Nazi phenomenon from the inside, so to speak, from the experience and testimony of those who lived through the period as victims, victimisers, bystanders, true believers, and members of the resistance.

To make a long story short, I was greatly surprised with the reaction of the students. I had asked for personal interpretations of moral relevant dilemmas. In their end of term papers, it was not a matter of indifference to Nazi oppressions that I found. Nobody attempted to minimise or explain Nazi excesses.

Rather what struck me most forcibly were the depressing fatalistic conclusions about major moral dilemmas facing the German people of that particular place and time in history.

Comments like these were frequent. 'And with the ever present threat of Gestapo terror, who would dare to speak out and resist? Would you? Would I? Probably not!'

Most disturbing of all to me was the end of the line of such arguments. This point was reached by a few students who seemed somehow to realise the moral peril of such exculpatory judgments. Their way out was to lessen the responsibility of any individual person by dispersing the guilt among all.

Clearly some trends of our times seemed to be running towards a no-fault, that is, a guilt-free society. One might say the virtues of responsible choice, paying the penalty, taking the consequences, all appear at low ebb today.

Next time I teach this course, I hope to stress more strongly my own belief in the contingencies, the open-endedness of history. Somehow, I have got to convey the meaning of moral decisions and their relation to significant outcomes. Most important, I want to point out that single acts of individuals and strong stands of institutions at an early date do make a difference in the long run. I am through with teaching no-fault history.[84]

The attitudes expressed by Dr Hunt's students become even more alarming when one stops to think that it is difficult to understand what is going on in one's own period of time with the same depth of perception that one has while looking back on history — as these students can do as they study Nazi Germany.

The euthanasia movement — that term is used in the broadest possible sense — is with us today in great strength and with great persuasive power. Many well-meaning people are attracted to what might seem to be the beneficial aspects of some sort of euthanasia programme, because they think they can be free of the guilt of responsibility. Yet undoubtedly many have not thought about where this may lead us.

Do not dismiss contemptuously our concern about the wedge principle. Historians and jurists are well aware of what we say. The first step is followed by the second. It is easy to see that if the first step is immoral, whatever follows it must be immoral. But even if the first step is moral, it does not necessarily follow that the second step will also be moral. We have to be consciously aware with each step as to what the next step is *likely* to be.

Semantic legerdemain can prepare us for accepting a horror. When the World Conference on Population Control in 1974 can refer to abortion as 'a retrospective method of fertility control', we know that the euphemisms for infanticide and euthanasia can be many indeed![85] In Britain, some call starving a child with spina bifida (cleft spine) putting it on a 'low calorie diet'!

Language itself is a subtle indicator and a powerful tool. Think of the deliberate changes in language that have been used to soften the stark impact of what is actually happening. Abortion is merely the 'removal of fetal tissue', or 'discontinuing' or 'termination' of pregnancy. Childless couples are now 'child free', a term that subtly establishes children as an unwanted burden. Language has power. The language we use actually forms the concepts we have and the results these concepts produce. Think of the Nazi use of the name *The Charitable Transport Company for the Sick* for the agency conveying people to the killing centres. But let us not be naive. Exactly the same language power is being used when the unborn baby is called 'fetal tissue'.[86]

We view what we are experiencing now as a critical situation which can accelerate month by month until the downhill momentum cannot be arrested. Times of monstrous inhumanity do not come about all at once; they are slipped into gradually. Often those who use certain emotional phrases or high-sounding moral tones about 'freedom of the individual' and appeal to 'rights' do not even know what they are starting. They see only some isolated condition they want to accomplish, but have not considered soberly the overall direction in which things are moving. At some later point they want to go backwards. But then it is too late. Mankind's selfishness and greed can be counted on to widen every breach, exploiting each to the fullest for selfish purposes.

Principal Concerns   Our concerns centre around several aspects of this issue. First of all, we must say that we are proponents of the sanctity of human life—*all* human life—born and unborn; old and young; black, white, brown, and yellow. We fear the attitude of the medical profession in sanctioning abortion and in moving inexorably down the road from abortion to infanticide and finally further on to what might be unthinkable today but acceptable in a very few years—such as a widespread euthanasia programme.

We are concerned that there is not more protest, outcry, or activism in regard to these issues of life and death. We can even recognise that there are people who are led to starve children to death, because they think they are doing something helpful for society. Lacking an absolute ethical standard, they have only the concept of what they think is beneficial for society to guide them. But we cannot understand why other people, those with a moral base—and we know there are many of them—do not cry out. We are concerned about this because, when the first German aged, infirm, and retarded were killed in gas chambers, there was likewise no perceptible outcry from the medical profession or from an apathetic population. It was not far from there to Auschwitz. Surely those who call themselves Christians, having a moral base, should make these things a principal issue and be willing, even at the risk of personal sacrifice, to strive privately and publicly for the dignity and sanctity of the individual.

Although at the moment the discussion is being conducted chiefly in terms of morals and ethics, another of our concerns is: What is going to happen with the addition of the economic factor? If you are a social burden *and* an economic burden, no matter how precious life might be to you, there will be little chance of your surviving.

Let it never be said by historians in the latter days of this century that—after abortion was legalised—there was no outcry from the medical profession and no outcry from many outside this profession. Let it never be said that the extermination programme for various categories of citizens could never have come about if physicians had stood for the moral integrity that recognises the worth of every human life. And above everything else, let it never be said that there was no outcry from Christians! All Christians know why people are different and have value as unique individuals—sick or well, young or old. People are unique because they are made in the image of God.

What *has* happened to the human race? Why are we afraid of being people, of being human? Of enjoying the greatest blessings that life can bring—being alive and being people of love, tenderness, gentleness, care, and concern?

It is vital that we put first *not* economics or efficiency charts and plans, but being *people*—real flesh and blood people. We are not to be materialistic robots who think and act like machines and will even kill to maintain their life-styles. This attitude is as stupid as it is wrong. It is stupid because such people have traded in their beautiful humanity for sawdust and ashes—for broken homes, for abortions, for starved children, and for old people locked away and even destroyed. Being a person has infinitely greater rewards for those who will consciously concentrate on being people—warm and loving people—rather than on their personal peace and affluence.

We challenge you to be a person in this impersonal age. Be human in this inhuman age. Put the people in your life first—whether perfect or marred. This is your once-in-a-lifetime chance of being 'people with people'. Come to your senses. You and those around you *are* people, made in their image of the personal God who created all people in His image.

We have seen how a people's world view affects how its individuals look at themselves and others. Your basic world view matters. It will have enormous results. A mild revulsion at people's inhumanity to one another will not change anything. Outward actions against such horrors must begin with the inward action of each individual's evaluating the basis for his standards and then assessing the application of those standards to the world around him.

In Old Testament days, God expressed special abhorrence for the Canaanite practice of infant sacrifice. With heathenism, this was not confined to the Canaanites. For example, the ancient Europeans also offered up their offspring to the gods. These people killed their offspring *in order to purchase from the gods, they hoped, their own personal peace and affluence.*

Today, indiscriminate abortion, infanticide, and euthanasia are also performed *for the personal peace and affluence of individuals.* People who destroy their own children and others', so that they can maintain their life-styles, are also sacrificing to the gods—the gods of a materialistic world view and practice, and the god of the 'self' as the egotistic centre and measure of all things.

In Nazi-occupied Holland, the Dutch people often distinguished themselves by the great personal sacrifices they made in defending, hiding, protecting, and *protesting for* their fellow citizens who were Jewish. Given a decree by the Nazis that they were to perform for Hitler as the German medical profession had done, Dutch physicians refused. As a result, the Dutch medical profession has no blot on its record of performance as physician-stewards. What would have happened if the *German* physicians had refused?

A resistance leaflet circulated by the underground at that time exhorted:

Protest against the detestable persecution of Jews!!! Organise self-defence in the factories and districts!!! Solidarity with the hard-hit Jewish section of

the working people!!!
Snatch the Jewish children from Nazi violence—take them into your family!!!
Strike!!! Strike!!! Strike!!!
Solidarity!!! Courage!!!
Fight proudly for the liberation of our country!!!

The Dutch resistance movement, armed only with great courage and a few typewriters, stood against the evil of its day. Let those of us who share a high view of people use wisely these days when we have influence and the freedom to strike a great blow for the humanity, dignity, and sanctity of individuals.

Alternatives   Christians and others who wish to see an end to inhumanities, in compassion and love must offer alternative solutions to the problems. What we are about to suggest does not by any means exhaust the inventory of practical proposals we must put forward—and for which we must sacrifice our own personal peace and affluence. Such a list would be impossible to complete, so we will just give examples.

Churches and other groups opposed to abortion must be prepared to extend practical help to both the unmarried woman who is pregnant and the married woman who may be faced with the question of abortion. Merely to say to either one, 'You must not have an abortion'—without being ready to involve ourselves in the problem—is another way of being inhuman.

The unmarried woman may need a place to stay. Time should be taken to tell her about the many couples who cannot have babies and who long to have a child to adopt. She will certainly need counsel about how to care for her child if she decides to keep the baby. Congenial accommodation should be available for unmarried women awaiting the birth of a baby, and each person who does not believe that abortion is right should personally be prepared to offer hospitality, financial aid, or other assistance.

Have you ever welcomed an unmarried mother in your home for the months before her baby was born? Are there babies now growing happily in homes that adopted them, or living with their mothers who have a changed outlook on life and death because of the months spent in your home? Hospitality, for a great number of us, should include some period of time in our lives when we care for a pregnant woman in her waiting months.

L'Abri has become known as an example of Christians practising community over a wide spectrum of life—intellectually and practically. In its twenty-five-year history, there has been a succession of unmarried mothers cared for, encouraged, and helped in a variety of ways. Because it has been a part of L'Abri life to make people in need a part of the family, there has been participation in some eager moments at the hospital, when a new baby is welcomed into the world as a wanted human being. L'Abri is not a 'work for unmarried mothers', but in all its branches a community of open homes—limited, of course, in space and in the possibility of giving personal attention. Yet L'Abri workers have been able to help a number of women who have chosen not to abort their babies.

For married women facing the problems that prompt them to consider abortion, support from a church can be a critical factor. If a mother must work, why shouldn't the church provide for her child's care? Surely such an arrangement could be worked out as an expression of the community which the church is supposed to be. The church might provide a child-care centre on its own premises (too many of our churches are only one-purpose buildings) or church members might take a child into their own families for a certain number of hours each week.

We are not trying to propose a universal formula, but to emphasise that saying that abortion is wrong immediately confronts us with a challenge to be willing to share in the consequences which our advice brings. For Christians who adhere to the truth of the Bible, the importance of doing what it teaches is imperative. We are to be compassionate about people's physical needs.

The same principle can be applied to infanticide. If a family resists letting a handicapped child die after birth, the church cannot just walk away from the family or the child. From the earliest days of the church, a part of its life and testimony has always been that its members care for one another in material ways as well as otherwise. Many of the best 'homes for the handicapped' had Christian beginnings. But we should also consider the practical possibility of our church's setting up a plan (to be overseen by some loving person) which schedules different church members to help in the home of a handicapped person for definite periods during the week, sharing in the hard work of this type of care.

In one of the churches Francis Schaeffer pastored in the United States, there were a mongoloid child and a mentally retarded youngster. The parents, far from wealthy, had no hope of providing special education for their children. Public services were poor. He began to spend a certain number of hours each week with the two children together. The leap forward in their achievements was a thing of joy for the whole congregation. In all his Christian work, Francis Schaeffer has never had a more satisfying ministry. Similarly, C. Everett Koop has placed many pregnant girls with Christian families in Pennsylvania. During this sheltering, ruptured father-daughter relationships have been healed, girls have become Christians, and unwanted babies have eventually brought joy to childless couples.

Again, we are offering no universal formula. The concept of being involved in hard situations and the practical outworking of that concept are the important things. It takes effort, concern, work, and often money. Christian love and humanness mean not only saying, 'Infanticide is wrong'. They also mean giving up part of our own personal peace and affluence to share in the results that morally correct decisions produce. That means not allowing the state to take all the responsibility. As Christians, we cannot slough off the whole burden on the state. In many cases, this means finding ourselves caring for handicapped people within the totality of the Christian community. Those in groups which are not Christian must likewise find ways of being human in the years following the birth of a handicapped child.

It is worth digressing here to insist that the positive aspects of the women's rights movement can be achieved without including abortion on the agenda. The linking of the women's movement with abortion is a deliberate strategem used by some to make this practice acceptable. This uses the women's rights movement as a vehicle to which abortion has no intrinsic relationship. Unhappily, at times the leadership of this movement has built an anti-human stance into its platform in regard to abortion-on-demand. This is hardly liberation, since—carried to its logical extreme—this arbitrary and inhuman stance can only lead to a further enslavement of women and of everyone else as well. Women cannot 'liberate' themselves by aborting their babies or killing their infants. The rights of women are fundamentally rooted in the biblical view of the value of each individual human being and the sacredness of human life.

Moral obligations fall to those who stand by the principle that there is no such thing as a life not worthy to be lived. We also have a responsibility toward people with terminal illnesses and toward the dying aged. St Joseph's Hospice in London and The Hospice Home Care Team of New Haven, Connecticut USA (both institutions that had Christian beginnings) can show us some ways of dying that can affirm and enhance life. We do not know the New Haven work personally, but are familiar with a representative hospice through a friend who spent a certain number of hours there each week—reading, talking, speaking of Christian beliefs, and just *being* with the dying patients. At most such hospices, three things are done. First, all possible medical knowledge is employed to keep pain under control. Second, patients are visited, read to, and kept in almost constant contact with a loving human being, so that they are not alone and deserted in that time when, of all times, being human means not being deserted. Third, families are treated as units; the family and its needs and the individual in his need are kept together as a human unit. These hospices are not in the business of dying, but of *living* right up to the end. Is this not the natural and rightful outflow of what we Christians believe about the abnormality of death and about the future resurrection victory we will experience through Christ?

If we oppose euthanasia, we must also share the weight of caring for lonely or incapacitated older people who are not terminally ill. One of us has personal knowledge about sharing such a burden. Francis Schaeffer's mother lived in his home in Switzerland for the last seven years of her life. At first she could come down to meals, go out for rides in the mountains, attend church, and so on. Gradually this changed, and she needed constant care, especially after breaking her hip. All this was taking place in the midst of the pressures at L'Abri. Students and others took turns playing draughts with her, reading to her, talking with her, and just being with her. The family could not have done this alone—it would have been a crushing strain upon them as well as upon the work. But in the united community, not only was she well cared for, but the caring was a thing of beauty. We are sure that some of those who gave of themselves in this way are still seeing their lives enhanced by this experience, as they are scattered over the face of the earth.

Our concern is more than *not killing* the elderly and the ill. *It is giving them real life.* Of course, there must be some facilities that care for the terminally ill. In fact, Christians and others should see to it that places like St Joseph's become models for many more such hospices. But, as long as possible and in spite of smaller apartments and the anti-family influences of our age, the old, infirm, and dying should be given the chance to be really alive in the midst of the whole spectrum of life. This includes being in relationship with the family and sharing in a Christian community. Christian doctors and others of the medical profession who stand for human life can make a special contribution in this whole area, but it is not their responsibility alone (and certainly not the responsibility

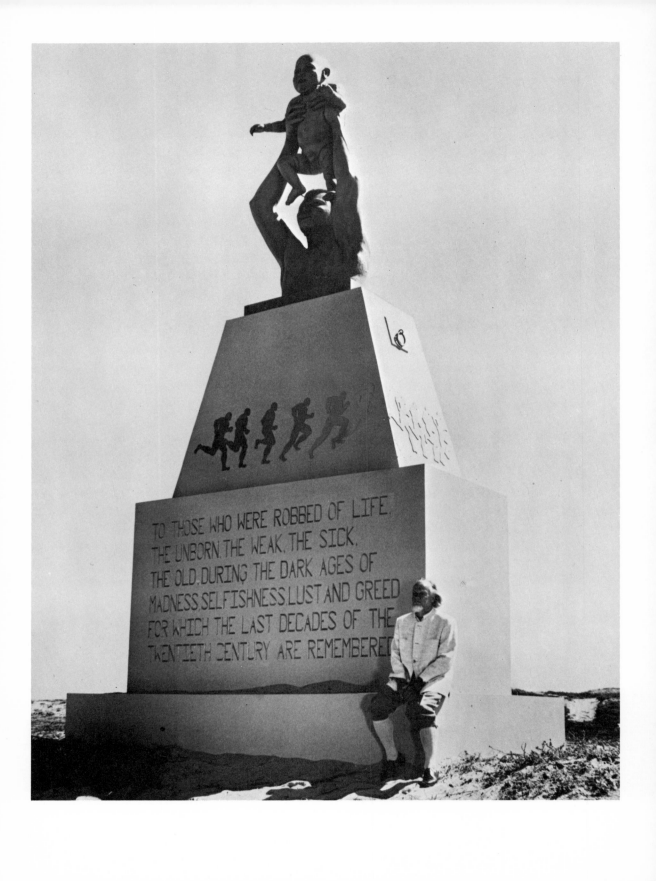

TO THOSE WHO WERE ROBBED OF LIFE,
THE UNBORN, THE WEAK, THE SICK,
THE OLD, DURING THE DARK AGES OF
MADNESS, SELFISHNESS, LUST AND GREED
FOR WHICH THE LAST DECADES OF THE
TWENTIETH CENTURY ARE REMEMBERED

of the state alone).[87] It becomes *our* responsibility when we quite properly say, 'Euthanasia is wrong.'

We must be realistic. The alternatives we have discussed will demand a high price. They will cost each of us some of our personal peace and affluence. But we must do them—first of all, because they are right. This is taught in the whole of the Bible and especially in the teachings of Christ. And, second, it will be a sharing of the burdens of life, and one day it will be *our* turn to be helped—and we will be glad when we are.

The question is not the worth of the imperfect infant, the retarded child, the defective adult, and the aging individual with physical and mental signs of the aging process. The question is this: Are we worthy enough to extend ourselves to meet their needs?

If we in the second half of the twentieth century wish to be remembered well, we need to do something to stop all the evils we have been speaking about. If we sit back and do nothing, our mere passivity and apathy will lead to actively evil results by removing resistance to those who *are* active and non-apathetic. That so many are doing so little should encourage more than a mild commitment to some vague idea of doing the 'right' thing, as opposed to the 'wrong' thing. As people, we are only as good as our deep inner principles; we are only as good as our world view.

In the chapters that follow, we will examine what to us is the ultimate basis for life, ethics, and an active moral stand against evil. We will look at biblical Christianity and the Bible itself. For, without a firm set of principles, without a firm world view, there cannot and will not be any firm and continued resistance to evil—or even any cohesive unity to our own lives and private moral decisions.

4
The Basis for Human Dignity

So far in this book we have been considering an evil as great as any practised in human history. Our society has put to death its own offspring, millions upon millions of them. Our society has justified taking their lives, even claiming it a virtue to do so. It has been said this is a new step in our progress toward a liberated humanity.

Such a situation has not come out of a vacuum. Each of us has an overall way of looking at the world, which influences what we do day by day. This is what we call a 'world view'. And all of us have a world view, whether we realise it or not. We act in accordance with our world view, and our world view rests on what to us is the ultimate truth.

Materialistic
Humanism:
The World View
of Our Age

What has produced the inhumanity we have been considering in the previous chapters is that society in the West has adopted a world view which says that all reality is made up only of matter. This view is sometimes referred to as philosophic materialism, because it holds that only *matter* exists; sometimes it is called naturalism, because it says that no supernatural exists. Humanism, which begins from man alone and makes man the measure of all things, usually is materialistic in its philosophy. Whatever the label, this is the underlying world view of our society today. In this view the universe did not get here because it was created by a 'supernatural' God. Rather, the universe has existed forever in some form, and its present form just happened as a result of chance events way back in time.

Society in the West has largely rested on the base that God exists and that the Bible is true. In all sorts of ways this view affected the society. The materialistic or naturalistic or humanistic world view almost always takes a superior attitude toward Christianity. Those who hold such a view have argued that Christianity is unscientific, that it cannot be proved, that it belongs simply to the realm of 'faith'. Christianity, they say, rests only on faith, while humanism rests on facts.

Professor Edmund R. Leach of Cambridge University expresses this view clearly:

> Our idea of God is a product of history. What I now believe about the supernatural is derived from what I was taught by my parents, and what they taught me was derived from what they were taught, and so on. But such beliefs are justified by faith alone, never by reason, and the true believer is expected to go on reaffirming his faith in the same verbal formula even if the passage of history and the growth of scientific knowledge should have turned the words into plain nonsense.[88]

So some humanists act as if they have a great advantage over Christians. They act as if the advance of science and technology and a better understanding of history (through such concepts as the evolutionary theory) have all made the idea of God and Creation quite ridiculous.

This superior attitude, however, is strange because one of the most striking developments in the last half-century is the growth of a profound pessimism among both well-educated and less-educated people. The thinkers in our society have been admitting for a long time that they have no final answers at all.

Take Woody Allen, for example. Most people know him as a comedian, but he has thought through where mankind stands after the 'religious answers' have been abandoned. In an article in *Esquire* (May 1977), he says that man is left with:

> . . . alienation, loneliness [and] emptiness verging on madness. . . . The fundamental thing behind *all* motivation and *all* activity is the constant

struggle against annihilation and against death. It's absolutely stupefying in its terror, and it renders anyone's accomplishments meaningless. As Camus wrote, it's not only that *he* (the individual) dies, or that *man* (as a whole) dies, but that you struggle to do a work of art that will last and then you realise that *the universe itself* is not going to exist after a period of time. Until those issues are resolved within each person—religiously or psychologically or existentially—the social and political issues will never be resolved, except in a slapdash way.

Allen sums up his view in his film *Annie Hall* with these words: 'Life is divided into the horrible and the miserable.'

Many would like to dismiss this sort of statement as coming from one who is merely a pessimist by temperament, one who sees life without the benefit of a sense of humour. Woody Allen does not allow us that luxury. He speaks as a human being who has simply looked life in the face and has the courage to say what he sees. If there is no personal God, nothing beyond what our eyes can see and our hands can touch, then Woody Allen is right: Life is both meaningless and terrifying. As the famous artist Paul Gauguin wrote on his last painting shortly before he tried to commit suicide: 'Whence come we? What are we? Whither do we go?' The answers are *nowhere, nothing,* and *nowhere.* The humanist H. J. Blackham has expressed this with a dramatic illustration:

> On humanist assumptions, life leads to nothing, and every pretence that it does not is a deceit. If there is a bridge over a gorge which spans only half the distance and ends in mid-air, and if the bridge is crowded with human beings pressing on, one after the other they fall into the abyss. The bridge leads nowhere, and those who are pressing forward to cross it are going nowhere. . . . It does not matter where they think they are going, what preparations for the journey they may have made, how much they may be enjoying it all. The objection merely points out objectively that such a situation is a model of futility.[89]

One does not have to be highly educated to understand this. It follows directly from the starting point of the humanists' position, namely, that everything is just matter. That is, that which has existed forever and ever is only some form of matter or energy, and everything in our world now is this and only this in a more or less complex form. Thus, Jacob Bronowski says in *The Identity of Man* (1965): 'Man is a part of nature, in the same sense that a stone is, or a cactus, or a camel.' In this view, men and women are by chance more complex, but not unique.

Within this world view there is no room for believing that a human being has any final distinct value above that of an animal or of non-living matter. People are merely a different arrangement of molecules. There are two points, therefore, that need to be made about the humanist world view. First, the superior attitude toward Christianity—as if Christianity had all the problems and humanism had all the answers—is quite unjustified. The humanists of the Enlightenment two centuries ago *thought* they were going to find all the answers, but as time has passed, this optimistic hope has been proved wrong. It is their own descendants, those who share their materialistic world view, who have been saying louder and louder as the years have passed, 'There are no final answers.'

Second, this humanist world view has also brought us to the present devaluation of human life—not technology and not overcrowding, although these have played a part. And this same world view has given us no limits to prevent us from sliding into an even worse devaluation of human life in the future.

So it is naïve and irresponsible to imagine that this world view will *reverse* the direction in the future. A well-meaning commitment to 'do what is right' will not be sufficient. Without a firm set of principles that flows out of a world view that gives an adequate reason for a unique value to all human life, there cannot be and will not be any substantial resistance to the present evil brought on by the low view of human life we have been considering in previous chapters. It was the materialistic world view that brought in the inhumanity; it must be a different world view that drives it out!

An emotional uneasiness about abortion, infanticide, euthanasia, and the abuse of genetic knowledge is not enough. To stand against the present devaluation of human life, a significant percentage of people within our society must adopt and live by a world view which not only hopes or intends to give a basis for human dignity but which really does. The radical movements of the sixties were right to hope for a better world; they were right to protest against the shallowness and falseness of our plastic society. But their radicalness lasted only during the life span of the adolescence of their members. Although these movements claimed to be radical, they lacked a sufficient root. Their world view was incapable of giving life to the aspirations of its adherents. Why? Because it, too—like the society they were condemning—had no sufficient base. So protests are not enough. Having the right ideals is not enough. Even those with a very short memory, those who can look back only to the sixties can see that there must be more than that. A truly radical alternative has to be found.

But where? And how?

The Search for an Adequate World View: A Question of Method

Before we consider various possibilities, we must settle the question of method. What is it we are expecting our 'answer' to answer?

There are a number of things we could consider, but at this point we want to concentrate on just two. The first is what we will call 'the universe and its form', and the second is 'the mannishness of man'. The first draws attention to the fact that the universe around us is like an amazing jigsaw puzzle. We see many details, and we want to know how they fit together. That is what science is all about. Scientists look at the details and try to find out how they all cohere. So the first question that has to be answered is: How did the universe get this way? How did it get this *form*, this pattern, this jigsaw-like quality it now has?

Second, 'the mannishness of man' draws attention to the fact that human beings are different from all other things in the world. Think, for example, of creativity. People in all cultures of all ages have created many kinds of things, from 'High Art' to flower arrangements, from silver ornaments to high-technology supersonic aircraft. This is in contrast to the animals about us. People also fear death, and they have the aspiration to truly choose. Incidentally, even those who in their writings say we only *think* we choose quickly fall into words and phrases that only make sense if they are wrong and we do truly choose. Human beings are also unique in that they verbalise. That is, people put concrete and abstract concepts into words which communicate these concepts to other people. People also have an inner life of the mind; they remember the past and make projections into the future. One could name other factors, but these are enough to differentiate people from the other things in the world.

What world view adequately explains the remarkable phenomenon of the distinctiveness of human beings? There is one world view which can explain the existence of the universe, its form, and the uniqueness of people— the world view given to us in the Bible. There is a remarkable parallel between the way scientists go about checking to see if what they think about reality does in fact correspond to it and the way the biblical world view can be checked to see if it is true.

Many people, however, react strongly against this sort of claim. They see the problem— Where has everything come from and why is it the way it is?—but they do not want to consider a solution which involves God. God, they say, belongs to 'religion', and religious answers, they say, do not deal with facts. Only science deals with facts. Thus, they say, Christian answers are not real answers; they are 'faith answers'.

This is a strange reaction, because modern people pride themselves on being open to new ideas, on being willing to consider opinions which contradict what has been believed for a long time. They think this is what 'being scientific' necessitates. Suddenly, however, when one crosses into the area of the 'big' and most basic questions (like those we are considering now) with an answer involving God, the shutters are pulled down, the open mind closes and a very different attitude, a dogmatic *rationalism*, takes over.[90]

This is curious—first, because few seem to notice that the humanist explanation of the big and most basic questions is just as much a 'faith answer' as any could be. With the humanist world view everything begins with only matter; whatever has developed has developed only within matter, a reordering of matter by chance.

Even though materialistic scientists have no scientific understanding of *why* things exist, nor any certain scientific understanding of *how* life began, and even though this world view leaves them with vast problems—the problems Woody Allen has described of 'alienation, loneliness and emptiness verging on madness'—many modern people still reject at once any solution which uses the word *God*, in favour of the materialistic humanist 'answer' which answers nothing. This is simply prejudice at work.

We need to understand, however, that this prejudice is both recent and arbitrary. Professor Ernest Becker, who taught at the University of California at Berkeley and San Francisco State College, said that for the last half-million years people have always believed in two worlds—one that was visible and one that was invisible. The visible world was where they lived their everyday lives: the invisible world was more powerful, for the meaning and existence of the visible world was dependent on it. Suddenly in the last century and a half, as the ideas of the Enlightenment have spread to the whole of Western culture, we have been told quite arbitrarily that there *is* no invisible world. This has become dogma for many secular people today.

Christians try to answer prejudices like these by pointing out that the biblical system does not have to be accepted blindly, any more than the scientific hypotheses have to be accepted blindly. What a scientist does is to examine certain phenomena in the world. He then casts about for an explanation that will make sense of these phenomena. That is the hypothesis. But the hypothesis has to be checked. So a careful checking operation is set up, designed to see if there is, in fact, a correspondence between what has been observed and what has been hypothesised. If it does correspond, a scientist accepts the explanation as correct; if it does not, he rejects it as false and looks for an alternative explanation. Depending on how substantially the statement has been 'verified'. it becomes accepted as a 'law' within science, such as the law of gravity or the second law of thermodynamics.

What we should notice is the method. It is rather like trying to find the right key to fit a particular lock. We try the first key and then the next and the next until finally, if we are fortunate, one of them fits. The same principle applies, so Christians maintain, when we consider the big questions. Here are the phenomena. What key unlocks their meaning? What explanation is correct?

We may consider the materialistic humanist alternative, the Eastern religious alternative, and so on. But each of these leaves at least a part of these most basic questions unanswered. So we turn to examine the Christian alternative.

Obviously, Christians do not look on the Bible as simply an alternative. As Christians we consider it to be objectively true, because we have found that it does give the answers both in knowledge and in life. For the purposes of discussion, however, we invite non-Christians to consider it as *an* alternative—not to be accepted blindly, but for good and sufficient reasons.

But note this—the physical scientist does something very easy, compared to those who tackle the really important and central questions for mankind. He examines a tiny portion of the real world—a leaf, a cell, an atom, a particle—and, because these things are not personal and obey very precise laws, he is able to arrive at explanations with relative ease. C. F. A. Pantin, who was professor of zoology at Cambridge University, once said: 'Very clever men are answering the relatively easy questions of the natural examination paper.' This is not to disparage physical science. It works consistently with its own principles of investigation, looking further and further into the material of the world around us. But it only looks at part of the world. As Professor W. H. Thorpe of Cambridge University says, it is 'a deliberate restriction to certain areas of our total experience—a technique for understanding certain parts of that experience and achieving mastery over nature.'

We are not then moving from definite things to indefinite things, when we look at those aspects of our experience which are more central than the study of an individual physical thing such as a leaf, a cell, an atom, or a particle. Rather, we are turning from a small part of reality to a larger part of reality. Picture a scientist for a moment: He is looking at a particular detail and carrying out his scientific investigation according to the recognised procedures. We have already discussed the method he uses to find the answers. Now we need to draw back and consider the whole phenomenon we are looking at, that is, the scientist carrying out his experiment. When the scientist is seated at his desk, he is able to find answers to his questions only *because* he has made two colossal assumptions about his situation, in fact about the entire world. He is assuming first of all that the things he is looking at do fit together somehow, even if some areas—such as particle physics—cannot at this time be fitted into a simple explanation. If the scientist did not assume that the things he is studying somehow fit together, he would not be trying to find an answer. Second, he is assuming that he as a person is able to find answers.

In other words, the *big* questions constitute the very framework within which the scientist is operating. To quote Thorpe again, 'I recently heard one of the most distinguished theoretical scientists state that his own scientific drive was based on two fundamental attitudes: a conviction of his own responsibility and an awe at the beauty and harmony of nature.' So we have to resist any suggestion that to be involved in answering the big questions is somehow to be getting further and further away from 'the real world'.

The opposite is the case. It is as we come to these big questions that we approach the real world that every one of us is living in twenty-four hours a day—the world of real persons who can think and so work out problems such as how to get to the other side of town, persons who can love, persons who can make moral decisions. These are, in other words, the phenomena which cry out for an adequate explanation. These are the things we know best about ourselves and the world around us. What world view can encompass them?

C. S. Lewis pointed out that there are only two alternatives to the Christian answer—the humanist philosophy of the West and the pantheist philosophy of the East. We would agree. We agree, too, with his observation that Eastern philosophy is an 'opposite' answer to the Christian system, but we shall look at that later. For the present our attention is directed toward the materialistic world view of the West.

From time to time we read in the press or hear on the radio that an oil tanker has run aground on rocks and that the crude oil is being driven by the wind and currents onto an otherwise beautiful coast. We can picture the problem of humanism in that way. There is a rock on which all humanist philosophy must run aground. It is the problem of relative knowledge and relative morality or, to put it another way, the problem of finiteness or limitation. Even if mankind now had perfect moral integrity regarding the world, people would still be finite. People are limited. This fact, coupled with the rejection of the possibility of having answers from God, leads humanists into the problem of relative knowledge. There *has* been no alternative to this relativity for the past two hundred years, and there can be no alternative within the humanist world view. That is what we want to show now.

How Do We Know We Know? During the early stages of modern philosophy (as distinguished from medieval philosophy)—that is, around the seventeenth century in Europe—the question that was troubling philosophers was this: *How do we know that we know?*

The early modern scientists had made advances in the physical sciences by rejecting previous human authority. For example, they rejected much of what had been inherited from the science of the Middle Ages. At that time, investigation had been governed and restrained by the concepts of Aristotle. In the field of astronomy, this had meant that the Ptolemaic system held sway. Suddenly, observations were made which cast doubt on that entire system of understanding the heavenly bodies. The result was, of course, the Copernican revolution: the discovery that the sun does not move around the earth but, rather, the earth around the sun. Thus, a general attitude was developed toward the ideas which had prevailed till then. The scientists said, 'We must not accept the ideas passed down to us or derived from various previous authorities. We must start from scratch and simply observe the world and see how it works. Otherwise, we may be hampered from seeing what is there.'

The early modern scientists did not, however, reject the knowledge that God gave in the Bible as they rejected previous human authority and opinion. For example, in *Novum Organum* (1620) Francis Bacon wrote: 'To conclude, therefore, let no man out of weak conceit of sobriety, or an ill applied moderation, think or maintain that a man can search too far or be too well studied in the book of God's word, or in the book of God's works.'[91] 'The book of God's word' is the Bible. 'The book of God's works' is the world which God has made.

Modern scientists in general lived, thought, and worked in the framework of rejecting human authority, while respecting what was taught in the Bible in regard to the cosmos—right up to the time of Michael Faraday and James Clerk Maxwell in the second half of the nineteenth century.

The *philosophers* (and later the materialistic scientists) went further. Their error was to confuse the escape from past human authority (which was indeed confining) with putting man at the centre and rejecting God's authority as well. They wanted to reject all outside authority. They wanted to establish everything only on human observation. That was how the question of epistemology (how we know we know) became so important in modern philosophy. It has remained so right up to our own day.

The philosopher who first raised these questions was René Descartes (1596–1650). Descartes wrote in *Meditations on First Philosophy:*

> How often it happened to me that in the night I dreamt that I found myself on this particular place . . . whilst in reality I was lying on my bed! At this moment it does seem that it is with eyes awake that I am looking at this paper. . . . But in thinking over this I remind myself that on many occasions I have in sleep been deceived by similar illusions, and in dwelling carefully on this reflection I see so manifestly that there are no certain indications by which we may clearly distinguish wakefulness from sleep that I am lost in astonishment. And my astonishment is such that it is almost capable of persuading me that I now dream.[92]

Here is the modern epistemological problem expressed three centuries ago! All knowledge comes through the senses, but how can we rely on our own senses? Sometimes, as in dreaming, we seem to be experiencing things very really, yet the reality is only in our heads.

We are reminded of the 1966 film by Michelangelo Antonioni called *Blow-Up*, in which one of the central issues was this same question. A photographer had taken a picture of a murdered man in a park in London and then became uncertain whether this was, in fact, part of reality or an experience of fantasy similar to a drug trip. Within the humanist world view there is no final way of telling. And Antonioni ends his film by making the point graphically. Tennis players play the game without a ball. The invisible 'ball' goes back and forth and the spectators watch its 'path' from side to side until finally the 'ball' (which does not exist) goes out over the surrounding wire and 'falls' at the photographer's feet. He pauses for a moment, uncertain about what he should do. (Is observation simply a matter of the majority? Does the reality of things come from the general agreement in society and nothing more?) Then the photographer stoops down, picks up the 'ball' and throws it back onto the court. Here, depicted brilliantly, is the problem of any system which builds its epistemology on man alone. This film was a philosophic statement of the period in which we are living.

Take another example out of the history of this new approach in philosophy, that of David Hume (1711–1776). In 1732 he shocked the world with *A Treatise of Human Nature*. John Locke (1632–1704) had already denied the concept of 'innate ideas' of right and wrong; that is, Locke denied that these ideas are inherent in the mind from birth. This had troubled many. Then Hume burst on the scene with a challenge which went further.

What was most startling was his progression beyond scepticism concerning God and other things of the 'invisible world' to a scepticism about the visible world as well. Among other things, he questioned the concept of causality. That is, Hume challenged the notion that there is a reality in the external world which leads us to speak about one thing as being the cause of another. When we see a tree bending and swaying and its leaves falling to the ground and racing off across the field, we naturally speak of the wind as *causing* this phenomenon. Hume challenged this.

Following on from Locke, who said that all knowledge comes only from the senses, Hume argued that causality is *not* perceived by the senses. What we *perceive* are two events following closely upon each other. It was custom, he argued, which led us to speak in terms of causality, not any objective 'force' working in the things themselves. Anyone can see where this thinking leads, and it was so understood at the time. If causality is not real, science becomes impossible — for what scientists are doing is tracing the path of cause and effect from one event to the next.

A modern British humanist, Kathleen Nott, has written perceptively about Hume in *Objections to Humanism* (1967): 'Among great philosophers, Hume . . . hung his nose as far as any over the nihilistic abyss.'[93] This is right. Hume was questioning the most basic elements of our experience. Yet he was trying to be consistent to his presuppositions (that is, his starting point). Where did this lead him? To a scepticism about knowledge itself. Hume wrote deliberately against the Christian world view which prevailed in England at the time. He wanted to dismantle the system of ideas which came out of the Bible, of a God before whom man was responsible, of people being more than matter, of a life after death which seemed to defy all natural law. Where he ended, though, was with uncertainty even about the ordinary things of life. As Kathleen Nott continues: 'Hume's philosophising was indeed a radical scepticism, which left no convincing logical grounds for believing that anything natural, let alone supernatural, was there at all.'[94]

But there is something even more striking about Hume. Scepticism was the direction in which his philosophy led him; yet he was not able to live with it himself. He 'hung his nose over the nihilistic abyss' — and we can picture him standing on the edge and peering over — but what then? Nott says, he 'withdrew it sharply when he saw the psychological risks involved'. Hume himself said in *A Treatise of Human Nature* (Volume I):

> Should it be asked me whether I sincerely assent to this argument which I have been to such pains to inculcate, and whether I be really one of those sceptics who hold that all is uncertain . . . I . . . should reply . . . that neither I nor any other person was ever sincerely and constantly of that opinion. . . . I dine, I play backgammon, I converse and am merry with my friends; and when, after 3 or 4 hours amusement, I would return to these speculations, they appear so cold and strained and ridiculous that I cannot find in my heart to enter into them any further. Thus the sceptic still continues to reason and believe, though he asserts that he cannot defend his reason by reason; and by the same rule, he must assent to the principle concerning the existence of body, though he cannot pretend, by any argument of philosophy, to maintain its veracity.[95]

We believe there are only two basic alternatives in the search for the source of knowledge. One is that a person attempts to find the answers to all his questions alone. The other is that he seeks revealed truths from God. We shall come to the second later. Now we are looking at the former, and we are suggesting that this is the basic problem with which all humanistic systems must wrestle: the problem of knowledge.

We could go into many other details concerning the subsequent history of the ideas we have dealt with, including in particular Immanuel Kant (1724–1804) and his own 'Copernican revolution' in philosophy and also the developments surrounding Ludwig Wittgenstein (1889–

1951) and linguistic philosophy in the twentieth century. We shall stop here, partly to keep the discussion of modern philosophy from becoming too technical, but mainly because the basic difficulties had already been expressed with a century of the birth of modern philosophy.

Starting with himself, a person cannot establish an adequate explanation for the amazing possibility that he can observe the world around him and be assured that his observations match up with reality. The problem is not just that a person cannot know everything. The need is not for exhaustive knowledge; the need is for a base for any knowledge at all. That is, even though we know we cannot exhaustively perceive even the smallest things in our experience, we want assurance that we have really perceived something— that this 'perception' is not simply an 'image' in our brain, a model or symbol of reality which we have projected out from ourselves. We want to know that we have had a *real* contact with reality. Even Hume had to admit that his philosophising did not make sense, that it did not fit into his own experience of the world. On the humanist side this is the great tension— to have no reason for reason and yet at the same time to have to live continuously on the reality of reason.

At this point, someone is bound to ask, 'But why is it necessary to have an "adequate explanation" for knowledge?' Agreeing that Descartes, Hume, and others could find no theoretical base which tied in with their experience, isn't it sufficient to just *reason?* Probably many of you have been wanting to ask this, as you have followed along. It is a good question, for the bulk of the world never bothers about the issues which Locke, Hume, and others like them raised. Most people simply live, going about their daily lives, never troubling themselves about reality and fantasy, the subject and the object, and so on. And we are not suggesting that their experience *in itself* is invalid, as if to imply that they are not perceiving and knowing the universe around them. They are. What we *are* saying is that— whether they know it or not— their experience is possible only because they are living in the universe the Bible describes, that is, in a universe which was created by God. Their internal faculty of knowing was made by God to correspond to the world and its form which He made and which surrounds them.

If, however, we attempt to bypass the question, 'Why is it possible for man to have knowledge in this way?' we must then remember the other two great problems of any system which starts only from man. Recall the illustration of the oil tanker and the rock. The rock is the problem of knowledge which we have been considering. That is the central problem. But there are two forms of pollution which flow from the broken ship of knowledge, first, the meaningless of all things and, second, the realitivity of morals.

The Meaninglessness of All Things

An overwhelming number of modern thinkers agree that seeing the universe and man from a humanist base leads to meaninglessness, both for the universe and for man—not just mankind in general but for each of us as individuals. Professor Steven Weinberg of Harvard University and the Smithsonian Astrophysical Observatory in the USA has written a book entitled *The First Three Minutes: A Modern View of the Origin of the Universe* (1976). Here he explains, as clearly as probably anyone has ever done, the modern materialistic view of the universe and its origin.

But when his explanation is finished and he is looking down at the earth from an aeroplane, as Weinberg writes, 'It is very hard to realise that this all is just a tiny part of an overwhelmingly hostile universe . . . [which] has evolved from an unspeakably unfamiliar early condition, and faces a future extinction of endless cold or intolerable heat. The more the universe seems comprehensible, the more it also seems pointless.'[96]

When Weinberg says that the universe seems more 'comprehensible', he is, of course, referring to our greater understanding of the physical universe through the advance of science. But it is an understanding, notice, within a materialistic framework, which considers the universe solely in terms of physics and chemistry—simply machinery. Here lies the irony. It is comprehension of a sort, but it is like giving a blind person sight, only to remove anything seeable. As we heard Woody Allen saying earlier, such a view of reality is 'absolutely stupefying in its terror, and it renders anyone's accomplishments meaningless'.

So, to the person who wants to be left alone without explanations for the big questions, we must say very gently, 'Look at what you are left alone with.' This is not merely rhetoric. As the decades of this century have slipped by, more and more have said the same thing as Steven Weinberg and Woody Allen. It has become an obvious thing to say. The tremendous optimism of the nineteenth century, which stemmed from the Enlightenment of the eighteenth century, has gradually ebbed away.

If everything 'faces a future extinction of endless cold or intolerable heat', all things are meaningless. This is the first problem, the first form of pollution. The second is just as bad.

The Relativity of Morals   The material universe in itself gives no basis for values. Those who begin with the material universe can *describe* but they can never *define*. They can speak only in the indicative, never in the imperative. They can describe, for example, what physical strength involves and how it works physiologically, but from the material universe alone they cannot derive any idea as to how strength *ought* and *ought not* to be used. The most they can do is argue that certain moral systems have been worked out through the passage of time on the basis of 'social contract'. This is what we call the 51 per cent view of morality—the majority has thought such and such is a good way to operate and so it becomes 'morality'. What confusion! What disaster! With this view any action can be justified, and our own very recent history has given us appalling examples.

Aldous Huxley said it all clearly in the thirties in his brilliant little novel *Brave New World*. In it he pictures a society which has reversed the morality of the present, especially in the area of sexual relationships. Faithfulness within a unique love relationship becomes 'evil'; promiscuity becomes 'good'.[97]

Here then is the humanist dilemma. We have to generate the answers to the big questions, but out of our own limited experience we can know *nothing* with certainty. If we were to add up the thinking of *all* of mankind, we would still have only limited knowledge. *Truth* with a capital *T*—explanations which would be true for all time and all people—would be impossible.

What is left, therefore, is 'relative' truth, and with relative truth, relative morality. Given time, even the 'certainties' of our ethical systems can be undone—the bills of rights, the charters of freedom, the principles of justice, everything. Alexander Solzhenitsyn understands this not only as a theoretical problem of a humanistic philosophy. He has suffered under its implications. He writes:

> Communism has never concealed the fact that it rejects all absolute concepts of morality. It scoffs at good and evil as indisputable categories.
> Communism considers morality to be relative. Depending upon circumstances, any act, including the killing of thousands, could be good or bad. It all depends upon class ideology, defined by a handful of people. . . .
> It is considered awkward to use seriously such words as good and evil. But if

we are to be deprived of these concepts, what will be left? We will decline to the status of animals.

We in the West must understand that it is not only Iron Curtain countries who operate on the basis of relative morality. Now the West does, too. The materialist world view has dominated the thinking of the West just as much. Therefore we can expect to see the same inhumanity here, just as Solzhenitsyn has warned. We must not sit back and think, *It could never happen here.* Worse still, we must not be confused into thinking the issue is principally or only military or economic power. The issue is more subtle, more immediate, a cancer-like growth which is in our midst right now — the materialist philosophy which underlies the Western humanistic world view. Marx may have proposed an economic system different from our own, but we have shared his basic world view.

The greatest dilemma for those who hold this world view, however, is that it is impossible to live consistently within it. We saw how this was true of David Hume. Likewise the playwright Samuel Beckett can 'say' that words do not communicate anything — and that everything, including language, is absurd — yet he must use words to write his plays, even plays about meaninglessness. If the words that Beckett uses did not convey meaning to his hearers, he could not say that everything, including words, is meaningless.

The list of contradictions can be extended endlessly. The truth is that everyone who rejects the biblical world view must live in a state of tension between ideas about reality and reality itself.

Thus, if a person believes that everything is only matter or energy and carries this through consistently, meaning dies, morality dies, love dies, hope dies. *Yet!* The individual does love, does hope, does act on the basis of right and wrong. This is what we mean when we say that everyone is caught, regardless of his world view, simply by the way things are. No one can make his own universe to live in.

The reason for this, as we have said all along, is that the individual is confronted with two aspects of reality that do not basically change: the universe and its form and the mannishness of man. Humanists argue that everything is finally only matter or energy and end up with no answers to the big questions. They arrive at only meaninglessness, relative morality, relative knowledge. But humanists actually live as if there *is* meaning and real morality. They act, for example, as if cruelty is not the same as non-cruelty, or justice the same as injustice. Also, humanists do have knowledge, knowledge of a world in which causality is real and science is possible.

Exactly the same dilemma exists with the other main alternative to Christianity: the philosophies of the East. Despite their many differences, all of these philosophies flow out of the view that ultimately everything is impersonal. The universe we are experiencing, the Eastern philosophers say, is simply an extension of God, but — and here we need to be careful — they do not mean that God is personal. 'God' means the 'impersonal everything', which has no final distinctions. So, within this view, the solution is to say we must get rid of those aspirations that are personal, those things that make us seem to be independent entities, entirely independent selves. Such an idea is *maya*, that is, 'illusion'.

In the Eastern thinking, the only reality is *one* beyond all distinctions and therefore impersonal: no 'male' or 'female', no 'you' or 'me', no 'good' or 'evil'. It is important to note that Eastern thinkers come to exactly the same place as those who begin by saying that everything is matter or energy. At first the two positions sound very different, but they result in the same final position.

And so we ask again: Can a person espousing this Eastern world view live consistently with it? In his 1974 novel *Zen and the Art of Motorcycle Maintenance*, Robert M. Pirsig relates an interesting anecdote. The author, who calls himself Phaedrus in the story, studied philosophy at Benares University for about ten years. He tells how his time there came to an end.

> One day in the classroom the professor of philosophy was blithely expounding on the illusory nature of the world for what seemed the fiftieth time and Phaedrus raised his hand and asked coldly if it was believed that the atomic bombs that had dropped on Hiroshima and Nagasaki were illusory. The professor smiled and said yes. That was the end of the exchange.
>   . . . . Within the traditions of Indian philosophy that answer may have been correct, but for Phaedrus and for anyone else who reads newspapers regularly and is concerned with such things as mass destruction of human beings that answer was hopelessly inadequate. He left the classroom, left India and gave up.[98]

There are, then, only two main alternative world views to Christianity, both of which begin with the impersonal. The West has a *materialistic* view and is non-religious. The East has an *immaterialistic* view and is religious. *But both are impersonal systems.* This is the important point;

by comparison, their differences pale into insignificance. The result is that, in both the West and the East, men and women are seen as abnormal aliens to the way things really are. In Eastern terms they are spoken of as *maya* or illusion; in Western terms, as absurd machines.

Relieving the Tension in the West

In both the East and the West, however, there are attempts to relieve the tension of seeming to be nothing, while in fact being something very real—a person in a real world which has a definite form. On the materialist side, Sir Julian Huxley (1887–1975) has clarified the dilemma by acknowledging, though he is an atheist, that somehow or other— against all that one might expect—a person functions better if he acts *as though God exists*. 'So,' the argument goes, 'God does not in fact exist, but act as if He does!' As observed by the Norwegian playwright Henrik Ibsen (1828–1906) in *The Wild Duck:* 'Rob the average man of his life-illusion, and you rob him of his happiness at the same stroke.' In other words, according to Huxley, you can function properly only if you live your whole life upon a lie. You act as if God exists, which to the materialist is false. At first this sounds like a feasible solution for relieving the tension produced by a materialistic world view. However, a moment's reflection shows what a terrible solution it is. You will find no deeper despair than this for a sensitive person. This is no optimistic, happy, reasonable, brilliant answer. It is darkness and death.

Another way the tension is relieved is through the theory of evolution, the idea that *by chance* there is an increasing advance. People are given an impression of progress—up from the primeval slime and the amoeba, up through the evolutionary chain, with life developing by chance from the simple carbon molecule to the complex, right up to the pinnacle, mankind.

This is not the place to discuss evolutionary theory, but it surprises us how readily people accept it, even on the scientific side, as if it had no problems. There are problems, even if these are not commonly realised or discussed (see Appendix 1). The primary point we are interested in, however, is not evolution itself but the illusion of 'progress' which has been granted by it. By chance, this amazing complexity called 'man' has been generated out of the slime. So, of course, there is progress! By this argument people are led into imagining that the whole of reality does have purpose even if, as we have said, there is no way that it really can have purpose within the humanistic world view.

Evolution makes men and women feel superior and at the top of the pile, but in the materialistic framework, the whole of reality is meaningless; the concept of 'higher' means nothing. Even if, within the humanist world view, people are more complex than plants and animals, both 'higher' and 'lower' have no meanings. We are left with everything being sad and absurd.

Thus, the concept of progress is an illusion. Only some form of mystical jump will allow us to accept that personality comes from impersonality.[99] No one has offered to explain, let alone demonstrate it to be feasible, how the impersonal plus time plus chance can give personality. We are distracted by a flourish of words — and, lo, personality has appeared out of a hat.

Imagine a universe made up of only liquids and solids, one containing no free gases. A fish is swimming in this universe. This fish, quite naturally, is conformed to its environment so that it is able to exist quite happily. Let us suppose, then, that by blind chance (as the evolutionists would have us believe) this fish developed lungs as it continued swimming in this universe without any gases. This fish would no longer be able to function and to fulfil its position as a fish. Would it then be 'higher' or 'lower' in its new state with lungs? Obviously it would be lower, for it would drown.

In the same way, if a person has been kicked up from the impersonal by chance, those things that make him a person — hope of purpose and significance, love, notions of morality and rationality and beauty — are ultimately unfulfillable and are thus meaningless. In such a situation, is man higher or lower? Mankind would then be the lowest creature on the scale, the least conforming to what reality is. Thus we see how hopeless is the illusion of meaning or purpose as derived from evolutionary thought.

Relieving the Tension in the East Within Eastern thinking, attempts to relieve the tension have been made by introducing 'personal gods'. To the uninitiated these gods seem to be real persons; they are said to appear to human beings and even have sexual intercourse with them. But they are not really personal. Behind them their source is the 'impersonal everything' of which they are simply emanations. We find a multitude of gods and goddesses with their attendant mythologies, like the *Ramayana*, which then give the simple person a 'feeling' of personality in the universe. People need this, because it is hard to live as if there is nothing out there in or beyond the universe to which they can relate personally. The initiated, however, understand. They know that ultimate reality is impersonal. So they submit themselves to the various techniques of the Eastern religions to eliminate their 'personness'. Their goal is to achieve a state of consciousness not bounded by the body and the senses or even by such ideals as 'love' or 'good'.

Probably the most sophisticated Eastern attempt to deal with the tension we are considering is the Bhagavad-Gita. This is a religious writing probably produced around 200 BC in India. It has been the inspiration for multitudes of Hindus through the centuries and most notably for the Indian spiritual and political leader Mahatma Gandhi. In it the individual is urged to participate in acts of charity. At the same time, however, the individual is urged to enter into these acts in 'a spirit of detachment'. Why? Because the proper attitude is to understand that none of these experiences really matter. It is the state of consciousness that rises above personality which is important, for personality is, after all, an abnormality within the impersonal universe.

Alternatively, the East proposes a system of 'endless cycles' to try to give some explanation for things which exist about us. This has sometimes been likened to the ocean. The ocean casts up waves for a time, but the waves are still a part of the ocean, and then the waves pull back into the ocean and disappear. Interestingly enough, the Western materialist also tries to explain the form of the universe by a theory of endless cycles. He says that impersonal material or energy always exists, but that this goes through endless cycles, taking different forms—the latest of which began with the 'big bang' which spawned the present expanding universe. Previously, billions and billions of years ago, this eternal material or energy had a different form and had contracted into the heavy mass from which came the present cycle of our universe. Both the Eastern thought and the Western put forth this unproved idea of endless cycles because their answers finally answer nothing.

We have emphasised the problems involved in these two alternatives because they are real. It is helpful to see that the only serious intellectual alternatives to the Christian position have such endless difficulties that they actually are non-answers. We do it, too, because we find people in the West who imagine that Christianity has nothing to say on these big issues and who discard the Bible without ever considering it. This superior attitude, as we said earlier, is quite unfounded. The real situation is very different. The humanists of the Enlightenment acted as if they would conquer all before them, but two centuries have changed that.

One would have imagined at this point that Western man would have been glad for a solution to the various dilemmas facing him and would have welcomed answers to the big questions. But people are not as eager to find the truth as is sometimes made out. The history of Western thought during the past century confirms this.

Reason is Dead   The hallmark of the Enlightenment had been 'Reason Is King'. The leading thinkers had consciously rejected the need for revelation. As Paul Hazard in *European Thought in the Eighteenth Century* says, they put Christianity on trial.[100]

Gradually, however, the problems of this enthronement of human reason emerged. The reason of man was not big enough to handle the big questions, and what man was left with was relative knowledge and relative morality. This noose around the humanist's neck tightened with every passing decade and generation. What would he do?

Ironically, even though the basis of the humanists' whole endeavour had been the central importance of man's reason, when faced with the problems of relative knowledge and relative morality they repudiated reason. Rather than admit defeat in front of God's revelation, the humanists extended the revolution further—and in a direction which would have been quite unthinkable to their eighteenth-century predecessors. Modern irrationalism was born.

We could go as far back as Immanuel Kant (1724–1804) in philosophy and to Friedrich Schleiermacher (1768–1834) in theology. Modern existentialism is also related to Søren Kierkegaard (1813–1855). However, our intention here is neither to go into the history of irrationalism, nor to examine the proponents of existentialism in our own century, but rather to concentrate on its main thesis. It is this that confronts us on all sides today, and it is impossible to understand modern man without understanding this concept.

Because we shall be using several terms a great deal now, we would ask the reader to attend carefully. When we speak of *irrationalism* or *existentialism* or *the existential methodology*, we are pointing to a quite simple idea. It may have been expressed in a variety of complicated ways by philosophers, but it is not a difficult concept.

Imagine that you are at the movies watching a suspense film. As the story unfolds, the tension increases until finally the hero is trapped in some impossible situation and everyone is groaning inwardly, wondering how he is going to get out of the mess. The suspense is heightened by the knowledge (of the audience, not the hero) that help is on the way in the form of the good guys. The only question is: *Will the good guys arrive in time?*

Now imagine for a moment that the audience is slipped the information that there are no good guys, that the situation of the hero is not just desperate, but completely hopeless. Obviously, the first thing that would happen is that the suspense would be gone. You and the entire audience would simply be waiting for the axe to fall.

If the hero faced the end with courage, this would be morally edifying, but the situation itself would be tragic. If, however, the hero acted *as if* help were around the corner and kept buoying himself up with this thought ('Someone is on the way!' — 'Help is at hand!'), all you could feel for him would be pity. It would be a means to keep hope alive within a hopeless situation. The hero's hope would change nothing *on the outside*; it would be unable to manufacture, out of nothing, good guys coming to the rescue. All it would achieve would be the hero's own mental state of hopefulness rather than hopelessness.

The hopefulness itself would rest on a lie or an illusion and thus, viewed objectively, would be finally absurd. And if the hero really knew what the situation was, but consciously used the falsehood to buoy up his feelings and go whistling along, we would either say, 'Poor guy!' or 'He's a fool.' It is this kind of conscious deceit that someone like Woody Allen has looked full in the face and will have none of.

Now this is what the existential methodology is about. If the universe we are living in is what the materialistic humanists say it is, then with our reason (when we stop to think about it) we could find absolutely no way to have meaning or morality or hope or beauty. This would plunge us into despair. We would have to take seriously the challenge of Albert Camus (1913–1960) in the first sentence of *The Myth of Sisyphus:* 'There is but one truly serious philosophical problem, and that is suicide.'[101] Why stay alive in an absurd universe? Ah! But that is *not* where we stop. We say to ourselves — 'There *is* hope!' (even though there is no help).

'We shall overcome!' (even though nothing is more certain than that we shall be destroyed, both individually at death and cosmically with the end of all conscious life). This is what confronts us on all sides today: the modern irrationalism.

Long Live Experience!   Another way to understand all this is to say that modern man has become a mystic. The word *mystic* makes people think immediately of a religious person—praying for hours, using techniques of meditation, and so on. Of course, mysticism includes this, but modern mysticism is different in a profound way. As the late Professor H. R. Rookmaaker of the Free University of Amsterdam said, modern mysticism is 'a nihilistic mysticism, *for God is dead*'.

The mystics within the Christian tradition (Meister Eckhart in the thirteenth century, for example) believed in an objective personal God. But, they said, though God is really there, the mind is not the way to reach Him. On the other hand, modern mysticism comes from a quite different background, and this we must be clear about.

When modern philosophers realised they were not going to be able to find answers on the basis of reason, they crossed over in one way or another to the remarkable position of saying, 'That doesn't matter!' Even though there are no answers by way of the mind, we will find them without the mind. The 'answer'—whatever that may be—is to be 'experienced', for it cannot be thought. Notice, the answer is not to be the experience of an objective and supernatural God whom, as the medieval mystics thought, it was difficult to understand with the mind. The developments we are considering came *after* Friedrich Nietzsche (1844–1900) had celebrated the 'death of God', *after* the materialist philosophy had worked its way throughout the culture and created scepticism about the supernatural.

The modern mystic, therefore, is not trying to 'feel' his way to a God he believes is really there (but whom he cannot approach by way of the mind). The modern mystic does not know if *anything* is there. All he knows is that he cannot know anything ultimate through the mind. So what is left is *experience as experience*. This is the key to understanding modern man in the West: Forget your mind; just experience! It may seem extreme—but we say it carefully—this is the philosophy by which the majority of people in the West are now living. For everyday purposes the mind is a useful instrument, but for the things of meaning, for the answers to the big questions, it is set aside.

'Whatever Reality may be, it is beyond the conception of the finite intellect; it follows that attempts at descriptions are misleading, unprofitable, and a waste of time.' That is a quotation from a modern Buddhist in the West. The secular existentialists may seem a long way from such an Eastern formulation about reality, but their rejection of the intellect as a means of finding answers amounts to the same thing. That is what the existentialist 'revolt', as it has been called, is. It is a revolt against the mind, a passionate rejection of the Enlightenment ideal of reason. As Professor William Barrett of New York University has put it: 'Existentialism is the counter-Enlightenment come at last to philosophic expression.'[102]

The way to handle philosophy, according to the existential methodology, is not by the use of the mind that considers (impersonally and objectively) propositions about reality. Rather, the way to deal with the big questions is by relying only on the individual's experience. That which is being considered is not necessarily an experience of something that really exists. What is involved is the experience *as an experience*, whether or not any objective reality is being experienced. We are reminded of our imaginary hero who said, 'Help is coming,' and therefore kept himself going, even though he had no reason to think any help existed. It is the experience as the experience that counts, and that is the end of it.

There are, of course, some valuable insights in what the existentialists have said. For one, they were right to protest against scientism and the impersonalism of much post-Enlightenment thought. They were right to point out that answers have to be 'lived' and not just 'thought'. (We will say more about this in chapter 6.) But their rejection of the mind is no solution to anything. It *seems* like a solution but is in fact a counsel of despair.

Having started with the apparently different positions of the Buddhist and the secular existentialist, we should now look at culture at large. One of the 'cultural breakpoints' was Haight-Ashbury in the sixties. There the counterculture, the drug culture, was born. Writing about the experience of Ken Kesey and his Merry Pranksters in the early days of Haight-Ashbury, Tom Wolfe says,

Gradually the Prankster attitude began to involve the main things religious mystics have always felt, things common to Hindus, Buddhists, Christians, and for that matter Theosophists and even flying-saucer cultists. Namely, the experiencing of an Other World, a higher level of reality. . . .

  Every vision, every insight . . . came out of the *new experience*. . . . And how to get it across to the multitudes who have never had this experience for themselves? *You couldn't put it into words.* You had to create conditions in which they would *feel* an approximation of that *feeling*, the sublime kairos (*italics* added).

Do you see what is involved here? We can agree this represents a wild-fringe element of the counterculture which is already behind us. But we must understand that the central ideas and attitudes are now part of the air we breathe in the West. 'Every insight . . . came out of the new experience.' *Experience!*—that is the word! And how to tell it? 'You couldn't put it into words.'

The New Mysticism

What about the spread of Eastern religions and techniques within the West—things like TM, Yoga, the cults? We have moved beyond the counterculture of the sixties, but where to? These elements from the East no longer influence just the beat generation and the dropouts. Now they are fashionable for the middle classes as well. They are everywhere.

  What has become important is not whether there is anything that causes an experience, but just the experience as such. What about modern theology in the churches? It is the same thing. Maybe the terminology is 'Christian', but the ideas are on the other side— experience is the important thing, not propositions about reality, about God, about salvation and all the rest. It does not matter if anything exists that has caused or conforms to the experience.

  What about the sudden growth of interest in UFOs and UFOlogy? Even though not a scrap of evidence exists to support Erich von Däniken's 'scientific' theories about spacemen who visited earth in the distant past, millions of people have been taken with these assumptions. He has given his ideas an aura of scientific plausibility, plenty of technical jargon, photographs, and so forth, and because this is a 'scientific age', people are impressed. But the real evidence is unconvincing. Is there conscious life in other parts of the cosmos? We do not know. If there is, it would pose no problem for Christianity. Still, at this time there is no proof at all that this is the case. Why then do people accept it? We suggest it is part of the swing to the irrational.

People are hungry for something which will give them hope in life. They are tired of the empty platitudes that politicians and theologians have made: endless exhortations to be good, to be good, to be good! They are also afraid. Things really do seem hopeless, even on the level of everyday life with its threats of a lower standard of living, of a growing authoritarianism, of famine and ecological disaster, of devastating war. And they are looking for *any* answer. So the UFOs are messengers of a friendly race from another planet. 'Do not fear — the Force is with you!' — to borrow from a current science-fiction film. And so people believe it irrationally. If they used their minds, they would see no evidence for friendly people from outside. But the feeling of experience as they read about this or see it on a screen is enough. It does not matter whether there is any reality to it.

What about the growth of occultism, witchcraft, astrology? Is it simply economics that has put the signs of the zodiac in shops from one end of our society to the other? In part it is economics, but, once again, the real reason is deeper. People are looking for answers — answers they can experience.

What about those who take drugs as a means of 'expanding their consciousness'? This, too, is in the same direction. Your mind is a hindrance to you: 'Blow it!' As Timothy Leary put it in *The Politics of Ecstasy* (1968): 'Our favorite concepts are standing in the way of a flood tide two billion years building up. The verbal dam is collapsing. Head for the hills or prepare your intellectual craft to flow with the current.' So we see again the rejection of the mind. The verbal dam, the concepts, the intellectual craft? These must be bypassed by the 'new man'.

Wherever we look, this is what confronts us: irrational experience. We must be careful not to be bewildered by the surface differences between these movements. We are not saying they are all the same. Of course there are differences. The secular existentialists, for example, disagree with one another. Then, too, secular existentialists differ with religious existentialists; the former tend to be pessimistic, the latter optimistic. Some of the movements are serious and command our respect. Some are just bizarre. There *are* differences. *Yet, all of them represent the new mysticism!*

The problem with mysticism of this sort is, interestingly enough, the same problem we considered earlier in relation to all humanistic systems. Who is going to say what is right?

As soon as one removes the checking mechanism of the mind by which to measure things, everything can then be 'right' and everything can also be 'wrong'. Eventually, anything and everything can be allowed! Take a simple example from life: If you are asking for directions in a city, you first listen to the directions your guide is giving and then you set off. Let us say the directions are: 'Take the first turn on the right, called Elvaston Place; then the next turn on the left, called Exhibition Road; and then keep going till you come to the park where you will see the art gallery just on your left by a big lake.' Armed with these directions, you go along—checking up on what you have been told: 'Yes, there is an Elvaston Place. Yes, there is an Exhibition Road,' and so on.

In other words, you are not just told words; you are able to see if these words relate to the outside world, the world you have to operate in if you are going to get from A to B. This is where your mind is essential. You can check to see if the information you have been given is true or false.

Imagine, on the other hand, that someone said, in answer to your request for directions, 'I don't know where or what B is. It is impossible to talk about an "art gallery". What is an "art gallery" anyway? We can only say of it that it is the "Unknowable".' How completely ridiculous for you to be told, 'Go *any* way—because this is the way!'

The trick in all these positions is to argue first of all that the End—Final Reality—cannot be spoken of (because it cannot be known by the mind) and yet to give the directions to find it. We should notice, however, that in this setting we can never ask questions ahead of time about the directions we receive. They are directions only for blindfolded experience, the blind 'leap of faith'.

We cannot ask, 'How will I know that it is truth or that it is the divine I am experiencing?' The answer is always, 'There is no way you can be told, for it is an answer beyond language, beyond categories, but take this path [or that one, or another one] anyway.'

Thus, modern man is bombarded from all sides by devotees of this or that *experience*. The media only compound the problem. So does the commercialism of our highly technological societies. The danger of manipulation from these alone is overwhelming. In the absence of a clear standard, they are a force for the control of people's minds and behaviour that is beyond anything in history. In fact, there are no clear standards in Western society now; and where there is an appearance of standards, very often there is insufficient motivation to lean against the enormous pressures. And why? In part, at least, because there is an inadequate basis for knowledge and for morality.

When we add to this that modern man has become a 'mystic', we soon realise the seriousness of the situation. For in all these mystical solutions no one can finally say anything about right and wrong. The East has had this problem for thousands of years. In a pantheistic system, whatever pious statements may be made along the way, ultimately good and evil are equal in God, the impersonal God. So we hear Yun-Men, a Zen master, saying, 'If you want to get the plain truth, be not concerned with right and wrong. Conflict between right and wrong is the sickness of the mind.'

Society can have no stability on this Eastern world view or its present Western counterpart. It just does not work. And so one finds a gravitation toward some form of authoritarian government, an individual tyrant or group of tyrants who take the reins of power and rule. And the freedoms, the sorts of freedoms we have enjoyed in the West, are lost.

We are, then, brought back to our starting point. The inhumanities and the growing loss of freedoms in the West are the result of a world view which has no place for 'people'. Modern humanistic materialism is an impersonal system. The East is no different. Both begin and end with impersonality.

We have looked at reasons for concluding not merely that these world views are uncomfortable because they lead to inhumanity, but because they are false. They do not fit into what we know best about ourselves and our environment. Ours is a universe which contains real personality. Neither the universe nor this personality is illusory. We will turn now to the Bible's claim to be the reliable source of information about the universe and mankind. But first, there are two very important introductory comments.

The Unveiling of Truth   The famous Hindu writer and statesman Sarvepalli Radhakrishnan once wrote, 'The altars erected to the unknown gods in the Graeco-Roman world were but an expression of man's ignorance of the divine nature. The sense of failure in man's quest for the unseen is symbolised by them. When asked to define the nature of God, the seer of the Upanishad sat silent, and when pressed to answer claimed that the Absolute is silence.'

By contrast, the apostle Paul, speaking in the context of the very same altars to unknown gods in Athens, said, '. . . Now what you worship as something unknown I am going to proclaim to you' (Acts 17:23).

And again, writing to the Corinthians not far away, 'However, as it is written: "No eye has seen, nor ear has heard, no mind has conceived. . . ." but God has revealed it to us. . . .' (1 Corinthians 2:9, 10). This claim is common to the whole Bible. God has not waited for us to stumble to Him in the dark (which would be impossible anyway), but has revealed Himself to us. The word *revelation* in Greek is *apokalupsis* which means literally 'unveiling'; so God has 'unveiled' to us the things we could not know because of our finiteness and sin.

This revelation or unveiling to finite and sinful people is the Bible as the *written Word*. This is the claim of the whole Bible. Moreover, through the Bible we learn of the life and teaching of the Second Person of the Trinity, who became man at a point in history and so became the *Living Word* of the Godhead: 'For in Christ all the fullness of the Deity lives in bodily form' (Colossians 2:9).

In this claim the dilemma of all humanistic systems is overcome at a stroke. The *infinite* God has spoken. None of the many finite attempts to define truth, doomed to failure as we have seen, is necessary. God has communicated to man, the infinite to the finite. God has communicated, in addition, in words that are understandable to us. The One who made man capable of language in the first place has communicated to man in language. Also, God has communicated truth about both spiritual reality and physical reality, about both the nature of God and the nature of man, about both events in past history and events in the future. Where all humanistic systems of thought are unable to give an adequate explanation of things, the Bible as God's statement is adequate.

It is equally important to note that the Bible's answer does not have to be believed blindly. There are good and sufficient reasons for seeing that it is true. It is the key that fits into the lock of what we know best about ourselves and the universe around us.

To change the metaphor: Imagine a book which has been mutilated, leaving just one inch of printed matter on each page. Although it would obviously be impossible to piece together and understand the book's story, few people would imagine that the printing which was left on those one-inch portions had come together by chance. However, if the torn pieces of each page were found in a trunk and were added in the right places, then the story could be read and would make sense.

So it is with Christianity. The ripped pages remaining in the book correspond to the universe and its form and to the mannishness of man. The parts of the pages discovered in the trunk correspond to the Scriptures, which are God's propositional communication to mankind. Neither the universe nor personality can give the answer to the whole meaning of the created order. Yet both are important as a testimony in helping us know that the Scriptures, God's communication to man, are what they claim to be. The question is whether the communication given by God completes and explains the portions we had before and especially whether it explains what was open to observation before (though without an explanation), that is, that the existence of the universe and its form and the mannishness of man are not just chance configurations of the printer's scrambled type.

This illustration is important for several reasons. First, it emphasises that Christians do not start out from themselves autonomously, as the humanists try to do. God gives the pages, and thus God gives the answers.

Second, it helps us see the proper place of man's reason. Just as a scientist does not create the order in the universe but does recognise it, so reason does not create the answer but simply recognises it. Of course this does not mean that reason will necessarily *receive* the answer. Each person has to *choose* to receive God's truth. But God's truth is clear. The individual must acknowledge that he (and mankind) is not autonomous, not the centre of all things, and he must acknowledge that he has many times done what he knows to be wrong and thus needs the work of Christ for himself. Those who refuse to back down from the position of autonomy make it impossible for themselves to receive the truth, even though there are good and sufficient reasons for knowing that it is the truth.

The Personal Origin of Man

The Scriptures tell us that the universe exists and has form and meaning because it was created purposefully by a personal Creator. This being the case, we see that, as we are personal, we are not something strange and out of line with an otherwise impersonal universe. Since we are made in the image of God, we are in line with God. There is a continuity, in other words, between ourselves, though finite, and the infinite Creator who stands behind the universe as its final source of meaning.

Unlike the evolutionary concept of an impersonal beginning plus time plus chance, the Bible gives an account of man's origin as a finite person made in God's image, that is, like God. We see then how man can have personality and dignity and value. Our uniqueness is guaranteed, something which is impossible in the materialistic system. If there is no qualitative distinction between man and other organic life (animals or plants), why should we feel greater concern over the death of a human being than over the death of a laboratory rat? Is man in the end any higher?

Though this is the logical end of the materialistic system, men and women still usually in practice assume that people have some real value. All the way back to the dawn of our investigations in history, we find that man is still man. Wherever we turn, to the caves of the Pyrenees, to the Sumerians in Mesopotamia, and even further back to Neanderthal man's burying his dead in flower petals, it makes no difference: Men everywhere show by their art and their accomplishments that they have been and have considered themselves to be unique. They *were* unique, and people today are unique. What is wrong is a world view which fails to explain that uniqueness. All people are unique because they are made in the image of God.

The Bible tells us also, however, that man is flawed. We see this to be the case both within ourselves and in our societies throughout the world. People are noble and people are cruel; people have heights of moral achievement and depths of moral depravity.

But this is not simply an enigma, nor is it explained in terms of 'the animal in man'. The Bible explains how man is flawed, without destroying the uniqueness and dignity of man. Man is evil and experiences the results of evil, not because man is non-man but because man is fallen and thus is *abnormal*.

This is the significance of the third chapter of Genesis. Some time after the original Creation (we do not know how long), man rebelled against God. Being made in the image of God as persons, Adam and Eve were able to make real choices. They had true creativity, not just in the area we call 'art' but also in the area of choice. And they used this choice to turn from God as their true integration point. Their ability to choose would have been equally validated if they had chosen not to turn away from God, as their true integration point, but instead they used their choice to try to make themselves autonomous. In doing this, they were acting against the moral absolute of the universe, namely, God's character—and thus evil among people was born.

The Fall brought not only moral evil but also the abnormality of (1) each person divided from himself or herself; (2) people divided from other people; (3) mankind divided from nature; and (4) nature divided from nature. This was the consequence of the choice made by Adam and Eve some time after the Creation. It was not any original deformity that made them choose in this way. God had not made them robots, and so they had real choice. It is man, therefore, and not God, who is responsible for evil.

We have to keep pointing out, because the idea is strange to a society by which the Bible has been neglected or distorted, that Christianity does not begin with a statement of Christ as Saviour. That comes later in its proper setting. Genesis 1:1 says, 'In the beginning God created. . . .' Christianity begins with the personal and infinite God who is the Creator. It goes on to show that man is made in God's image but then tells us that man is now fallen. It is the rebellion of man that has made the world *abnormal*. So there is a broken line as we look back to the creation of man by God. A chasm stands there near the beginning, the chasm which is the Fall, the choice to go against God and His Word.

What follows from this is that not everything that happens in the world is 'natural'. Unlike modern materialistic thought on both sides of the Iron Curtain, Christianity does not see everything in history as equally 'normal'. Because of the abnormality brought about by man, not everything which occurs in history should be there. Thus, not all that history brings forth is right just because it happens, and not all personal drives and motives are equally good. Here, then, is a marked difference between Christianity and almost all other philosophies. Most other philosophies do not have the concept of a present abnormality. Therefore, they hold that everything now is normal; things are now as they always have been.

By contrast, Christians do *not* see things as if they always have been this way. This is of immense importance in understanding the evil in the world. It is possible for Christians to speak of things as absolutely wrong, for they are not original in human society. They are derived from the Fall; they are in that sense 'abnormal'. It also means we can stand against what is wrong and cruel without standing against God, for He did not make the world as it now is.

This understanding of the chasm between what mankind and history are now and what they could have been—and should have been, from the way they were made—gives us a real moral framework for life, one which is compatible with our nature and aspirations. So there are 'rules for life', like the signs on cliff tops which read: DANGER—KEEP OUT. The signs are there to help not hinder us. God has put them there because to live in this way, according to His rules, is the way for both safety and fulfilment. The God who made us and knows what is for our best good is the same God who gives us His commands. When we break these, it is not only wrong, it is also not for our best good; it is not for our fulfilment as unique persons made in the image of God.

Freedom Within Form   We should not allow ourselves to hurry past this point, because it is of tremendous importance in relation to the problems we outlined in the first three chapters of this book. Knowing what is right and wrong, we have a way to have order and freedom simultaneously. It is relatively easy to attain order in society and not have any freedom. There are plenty of examples of that today. Likewise, it is easy to practise freedom without any order. There are examples of that, too, in the Western societies most of us live in. But how do we get both together? That is the problem.

The Bible gives a world view that provides order and yet at the same time freedom. God's rules are like a perimeter fence. We must stay within that fence if we are to avoid getting messed up. But inside the fence we have an almost endless *variety·of possibilities for freedom*. These touch every area of human life.

A good example is the pursuit of science. The Christian world view gives us a base for science, yet (since we are made in the image of God) a freedom to pursue science. The birth of modern science is generally conceded to be heavily indebted to the Christian world view. The Bible tells us that the universe is ordered, because God made it to cohere in all sorts of amazing ways. At the same time it tells us that we are persons. We are able to know what is around us; the subject can know the object.

It may seem rather obvious to say we can know what is around us, for everyone lives like this, day in and day out. We drive the car, use the stove, and so forth. Even though we cannot completely know any single detail of what is around us, we can still have accurate knowledge. This is what makes science possible, too. But, for the materialistic philosophers, this is still a problem.

Why is it that the noises we make from our mouths, for example, 'cat', 'dog', 'glass', 'hand', have a correspondence with objects in the outside world? That is the problem with which modern philosophers are still struggling. But within the Christian view the answer is simple and obvious: the world was made that way in the first place. Without the Bible's answer of a personal God who has made the universe—and at the same time persons within it to have a relationship with what has been made—people can still know the objects, *but they do not know why they can know them*.

The Importance of Genesis   So the Bible is the key to understanding the universe and its form and the mannishness of man. Without this key our observations are out of perspective; we do not know what we are looking at. This being the case, our conclusions about what we are seeing can be massively in error.

Unless we are told about our beginnings, we cannot make sense of our present history. And secular study is incapable of doing that. This is not to say that the study of history and science is irrelevant or useless, but when secular study is finished, the most important questions are left unanswered. It can tell us much of patterns and statistics, but not the reason or meaning or significance of it all. Twentieth-century people know something exists, but have no way of saying what that something amounts to.

This is where the early chapters of Genesis are so important. These chapters give the history that comes before anything that secular historians have been able to ascertain, and *it is this presecular history which gives meaning to mankind's present history*.

Some people mistakenly believe that one can 'spiritualise' away the history of the first chapters of Genesis and that this will make no difference. They argue that these chapters are not history but something like parables. This type of thinking depreciates the factual content, which gives information about history and the cosmos. Those who do this sometimes imagine that doing this makes little or no difference. But it changes everything. For these chapters tell us the *why* (the significance and meaning) of all the subsequent history which historians can know through their investigations. These chapters tell us also the *why* of our own personal history.

For this reason we can say that in this sense the early chapters of Genesis are more important than anything else we could have. They are the very foundation on which *all* knowledge rests. So we learn from them that before the creation of the universe, the infinite-personal God existed and that He created the universe (the space-time continuum) by choice, out of nothing. The Creation was not without a cause.

The infinite-personal God was its cause. He chose to create, He willed to create, and 'it was' — it came into being.

> You are worthy, our Lord and God,
>   to receive glory and honour and power,
> for you created all things,
>   and by your will they were created
>   and have their being.
> Revelation 4:11

As we have seen already, we learn also about the fact that man was made 'in the image of God', a person, and that then there was a space-time Fall.

All the information given by the Bible flows out of the information given in the early chapters of Genesis. If we are to understand the world as it is and ourselves as we are, we must know the flow of history given in these chapters. Take this away and the flow of history is lost. Take this away and even the death of Christ has no meaning.

So the Bible tells us who we are and who other people are. It tells us how people are differentiated from all other things. We do not need to be confused, as is much of modern mankind, about people's distinction from both animal life and the complicated machines of the second half of the twentieth century. Suddenly people have unique value, and we can understand how it is that each of us is different as a person.

Furthermore, we can see that *all* people are similarly to be distinguished from non-man and that therefore we ourselves must look on others as having great value. Anyone who kills a person is not killing just another member of the same biological species, but one of overwhelming value, one made in the image, the likeness, of God.

Any person, no matter who he or she is—a stranger or a friend, a fellow believer or someone who is still in rebellion against God, anyone of any age, before or after birth—*any and every person is made after the likeness of God.*

Each man, woman, and child is of great value, not for some ulterior motive such as self-gratification or wealth or power or as a sex object or for 'the good of society' or the maintenance of the gene pool—but simply because of his or her origin.

This flow of history that springs from Genesis has implications for every aspect of our lives. Each of us stands in the flow of history. We know our origin—a lineage more ancient than the Queen of England's or the Pilgrim Fathers'. As we look at ourselves in the flow of space-time reality, we see our origin in Adam and Eve, and we know that God has created every human being in His own image.

5
Truth and History

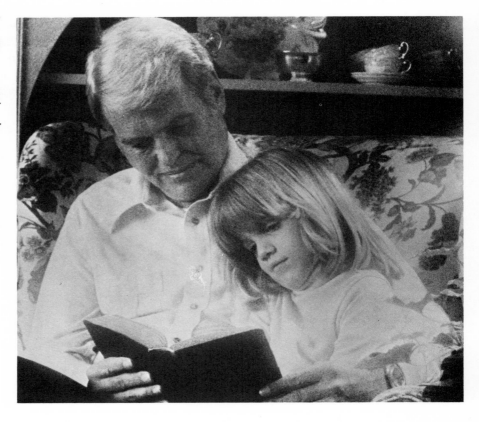

In the previous chapter we saw that the Bible gives us the explanation for the existence of the universe and its form and for the mannishness of man. Or, to reverse this, we came to see that the universe and its form and the mannishness of man are a testimony to the truth of the Bible. In this chapter we will consider a third testimony: the Bible's openness to verification by historical study.

Christianity involves history. To say only that is already to have said something remarkable, because it separates the Judaeo-Christian world view from almost all other religious thought. It is rooted in history.

The Bible tells us how God communicated with man in history. For example, God revealed Himself to Abraham at a point in time and at a particular geographical place. He did the same with Moses, David, Isaiah, Daniel and so on. The implications of this are extremely important to us. Because the truth God communicated in the Bible is so tied up with the flow of human events it is possible by historical study to confirm some of the historical details.

It is remarkable that this possibility exists. Compare the information we have from other continents of that period. We know comparatively little about what happened in Africa or South America or China or Russia or even Europe. We see beautiful remains of temples and burial places, cult figures, utensils, and so forth, but there is not much actual 'history' that can be reconstructed, at least not much when compared to that which is possible in the Middle East.

When we look at the material which has been discovered from the Nile to the Euphrates that derives from the twenty-five-hundred-year span before Christ, we are in a completely different situation from that in regard to South America or Asia. The kings of Egypt and Assyria built thousands of monuments commemorating their victories and re-counting their different exploits. Whole libraries have been discovered from places like Nuzu and Mari and most recently at Ebla, which give hundreds of thousands of texts relating to the historical details of their time. It is within this geographical area that the Bible is set. So it is possible to find material which bears upon what the Bible tells us.

The Bible purports to give us information on history. Is the history accurate? The more we understand about the Middle East between 2500 BC and AD 100, the more confident we can be that the information in the Bible is reliable, even when it speaks about the simple things of time and place (see Appendices 2, 3, 4).

Moses and Joshua   Mount Sinai is one of the most important sites of the entire Bible. It was here that the Hebrew people came shortly after their flight from Egypt. Here God spoke to them through Moses, giving them directions for their life as a newly formed nation and making a covenant with them.

The thing to notice about this epochal moment for Israel is the emphasis on history which the Bible itself makes. Time and time again Moses reminds the people of what has happened on Mount Sinai:

> You came near and stood at the foot of the mountain while it blazed with fire to the very heavens, with black clouds and deep darkness. Then the LORD spoke to you out of the fire. You heard the sound of words but saw no form; there was only a voice.
>
> Deuteronomy 4:11, 12

Moses emphasises that those alive at the time had actually heard God's direct communication in words. They also were eyewitnesses of what had occurred—they saw the cloud and the mountain burning with fire. They saw and they heard. In the same way they had been eyewitnesses of the remarkable events which had accompanied their escape from Egypt shortly before: 'But it was your own eyes that saw all these great things the LORD has done' (Deuteronomy 11:7). Therefore, Moses says, on the basis of what they themselves have seen and heard in their own lifetime, they are not to be afraid of their present or future enemies.

> But do not be afraid of them; remember well what the LORD your God did to Pharaoh and to all Egypt. You saw with your own eyes the great trials, the miraculous signs and wonders, the mighty hand and outstretched arm, with which the LORD your God brought you out. The LORD your God will do the same to all the peoples you now fear.
>
> Deuteronomy 7:18, 19

On the same basis too, Moses urges them to obey God: 'Only be careful, and watch yourselves closely so that you do not forget the things your eyes have seen . . .' (Deuteronomy 4:9).

Thus the people's confidence and trust in God and their obedience to Him are alike rooted in truth that is historical and observable. Therefore, the historical records are subject to factual study; the historical records are not only open to verification but to falsification as well. The relationship between God and His people was not based on an inward experience inside their own heads, but upon a reality which was seen and heard. They were called to obey God not because of a leap of faith, but because of God's real acts in history. For God is the *living* God. The universe within which man lives is not a 'closed' system of natural causes. The universe is God's creation and it is 'open' to Him. God has acted into history, into a history which is seeable.

'Religious truth' according to the Bible involves the same sort of truth which people operate on in their everyday lives. If something is true, then its opposite cannot also be true. For example, if the Israelites were slaves in Egypt under the Egyptian pharaohs at a particular moment in history, then it cannot also be true that at the same time the Israelites were *not* slaves in Egypt. Likewise, if Jesus was raised from the dead, His body will not be able to be found where He was buried near Jerusalem.

This is the Bible's view of truth: Certain things are true whose opposites are not true. It is important to understand that this concept of truth did not begin with the Greeks, as some people suggest. God made the human mind itself so that we all act on this. Even those who deny the concept act on it in practice. If someone says that all truth is relative, he is saying absolutely that this is true. The necessities of everyday life give the lie to relativistic thought.

From the Bible's viewpoint, all truth finally rests upon the fact that the infinite-personal God exists in contrast to His not existing. This means that God exists objectively; He exists whether or not people say He does. The Bible also teaches that God is personal. That means, therefore, that the statements 'God does *not* exist' and 'God is *im*personal' are false.

Three things should be emphasised about the Hebrew (and biblical) view of truth.

1. In the Hebrew (and biblical) view, truth is grounded ultimately in the existence and character of God and what has been given to us by God in creation and revelation. Because people are finite, reality cannot be exhausted by human reason. Mankind, being limited, can know many things only through revelation. (Biblical truth is bountifully full. Thus, while what the Bible teaches can be put into words and discussed, it so gives things in balance that its teaching as a whole is often richer than any single statement quoted as a proof text.)

2. The biblical view of truth is not a lesser view of truth than the Greek view, but a far higher one. The Judaeo-Christian world view is not merely a philosophic system to be reasoned about abstractly as a nicely balanced system as the Greeks did. It is certainly a world view, one that makes sense of our experience. But it is more; *it is a world view related to history* and therefore at crucial points open to confirmation through what can be touched and seen.

3. It is a view of truth that involves the whole person; it is to be enjoyed; it is to be upheld through opposition and denial. It demands choice and commitment. Why? Because it is objectively true. It is truth both to God and to us. Thus, the Hebrew (and biblical) view of truth, rather than being similar to the modern relativistic (or dialectical or existential) concept of truth, is completely contrary to it.

It is within this Judaeo-Christian view of truth that, by its own insistence, we must understand the Bible. Moses could appeal to real historical events as the basis for Israel's confidence and obedience into the future. He could even pass down to subsequent generations physical reminders of what God had done, so that the people could see them and remember. So, for example, he gave the Ten Commandments on the two tablets of stone to be kept in the Ark of the Covenant. Likewise he gave them a pot of manna (the food provided by God during the wilderness wanderings), and the rod belonging to Aaron, Moses' brother, which had been used in Egypt and later as a sign of God's power

and presence. These were kept as silent witnesses of truth; they were observable in history from generation to generation within the Jewish sanctuary.

At the time of Joshua, who followed Moses in the leadership of the Jews, we find the same emphasis on historic testimony as in the writings of Moses: 'Joshua set up the twelve stones that had been in the middle of the Jordan at the spot where the priests who carried the ark of the covenant had stood. And they are there to this day' (Joshua 4:9). God is not an abstract force or idea. Man's experience of God is not just within his head. God is active in history. And just as in the time of Moses God commanded various items to be kept as physical reminders of what He had done, so God did the same thing in the time of Joshua.

God temporarily dried up the Jordan River so that the Jews could pass. As a memorial of that fact — so that it could be observed through subsequent generations — two piles of twelve stones each were made. The first pile was made in the riverbed of the Jordan itself while the people were actually crossing. There they could be seen for centuries when the water in the Jordan was low. The second pile was made out of rocks which the Jews lifted from the river as they passed by and then piled on the dry land at their camp in Gilgal: 'And Joshua set up at Gilgal the twelve stones they had taken out of Jordan'' (Joshua 4:20).

Abraham and Isaac   The Bible's account of Abraham's life also emphasises historic events as real events. This becomes especially obvious — and important — in the account of Abraham's sacrifice of his son, Isaac.

The Bible sets this event in a definite framework. We are told, for example, that Abraham was directed by God to take Isaac to a particular mountain, Mount Moriah — a long three-day journey from where Abraham and Isaac were. This is important, not just an incidental detail. This was the site on which Solomon many years later built the temple. And the New Testament tells us that Jesus died not far from this same spot.

None of this is by chance. Jesus died as the promised Lamb of God, as John the Baptist calls Him. He died to take away the sin of the world. As such He is the fulfilment of what was prefigured in the 'almost sacrifice' of Isaac a bit less than two thousand years earlier. And as such, too, Jesus is the fulfilment of all the sacrifices associated with the tabernacle and temple. God was indicating in 'the sacrifice of Isaac' that it is not an animal which delivers people from their sin, but a Person.

This also helps us to understand why something which the rest of the

Bible tells us is abhorrent to God, human sacrifice, could have been used as the supreme test of Abraham's trust in God's promises to him. It was not because God wished Isaac to die (and, of course, Isaac did not die), but because God wished to make clear that He Himself would provide the sacrifice and that that sacrifice would not be an animal but a very special *Person*.

Let us notice in particular that God did not ask Abraham for a 'leap of faith', any more than He asked the people of Israel for a leap of faith at the time of Moses. Abraham had already been given many evidences of God's reality and of His reliability. God had spoken to him over and over again before this time:

> The Lord had said to Abram, 'Leave your country, your people and your father's household and go to the land I will show you.
>
> 'I will make you into a great nation
>   and I will bless you;
> I will make your name great,
>   and you will be a blessing.
> I will bless those who bless you,
>   and whoever curses you I will curse;
> and all peoples on earth
>   will be blessed through you.'
>
> Genesis 12:1–3

Then again, when Abraham came into Canaan: 'The LORD said to Abram after Lot had parted from him, "Lift up your eyes from where you are and look north and south, east and west. All the land that you see I will give to you and your offspring forever . . ."' (Genesis 13:14, 15).

God promised to give Abraham a new country and descendants. However, where was the son and heir? Abraham was old, and in his concern to provide an heir he had first chosen a servant called Eliezer who came from Damascus. Here are the key passages from Genesis which record Abraham's experience in getting a proper heir:

> Then the word of the LORD came to him: 'This man will not be your heir, but a son coming from your own body will be your heir.' He took him outside and said, 'Look at the heavens and count the stars—if indeed you can count them.' Then he said to him, 'So shall your offspring be.'
>   Abram believed the LORD, and he credited it to him as righteousness.
>
> Genesis 15:4–6

When Abram was ninety-nine years old, the LORD appeared to him and said, 'I am God Almighty; walk before me and be blameless. I will confirm my covenant between me and you and will greatly increase your numbers.'

Abram fell facedown, and God said to him, 'As for me, this is my covenant with you: You will be the father of many nations. No longer will you be called Abram; your name will be Abraham, for I have made you a father of many nations.   Genesis 17:1–5

The LORD appeared to Abraham near the great trees of Mamre while he was sitting at the entrance to his tent in the heat of the day. Abraham looked up and saw three men standing nearby. When he saw them, he hurried from the entrance of his tent to meet them and bowed low to the ground.

He said, 'If I have found favour in your eyes, my lord, do not pass your servant by. . . .'

'Where is your wife Sarah?' they asked him.

'There, in the tent,' he said.

Then the LORD said, 'I will surely return to you about this time next year, and Sarah your wife will have a son.'

Now Sarah was listening at the entrance to the tent, which was behind him. Abraham and Sarah were already old and well advanced in years, and Sarah was past the age of childbearing. So Sarah laughed to herself as she thought, 'After I am worn out and my master is old, will I now have this pleasure?'

Then the LORD said to Abraham, 'Why did Sarah laugh and say, "Will I really have a child, now that I am old?" Is anything too hard for the LORD? I will return to you at the appointed time next year and Sarah will have a son.'   Genesis 18:1–3, 9–14

Thus, in this remarkable way Abraham came to have an heir, just as God had said. Abraham also saw God's remarkable deliverance of his nephew Lot from Sodom and Gomorrah.

Therefore, the certainty that God was both real and trustworthy had been established to Abraham through a number of revelations and events. He had heard God, he had talked with Him, he had received propositional revelation from God. He had seen God keep His promises, both in regard to a son (even though he and Sarah were old) and in regard to Lot's rescue. When we read the following account of the sacrifice of Isaac, we must keep these facts in mind. Abraham knew God was both real and trustworthy.

Some time later God tested Abraham. He said to him, 'Abraham!'

'Here I am,' he replied.

Then God said, 'Take your son, your only son Isaac, whom you love, and go to the region of Moriah. Sacrifice him there as a burnt offering on one of the mountains I will tell you about.'

Early the next morning Abraham got up and saddled his donkey. He took with him two of his servants and his son Isaac. When he had cut enough wood for the burnt offering, he set out for the place God had told him about.

On the third day Abraham looked up and saw the place in the distance. He said to his servants, 'Stay here with the donkey while I and the boy go over there. We will worship and then we will come back to you.'

Abraham took the wood for the burnt offering and placed it on his son Isaac, and he himself carried the fire and the knife. As the two of them went on together, Isaac spoke up and said to his father Abraham, 'Father?'

'Yes, my son?' Abraham replied.

'The fire and wood are here,' Isaac said, 'but where is the lamb for the burnt offering?'

Abraham answered, 'God himself will provide the lamb for the burnt offering, my son.' And the two of them went on together.

When they reached the place God had told him about, Abraham built an altar there and arranged the wood on it. He bound his son Isaac and laid him on the altar, on top of the wood. Then he reached out his hand and took the knife to slay his son. But the angel of the LORD called out to him from heaven, 'Abraham! Abraham!'

'Here I am,' he replied

'Do not lay a hand on the boy,' he said. 'Do not do anything to him. Now I know that you fear God, because you have not withheld from me your son, your only son.'

Abraham looked up and there in a thicket he saw a ram caught by its horns. He went over and took the ram and sacrificed it as a burnt offering instead of his son. So Abraham called that place 'The LORD will provide.' And to this day it is said, 'On the mountain of the LORD it will be provided.'

Genesis 22:1–14

Far from Abraham being asked to make a blind leap of faith, the Bible indicates that it would have been unreasonable and disobedient on Abraham's part for him not to obey God. He had previously had ample evidence of God's reliability. Therefore he had said to the servants, with real assurance, '. . . we will come back to you' (Genesis 22:5).

This is not to minimise his difficulty as a human father, as he stood there with his much loved son at his side. Nor is it to minimise the profound obedience he showed toward God as he followed along toward the sacrifice of that son until God stopped him. But any idea that Abraham's faith was contrary to reason overlooks all that had gone before.

Paul in Corinth   This emphasis—that faith is not contrary to reason—is presented in both the Old and the New Testaments. The entire Bible makes plain that the history it records is to be seen as real history. Consider the apostle Paul in Greece. Paul visited Corinth and stayed there for a year and a half.

> There he met a Jew named Aquila, a native of Pontus, who had recently come from Italy with his wife Priscilla, because Claudius had ordered all the Jews to leave Rome. Paul went to see them, and because he was a tentmaker as they were, he stayed and worked with them. Every Sabbath he reasoned in the synagogue, trying to persuade Jews and Greeks. . . . So Paul stayed for a year and a half, teaching them the word of God.
>
> Acts 18:2–4, 11

We have now left far behind the great powers of Assyria and Babylon and Egypt. Alexander the Great has also come and gone. Though the Greek language is still used through the Mediterranean world, it is now Rome who rules and Claudius who is emperor. This is our setting; we are in a real moment of history and the people we read about in the Bible are as real as ourselves.

There are a number of interesting things about Corinth. We learn from Acts 18:2 that while Paul was here he met a Jewish couple, Priscilla and Aquila, who had recently come from Italy, and he stayed with them and, in fact, supported himself financially by helping them in their craft of tentmaking. Priscilla and Aquila had had to leave Italy, Acts tell us, because Claudius had commanded all Jews to depart from Rome.

What we should notice is that the Book of Acts gives us here, in the midst of an account of Paul's preaching in Corinth and his trials and deliverances, a statement about the Roman Emperor Claudius and a decree of his against the Jews. We are immediately conscious that this is the same type of world view we have become accustomed to throughout the Old Testament. This is real history again.

The Roman biographer Suetonius tells us more about that expulsion of the Jews, and the occasion can be dated from another source to the year AD 49. Acts tells us that the governor in Corinth while Paul was there was a man named Gallio. Now Gallio was a famous man, the brother of Seneca, who was a prominent Roman philosopher and writer and who later became tutor to the future Emperor Nero. Seneca wrote about his brother Gallio, and some of his letters have been preserved down to the present. He mentioned, for example, Gallio's year of office in Corinth. This has also been attested by several fragments of an inscribed stone from Delphi (which is across the isthmus from Corinth). This gives the dates when Gallio held his governorship: the summer of AD 51 to the summer of AD 52. It also gives his title as 'Proconsul of Achaia' (that is, southern Greece) which is exactly the title used of him in Acts 18:12.

Here, then, are a number of historical strands inside and outside the

Bible which run together naturally and easily. Archaeology has even identified the Governor's palace at Corinth, and we can see the very place where Paul is likely to have appeared before Gallio.

Resurrection and History

Later we find Paul writing a letter to the church at Corinth. In it he presents what he preached and taught throughout the Roman Empire:

> Now, brothers, I want to remind you of the gospel I preached to you, which you received and on which you have taken your stand. By this gospel you are saved, if you hold firmly to the word I preached to you. Otherwise, you have believed in vain.
>
> For what I received I passed on to you as of first importance: that Christ died for our sins according to the Scriptures, that he was buried, that he was raised on the third day according to the Scriptures, and that he appeared to Peter, and then to the Twelve. After that, he appeared to more than five hundred of the brothers at the same time, most of whom are still living, though some have fallen asleep. Then he appeared to James, then to all the apostles, and last of all he appeared to me also, as to one abnormally born.
>
> For I am the least of the apostles and do not even deserve to be called an apostle, because I persecuted the church of God. But by the grace of God I am what I am, and his grace to me was not without effect. No, I worked harder than all of them—yet not I, but the grace of God that was with me. Whether, then, it was I or they, this is what we preach, and this is what you believed.
>
> But if it is preached that Christ has been raised from the dead, how can some of you say that there is no resurrection of the dead? If there is no resurrection of the dead, then not even Christ has been raised. And if Christ has not been raised, our preaching is useless and so is your faith. More than that, we are then found to be false witnesses about God, for we have testified about God that he raised Christ from the dead. But he did not raise him if in fact the dead are not raised. For if the dead are not raised, then Christ has not been raised either. And if Christ has not been raised, your faith is futile; you are still in your sins. Then those also who have fallen asleep in Christ are lost. If only for this life we have hope in Christ, we are to be pitied more than all men.
>
> But Christ has indeed been raised from the dead, the firstfruits of those who have fallen asleep. For since death came through a man, the resurrection of the dead comes also through a man. For as in Adam all die, so in Christ all will be made alive. But each in his own turn: Christ, the firstfruits; then, when he comes, those who belong to him. Then the end will come, when he hands over the kingdom to God the Father after he has destroyed all dominion, authority and power.
>
> 1 Corinthians 15:1–24

In this section of his First Letter to the Corinthians, Paul asserts unequivocally that Jesus has been raised from the tomb and that we shall ourselves be raised like Him in the future. Jesus' body was placed in the tomb, but it did not remain there. Jesus rose from the dead. It was not simply a subjective experience by which the disciples were deceived. Jesus rose from the dead as a space-time fact and then He appeared to the disciples.

But we should notice particularly the other side of Paul's argument. He says, 'Suppose that Jesus did not rise from the dead.' That is not what he believes, of course, for he knows on objective grounds that Jesus has been raised; he himself had met Jesus and heard Him speak to him in the Hebrew language. And there were many other eyewitnesses to the resurrected Christ. Paul is saying, 'Let us just suppose for the sake of seeing what follows that Jesus was not resurrected. What would happen then?' Paul is quick to reply: 'If this did not happen, everything is finished from Christianity's point of view. We may as well "eat and drink, for tomorrow we die". If Christ did not rise from the dead as a historical fact, we have no Saviour. Therefore we are "still in our sins"; we shall have to face God's judgment and bear the penalty for our sin alone.'

What he does *not* say is the sort of thing one hears all over the world today from churchmen who have been influenced by existential thought. They say, 'Even if Jesus did *not* rise from the dead, Christianity is untouched.' One such theologian said that the Resurrection took place—but if a television crew had visited the tomb that morning, it could not have recorded the event. In other words, the body of Christ was still there! But this is unthinkable to Paul. Either Christ rose from the dead as an objective fact of history, or He did not. If He did not, Christianity is finished.

When we examine the actual account of the Resurrection of Jesus in the Gospels, we find the same emphasis. The Garden Tomb in Jerusalem may not be the precise place where Jesus was buried, but certainly it must have been a tomb very like it and somewhere near that site. On the third day after the burial, Jesus rose from the dead. Here is how the Gospel of John records the events:

> Early on the first day of the week, while it was still dark, Mary of Magdala went to the tomb and saw that the stone had been removed from the entrance. . . . Then Simon Peter, who was behind him [the other disciple, John] arrived and went into the tomb. He saw the strips of linen lying there,

as well as the burial cloth that had been around Jesus' head. The cloth was folded up by itself, separate from the linen.

John 20:1, 6, 7

Notice that Mary Magdalene and Peter and John observed something *with normal observation*—the stone was rolled away; the linen cloth and the headcloth in which Jesus had been wrapped at His burial were still lying in the empty tomb. We read in Luke 24 that Jesus later appeared to all the disciples as they were gathered together. Evidently they were in some agitation, both from what they had witnessed at Christ's death and by the reports that Jesus had risen from the dead:

> While they were still talking about this, Jesus himself stood among them and said to them, 'Peace be with you.'
> They were startled and frightened, thinking they saw a ghost. He said to them, 'Why are you troubled. and why do doubts rise in your minds? Look at my hands and my feet. It is I myself! Touch me and see; a ghost does not have flesh and bones, as you see I have.'
> When he had said this, he showed them his hands and feet. And while they still did not believe it because of joy and amazement, he asked them, 'Do you have anything here to eat?' They gave him a piece of broiled fish, and He took it and ate it in their presence.

Luke 24:36–43

The Resurrection of Christ is presented in the Gospels as verifiable history. It is given in the same frame of reference as applies in science—when Christ arose, He did not leave His body in the grave. The Resurrection was open to normal observation. There were the graveclothes. Jesus spoke to the disciples. He could be touched. He ate before them.

Thomas and the Resurrected Christ

Perhaps the most striking incident recorded involves Thomas:

> Now Thomas (called Didymus), one of the Twelve, was not with the disciples when Jesus came. When the other disciples told him that they had seen the Lord, he declared, 'Unless I see the nail marks in his hands and put my finger where the nails were, and put my hand into his side, I will not believe it.'
> A week later his disciples were in the house again, and Thomas was with them. Though the doors were locked, Jesus came and stood among them and said, 'Peace be with you!' Then he said to Thomas, 'Put your finger here; see my hands. Reach out your hand and put it into my side. Stop doubting and believe.'
> Thomas said to him, 'My Lord and my God!'

> Then Jesus told him, 'Because you have seen me, you have believed;
> blessed are those who have not seen and yet have believed.'
>
> John 20:24-29

Just as Moses said, well over a thousand years before, 'You saw, you heard,' so the Gospels say, 'You saw, you heard!' God acted in history, and this was observed and was able to be described in ordinary language.

If Jesus did not live, or if He did not rise from the dead, Christianity cannot continue. It cannot live on as a mere *idea*, because Christianity is about objective truth and not merely religious experiences. Both the Old Testament and the New Testament claim to be truth, in contrast to that which is not true, and this truth is rooted in history. We have only one hope, and it rests on a serious commitment to the existence of God and the reliability of His Word, the Bible, in all the areas in which it speaks.

There is truth that can be known and before which we can bow with joy—truth that in a very real way is climaxed in the physical Resurrection of Christ. If the tomb was not empty—so that a camera crew could have recorded the absence of Jesus' body, at the same time that they could have filmed the linen strips and headcloth in which His body had been wrapped—we have no hope.

Thomas should have believed on the basis of the evidence that he had from the other disciples and that was quite sufficient. Jesus rebuked him when He appeared to him and said, 'Put your finger here; see my hands. Reach out your hand and put it into my side. Stop doubting and believe.' After Thomas had said, 'My Lord and my God!' Jesus said, 'Because you have seen me, you have believed; blessed are those who have not seen and yet have believed.'

Is Jesus saying by this that believing is a blind leap of ungrounded faith? Quite the opposite! Because Thomas insisted on seeing and touching Jesus in His resurrected body, we have been given in the Gospels an even clearer evidence of the Resurrection than we would otherwise have had. But Jesus is saying that Thomas should have believed without this additional evidence, because the evidence available to Thomas before was in itself sufficient. In other words, before Thomas saw and heard Jesus in this way, he was in the same position as we are today. Both he at that time and we today have the same sufficient witness of those who have seen and heard and who have had the opportunity to touch the resurrected Christ. In fact, in the light of this sufficient and sure witness we, like Thomas, are disobedient if we do not bow. We are without excuse.

After telling about Thomas, the Gospel of John then turns to another appearance of Jesus:

> Afterward Jesus appeared again to his disciples by the Sea of Tiberias. It happened this way: Simon Peter, Thomas (called Didymus), Nathanael from Cana in Galilee, the sons of Zebedee, and two other disciples were together. 'I'm going out to fish,' Simon Peter told them, and they said, 'We'll go with you.' So they went out and got into the boat, but that night they caught nothing.
>
> Early in the morning, Jesus stood on the shore, but the disciples did not realise that it was Jesus.
>
> He called out to them, 'Friends, haven't you [caught] any fish?'
>
> 'No,' they answered.
>
> He said, 'Throw your net on the right side of the boat and you will find some.' When they did, they were unable to haul the net in because of the large number of fish.
>
> Then the disciple whom Jesus loved said to Peter, 'It is the Lord!' As soon as Simon Peter heard him say, 'It is the Lord,' he wrapped his outer garment around him (for he had taken it off) and jumped into the water. The other disciples followed in the boat, towing the net full of fish, for they were not far from the shore, about a hundred yards. When they landed, they saw a fire of burning coals there with fish on it, and some bread.
>
> Jesus said to them, 'Bring some of the fish you have just caught.'
>
> Simon Peter climbed aboard and dragged the net ashore. It was full of large fish, 153, but even with so many the net was not torn. Jesus said to them, 'Come and have breakfast.' None of the disciples dared ask him, 'Who are you?' They knew it was the Lord. Jesus came, took the bread and gave it to them, and did the same with the fish. This was now the third time Jesus appeared to his disciples after he was raised from the dead.
>
> John 21:1–14

The resurrected Jesus stood there on the beach of the Sea of Galilee. Before the disciples reached the shore, he had already prepared a fire with fish cooking on it for them to eat. It was a fire that could be seen and felt; it cooked the fish, and the fish and bread could be eaten for breakfast.

When the fire died down, it left ashes on the beach; the disciples were well fed with bread and fish. There is no reason to suppose that Christ's footprints were not visible on the beach.

We must respond with Thomas: 'My Lord and my God!'

6
Our Personal Response and Social Action

The relationship of chapters 4, 5, and 6 to chapters 1, 2, and 3 is direct and far-reaching. In the flood of the loss of humanness in our age — including the flow from abortion-on-demand to infanticide and on to euthanasia — the only thing that can stem this tide is the certainty of the absolute uniqueness and value of people. And the only thing which gives us this is the knowledge that people are made in the image of God. We have no other final protection. And the only way we know that people are made in the image of God is through the Bible and the Incarnation of Christ, which we know from the Bible.

If people are not made in the image of God, the pessimistic, realistic humanist is right: The human race is indeed an abnormal wart on the smooth face of a silent and meaningless universe. In this setting, abortion, infanticide, and euthanasia (including the killing of mentally deranged criminals, the severely handicapped, or the elderly who are an economic burden) are completely logical. Any person can be obliterated for what society at one moment thinks of as its own social or economic good. Without the Bible and without the revelation in Christ (which is only told to us in the Bible) there is nothing to stand between us and our children and the eventual acceptance of the monstrous inhumanities of the age.

In chapters 4 and 5 we saw reasons why we can know that the Bible is truth. The existence of the universe and its form and the uniqueness of man testify to the truth of Scripture, and historical study likewise testifies to the truth of Scripture. The Bible gives us a solid and certain basis on which we can begin to act toward stemming the tide of inhumanity. The solution to the inhuman drift begins, however, with each of us as individuals. It begins with you, with me—with each of us.

First Steps Towards Solving the Problem

First, Christianity must be acknowledged to be the truth. Christianity and Christ must not be accepted merely to change society and stop the drift of our culture toward the loss of humanness.

Unhappily, it is possible for people to reject the truth of Christianity and the claims of Christ and yet to hope that others will accept Christianity so that the drift of society will be halted. They think that some kind of Christian revival would be useful in order to affect human behaviour and thus protect their own political and economic comfort, allowing them to keep their personal peace and affluence. Biblical Christianity and Christ will indeed stop the drift, but not if Christianity is only used for manipulation by those who think it is not true—but only useful.

In contrast to this attempted utilitarian use of Christianity, what must we do? First, we should see that, for what are good and sufficient reasons, Christianity is true. Then we should personally bow as finite creatures before our infinite-personal Creator. And then we should accept Christ as Saviour to remove our personal moral guilt before God. We need that true moral guilt removed because there is the absolute of the Creator's character, and over and over again we have deliberately done what we know to be wrong.

God's promise of a solution to mankind's revolt against Him was first given in the third chapter of Genesis. This promise was expanded with increasing clarity right through the Old Testament. A Messiah, a Saviour, was coming. He would take upon Himself the punishment of our sins. As Isaiah said, some 700 years before Christ came:

> We all, like sheep, have gone astray,
>   each of us has turned to his own way;
> and the LORD has laid on him
>   the iniquity of us all.
>
> Isaiah 53:6

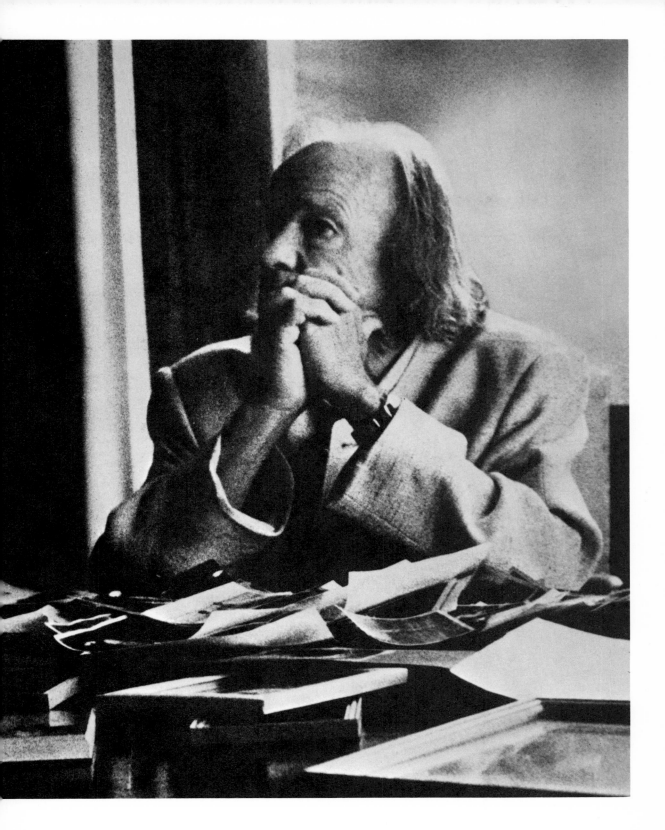

And we are told that the work of Christ as the dying and resurrected Lamb of God was sufficient to reconcile us to God, that we do not have to add any 'works' of our own, that we are saved by the infinite value of what Christ has done—plus *nothing*. Salvation is a gift that we receive with empty hands. This is what it means to have faith in Christ, or to accept Christ as Saviour.

The Lordship of Christ

But when we accept Christ as Saviour, we must also acknowledge and then act upon the fact that if He is our Saviour, He is also our Lord in *all* of life. He is Lord not just in religious things and not just in cultural things such as art and music, but in our intellectual lives and in business and our attitude toward the devaluation of people's humanness in our culture. Acknowledging Christ's Lordship and placing ourselves under what is taught in the whole Bible includes thinking and acting as citizens in relation to our government and its laws. We must know what those laws are and act responsibly to help to change them if they do not square with the Bible's concepts of justice and humanness. The biblical answers have to be lived and not just thought.

We must live under the Lordship of Christ in all the areas of life—at great cost, if need be. It is moving to think of the Christians in China, paying a great price for their loyalty to Christ, but that does not relieve each of us from being under the Lordship of Christ in regard to our own country.

Who is on the cutting edge here? The doctor who pays the price of having certain hospitals closed to him because he will not perform abortions. The businessman who knows he is forfeiting advancement in his company because he will not go along with some inhuman practice of his company. The professor of sociology who is willing to lose his post because he will not teach sociology on the basis of determinism. The pastor who loses his church rather than follow the dictates of a liberal theology or a 'trashy Christianity'. Or the pastor who preaches the Bible, stressing that today's people are called to sacrificial action, rather than keeping his congregation comfortable while death, spiritual and physical, is built up year after year for the children and grandchildren. Examples could be endlessly multiplied.

Faithfulness to the Lordship of Christ means using the constitutional processes while we still have them. We live in a shrinking island of free constitutional practice. Only a small percentage of countries in the world still possess this. The Lordship of Christ means using these processes to speak and to act on the basis of the principles set forth in the Bible.

With Christ as Saviour and Lord, we must do all we can to lead others to Christ. And simultaneously we must use every constitutional practice to offset the rise of authoritarian governments and the loss of humanness in our society. But there is no use in talking of offsetting the loss of humanness in society if we do not act humanly to all people about us in the contacts of our individual lives. We must practise the human alternatives set forth at the end of chapter 3. We ourselves must act humanly, even when it is costly.

We implore those of you who are Christians to exert all your influence to fight against the increasing loss of humanness—through legislation, social action, and other means at your disposal, both privately and publicly, individually and collectively, in all areas of your lives.

Without the uniqueness and inherent dignity of each human being, no matter how old or young, sick or well, resting on the fact that each person is made in the image of God, there is no sufficient foundation to build on as we resist the loss of humanness in our generation. So we would say again to those of you who are Christians, do not allow your only base, your only hope to be able to stand—namely, the Bible—to be weakened by however subtle means. The Bible is truth in all its parts, and provides, if taken as a whole, the truth of salvation and also a base to work from in our daily lives, a base to stand on morally.

So we who are Christians must, on the one hand, fight with determination and sacrifice for the individual in society, and on the other, provide the loving care of people as individuals. Thus the world will truly feel our presence in its midst as the true salt of the earth. That salt will be a true preservative, both showing forth the beauty of care in the midst of utilitarian ugliness and also helping to remove the festering malignancy of evil that surrounds us.

The Challenge Before Us As a result of being made in the image of God, each man and woman has a conscience. That built-in monitor, coupled with the advantages of being raised in a society that has had until recently a Judaeo-Christian tradition, permits the understanding of the worth of human life to surface periodically, even subconsciously—as, for example, in the recent preoccupation with the special needs of the handicapped adult. But

that memory will not last forever without the Judaeo-Christian base. Recent history shows us that the conscience can be so corrupted and manipulated that today's unthinkable becomes tomorrow's thinkable with remarkable speed.

People are special and human life is sacred, whether or not we admit it. Every life is precious and worthwhile in itself—not only to us human beings but also to God. Every person is worth fighting for, regardless of whether he is young or old, sick or well, child or adult, born or unborn, or brown, red, yellow, black, or white.

If, in this last part of the twentieth century, the Christian community does not take a prolonged and vocal stand for the dignity of the individual each person's right to life—for the right of each individual to be treated as created in the image of God, rather than as a collection of molecules with no unique value—we feel that as Christians we have failed the greatest moral test to be put before us in this century.

Future generations will look back, and many will either scoff or believe in Christ on the basis of whether we Christians of today took a sacrificial stand in our various walks of life on these overwhelmingly important issues. If we do not take a stand here and now, we certainly cannot lay any claim to being the salt of the earth in our generation. We are neither preserving moral values and the dignity of the individual nor showing compassion for our fellow human beings.

Will future generations look back and remember that—even if the twentieth century *did* end with a great surge of inhumanity—at least there was one group who stood consistently, whatever the price, for the value of the individual, thus passing on some hope to future generations? Or are we Christians going to be merely swept along with the trends—our own moral values becoming increasingly befuddled, our own apathy reflecting the apathy of the world around us, our own inactivity sharing the inertia of the masses around us, our own leadership becoming soft?

What can we do concerning these issues that we are not doing now?

On the basis of an unweakened Bible, we must teach and act, in our individual lives and as citizens, on the fact that every individual has unique value as made in the image of God. This is so from a child just conceived in the womb to the old with their last gasping breath and beyond; for death does not bring the cessation of life, but all people will spend eternity somewhere . . . with God or not, depending on their relationship to Christ as Saviour.

If we ache and have compassion for humanity today in our own country and across the world, we must do all that we can to help people see the truth of Christianity and accept Christ as Saviour. And we must stand against the loss of humanness in all its forms. It is God's life-changing power that is able to touch every individual, who then has a responsibility to touch the world around him with the absolutes found in the Bible. In the end we must realise that the tide of humanism, with its loss of humanness, is not merely a cultural ill, but a spiritual ill that Christ alone can cure.

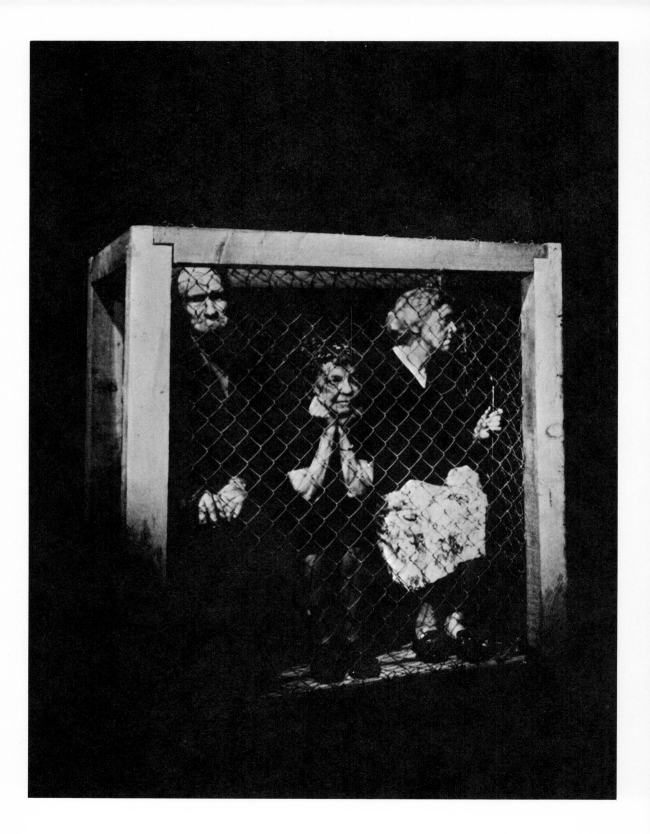

Notes

Chapter 1   1. The barbarism of the holocaust was not limited to European Jewry. Gypsies, Slavs, Russians, German dissidents for political and religious reasons, resistance leaders from occupied European countries, ordinary captives in the course of war, and even children of some of these former categories were eliminated. However, the Jews were especially slated for total elimination. Heinrich Himmler delivered an address on 10 October, 1943, to an assembly of SS generals at Poznan. By this time both Himmler and his audience must have known that Germany could not win the war. Himmler stated: 'Among ourselves it should be mentioned quite frankly, and yet we will never speak of it publicly . . . I mean . . . the extirpation of the Jewish race . . . this is a page of glory in our history which has never been written and is never to be written.'

2. The following is contained in the standard form of the Oath of Hippocrates:

> I will follow that method of treatment which, according to my ability and judgment, I consider for the benefit of my patients, and abstain from whatever is deleterious and mischievous. I will give no deadly medicine to anyone if asked, nor suggest any such counsel; furthermore, I will not give to a woman an instrument to produce abortion.

3. According to Mr John Marks in a letter to the *Guardian,* 12 July, 1979, where he quoted the BMA's Representative Body as passing a resolution in 1978, '. . . deploring the persistent attacks on the 1967 Act and reaffirming its belief that it (the Act) is a practical and humane piece of legislation'.

4. George F. Will, *Newsweek*, 4 April, 1977.

5. David Steel in a speech to the Abortion Law Reform Association as reported in the Medical Tribune, 31 October, 1968. It is also worth remembering that the Royal College of Obstetricians and Gynaecologists, those most to be affected by the Act, were opposed to it. RCOG Report by the Council, 'Legalised Abortion' 1966, 1:850.

6. *Time* magazine, 1 August, 1977.

7. Edward O. Wilson wrote *Sociobiology: The New Synthesis* in 1975 (Belknap Press of Harvard University). His more recent book (1978)—*On Human Nature* (Harvard University Press)—applies his ideas specifically to human behaviour.

8. *Time* magazine, 1 August, 1977.

9. Joan Hutchison, writing in *Challenge* (USA) for May/June 1976, started her essay dealing with the history of child abuse in the following way: 'Burned, bashed, beaten, stomped, suffocated, strangled, poisoned, choked, ripped, steamed, boiled, dismembered, bitten, raped, clubbed, banged, torn. Ignored, starved, abandoned, exploited, demeaned, ridiculed, treated with coldness and indifference or unreasonable demands.'

10. Gay Pauley, 'Of Cries, Whispers, and Incest', *Philadelphia Evening Bulletin* (USA), 3 October, 1977.

11. Gay Pauley, 'Incest: Healing Taboos, Harsh Wounds', *Philadelphia Evening Bulletin*, 4 October, 1977.

12. A number of forces at work in America and Britain are anti-family. Among these are the constantly climbing divorce rate, the gay-liberation movement, extreme forms of women's lib, and abortion on demand. Increasingly children live in single parent families. In the United States the figure is one child in six, while in Britain it is one child in ten. Also in both countries the proportion of women with children who are in full time work is increasing.

13. Mothers who have had several abortions are more likely than others to beat their children, according to a study conducted in the United States by Dr Burton G. Schoenfeld, a child psychiatrist of Prince Georges County General Hospital in Maryland.

14. In the National Right to Life *News* (USA) of January 1977, Jesse L. Jackson had this to say on the right of privacy: 'There are those who argue that the right to privacy is of higher order than the right to life . . . that was the premise of slavery. You could not protest the existence or treatment of slaves on the plantation because that was private and therefore outside your right to be concerned. . . . The Constitution called us three-fifths human and the whites further dehumanised us by calling us "niggers". It was part of the dehumanising process. . . . These advocates taking life prior to birth do not call it killing or murder, they call it abortion. They further never talk about aborting a baby because that would imply something human. . . . Fetus sounds less than human and therefore can be justified. . . .

'What happens to the mind of a person, and the moral fabric of a nation, that accepts the aborting of the life of a baby without a pang of conscience? What kind of a person and what kind of a society will he have twenty years hence if life can be taken so casually? It is that question, the question of our attitude, our value system, and our mind set with regard to the nature and worth of life itself that is the central question confronting mankind. Failure to answer that question affirmatively may leave us with a hell right here on earth.'

15. John T. Noonan, Jr, 'Why a Constitutional Amendment?' *Human Life Review* (USA), 1:28 (1975).

16. Ibid.

Did the Court really go so far? Here is what it held:

Until a human being is 'viable' or 'capable of meaningful life', a state has no 'compelling interest' that justifies it in restricting in any way in favour of the fetus a woman's fundamental personal liberty of abortion. For six months, or 'usually' for seven months (the Court's reckoning), the fetus is denied the protection of law by virtue of either the Ninth Amendment or the Fourteenth Amendment of the American constitution.

After viability has been reached, the human being is not a person 'in the whole sense', so that even after viability he or she is not protected by the Fourteenth Amendment's guarantee that life shall not be taken without due process of law. At this point he or she is, however, legally recognisable as 'potential life'.

. . . The state may require that after the first trimester abortions be performed in licensed 'facilities', and that after viability they be regulated so long as 'health' abortions are not denied. The state is constitutionally barred, however, from requiring review of the abortion decision by a hospital committee or concurrence in the decision by two physicians other than the attending physician. The Constitution also prohibits a state from requiring that the abortion be in a hospital licensed by the Joint Committee on Accreditation of Hospitals or indeed that it be in a hospital at all.

At least in Britain the consent of two physicians and the use of Government inspected clinics is required although pro-abortion forces want this ended.

17. Archibald Cox, *The Role of the Supreme Court in American Government* (Oxford University Press, 1976).

18. It is interesting to note that while in the United States over a million unborn babies were being destroyed in the womb each year, the same Supreme Court which made that slaughter possible stopped the construction of the $116,000,000 Tellico Dam in Tennessee—because it might wipe out the snail darter, a 3-inch fish. Since then, the threat to the lousewort plant has raised legal questions about building a power plant in Maine, and the orange-bellied mouse has complicated siting requirements for a power plant near San Francisco. A $340,000,000 dam on the Stanislaus River in California ran into legal difficulties because a 5/8-inch daddy-long-legs spider dwells there. There are quotas on whales and porpoises, but it is always open season on unborn babies. Although we can applaud the efforts to preserve our environment, it seems that we have confused our priorities.

19. The radical change caused by the 1967 Act was not apparently fully intended. For example, David Steel said before the Act, 'it is not the intention of the promotion of the Bill to leave a wider door open for abortion on request' (Hansard, House of Commons, 22 July, 1966, Col. 1075). However, Keith Hindell and Madeleine Simms in an article, 'How the abortion lobby worked' (*Political Quarterly*, 1968, 39.269) showed how the clauses of the Act were vague enough to be loosely interpreted. Some argue, for example Glanville Williams in chapter 11 of his *Textbook of Criminal Law* 1978, that part of the blame for this lay with those who tried to tighten the Act. It is said they believed

their own propaganda that abortion was a more dangerous procedure for the mother than childbirth. And this was why the Act was worded so that abortion could only be carried out when the risk of birth was greater than for abortion. When it was then 'discovered' after the Act that as far as the safety of the mother was concerned abortion was relatively safe, safer than childbirth, the door for abortion on demand swung open. Some doctors took the view that after all, any emotional upset over an unwanted birth was worse than an abortion. The intentions of the Act have thus been ignored.

However, whatever the merits of this point it is important to see the background and details of the Act. Before 1967 the situation had been as follows: the 1861 Offences Against the Person Act had made abortion a felony punishable by life imprisonment. In 1929 the Infant Life Preservation Act in the process of defining the offence of child destruction allowed abortion for the sole purpose of saving 'the life of the mother'. Then in 1938 the Bourne Case judgment liberalised the law a little. A Doctor Bourne was acquitted after aborting a fourteen year old who had been involved in a particularly savage rape case. The judge took the view that the 'life of the mother' should not be interpreted literally and thus a slightly wider criterion became in practice accepted, enabling 'therapeutic' abortions. However, the number of these remained relatively few until the Abortion Act of 1967. This then legislated that abortion was no longer an offence when two doctors decided that:

a) the life of the mother was at risk

b) there would be a risk of injury to the mental and physical health of the woman and any existing children, which was greater than if an abortion was carried out; and in determining this, the woman's actual or forseeable environment (social conditions) could be taken into account.

c) there would be a substantial risk of a seriously handicapped child, either physically or mentally.

It is easy to see how despite the intentions of the Act it became vulnerable to abuse. The 'risks' were capable of wide definition especially when child birth came to be regarded as a greater risk to the mother than abortion. Abortion on demand became normal practice and when the Lane Report reviewed the workings of the Act in 1974 it raised no objection. It was this that earned the Report the jibe from Malcolm Muggeridge of 'a whitewash'. So now the only real restriction of the 1967 Act is that the 1929 Act remains in force and one of its clauses forbade abortion after 28 weeks. This was because it wanted to outlaw the abortion of babies 'capable of being born alive' and at that time 28 weeks of pregnancy was the earliest that was considered possible.

20. Confusion of thought is further evidenced in the United States by organisations like Planned Parenthood who see abortion as a way of planning parenthood! Fuelled with millions of taxpayers' dollars, not intended for the purpose, they promote abortion alongside family planning.

21. It is worth appreciating the scale and the rate of increase of abortions in Britain. In 1969 there was a total of 54,819 of which 4,990 were for non-residents, in 1970 the total was 86,565 of which 10,603 were non-residents; by 1978 the total was 142,343 of which 30,288 were for non-residents (Figures for England and Wales).

22. Harold O. J. Brown, in comparing the action of the United States Supreme Court with that of the West German Federal Constitutional Court (in action the latter took in June 1974) had this to say: 'The West German Federal Constitutional Court dealt with the question of unlimited right to abortion on demand on the basis of an evaluation of fundamental questions concerning the nature of man and the requirements of justice. No one familiar with *Roe* v. *Wade* can fail to recognise that in it the highest American court has evaded the basic moral issue and resolved a fundamental question only on the basis of technical legal construction.' (*See* Harold O. J. Brown, 'Abortion: Rights or Technicalities', *Human Life Review*, Vol. 1 No. 3, 1975, pp. 72–73.)

23. Harold O. J. Brown, 'Abortion and Child Abuse', *Christianity Today* (USA), 7 October, 1977, p. 34.

24. In 1967, at the First International Conference on Abortion, a purely secular group of people said, 'We can find no point in time between the union of sperm and egg and the birth of an infant at which point we can say that this is not a human life' (Washington, DC: conference sponsored by Harvard Divinity School and Joseph P. Kennedy, Jr, Foundation).

25. According to nurses' testimony after the uterus was opened at the time of hysterotomy, Dr Edelin purportedly cut off the blood supply of an allegedly viable fetus by detaching the placenta and waiting three minutes before removing the fetus from the uterus. A number of emotional factors were introduced by the media during this trial. One of these factors was that Dr Edelin was black and therefore the trial was seen to be racist. The final conclusion of the case was that a higher court reversed the lower court's decision and Dr Edelin was not only free but went on to become the president of a national medical organisation.

26. *Markle* v. *Abele* (1972), Supreme Court of the United States, No. 72–56, 72–730, p. 72.

27. Waddill was charged with strangling a baby girl at Westminster Community Hospital, 2 March, 1977, after an unsuccessful abortion attempt. At a preliminary hearing in April 1977 before the jury trial in January 1978, Dr Ronald Cornelsen testified that Dr Waddill throttled the infant's neck and complained about what would happen if the baby survived. According to Cornelsen's testimony, Waddill said that there would be lawsuits, that the baby would be brain damaged, and talked about stopping respiration by drowning or injecting potassium chloride.

At the trial in January 1978, Mrs Joanne Griffith, a nurse at the hospital where the abortion was performed, testified that another nurse had quoted Dr

Waddill on the telephone as ordering everyone involved not to do anything, and to leave the baby alone. Dr Cornelsen testified at the trial that when he first examined the baby, and the heart was beating sixty to seventy times a minute with a regular rhythm, there was some discolouration on the baby's neck (allegedly from the first attempt at strangling) and further testified that while he was examining the baby, Dr Waddill '. . . stuck his hand back in [the isolette] and pressed the baby's neck again' (from *The Los Angeles Times,* 26 January, 8 February, 1978).

Dr Waddill was brought to trial again on the same charges in the same case in 1979.

28. *Medical World News* (USA), 14 November, 1977.

29. Ibid.

30. Ibid.

31. Ibid.

32. The law in Britain is not completely clear, yet it would seem reasonable to argue that a live birth means an illegal abortion, since the 1929 Infant Life Preservation Act forbade abortion where 'a child is capable of being born alive'. (The 28 week limitation did not exclude that a child born before this period was not 'capable of being born alive', only that after 28 weeks, there was *prima facie* proof that it could be.) To introduce some poison like urea to kill the fetus would moreover appear to be an admission that the baby might be born alive. Further, the fact that a child might be handicapped is no defence, when the child is capable of 'being born alive'. This is unlike America where abnormality can justify abortion right up until birth. Given that tests taken, for example, for spina bifida, may not be completed until it is possible for the fetus to be 'born alive', this would seem to mean that abortions in these cases are illegal. The practice of nurses administering prostaglandin at intervals to induce abortion would seem to be another example of illegality, since only doctors are supposed to carry out abortions. Perhaps given that the law has already legalised killing, it is not surprising that no action is taken on such matters.

33. *Fort Lauderdale News* (USA), 13 November, 1977.

34. This has not always been the case. The *Sunday Mirror*, 10 December, 1978 reported how eleven nurses at Hairmyres Hospital, East Kilbride in Scotland walked out and forced the hospital to negotiate so that they would not be involved in abortions and would be sure that the conscience clause was respected.

35. Ibid. These are chilling words yet in Britain some at least of the lay public are not easily upset. The National Abortion Campaign according to their Newsletter, summer 1977, and the Abortion Law Reform Association in their evidence to the National Tribunal on Abortion Rights, 1 January, 1977 show that they want an amendment to the 1929 Infant Life Preservation Act which would eventually lead to abortion up until birth. The NAC also want to

end the conscience clause at present in the 1967 Act leading to the dismissal of anti-abortion doctors.

36. 'You Be the Judge', *National Newsline* (USA), February 1975 (Dayton, Ohio: Nurses Concerned for Life, Inc.).

37. More recently it has been reported by the *Guardian,* 8 September, 1979, that Mr Steptoe has suggested that a fertilised egg be placed in a 'stand-in mother' if the real mother could not undertake the pregnancy. That such a distorted view of human relationships should come out of such research is perhaps not surprising. One wonders to whom the child will belong and would the 'stand-in' be paid?

38. Leon Kass, as quoted by George F. Will in 'Discretionary Killing', *Newsweek,* 20 September, 1976.

39. The Akron ordinance regulating abortion was put together and guided through Akron City Council by a twenty-three-year-old Orthodox Jew named Marvin Weinberger, a Boston University law student. He took leave from Boston University Law School and formed a group called Citizens for Informed Consent and guided the ordinance from its original draft and early public hearings to a 7:6 City Council victory.

40. Dr Matthew Bulfin, onetime president of Pro-Life Obstetricians and Gynaecologists in the USA, has done a study on more than 300 patients who previously had legal abortions and later saw him as gynaecological patients. He developed a set of questions that he asked this selected group of patients. Here are some of the things he learned:

The vast majority of women would not have had an abortion if it were illegal to do so.

For 90 per cent of the women, a physician apparently never entered into the decision to have an abortion.

The majority of women did not even know the name of the doctor who performed the abortion.

The great majority of patients did not seem to recall any discussion of the risks of the abortion itself or the possible risks of future childbearing.

Not one patient admitted to having any kind of thorough examination until the actual pelvic exam that was done as the abortion was about to be started.

When complications occurred after the abortion, most women reported they did not know the name of the doctor nor had they any confidence in him and therefore usually called their own gynaecologist or went to the emergency room of the nearest hospital.

Dr Bulfin used to ask this question: 'Were you aware at any time that you might be destroying a human life when you had your abortion?' The reason he stopped asking the question is that too many patients either broke down in tears or became upset because they thought he might be about to impose a religious prejudice on them (*Newsletter:* Pro-Life Obstetricians and Gynaecologists).

41. In Britain nearly half of all abortions are carried out in the private sector through pregnancy counselling services which are registered as charities no less. The degree of their 'advice' can be gathered by the fact that in 1976 the British Pregnancy Advisory Service, one of the largest, gave pregnancy counselling to 22,824 and of those, referred 21,257 for abortion. One wonders how far their clients were given full and adequate advice.

In a letter to the *Guardian*, 19 July, 1979, one woman wrote about the lack of advice she had obtained. 'I was quite unprepared, indeed I had found it difficult to obtain information. The mental backlash has been enormous . . . and not one person warned me of this. Even with the support of a firm marriage and a loving family, I came as close to a mental breakdown as I am ever likely to come.'

42. It is very difficult to obtain statistics in the United States that illuminate the effects of abortion on the woman. The 1973 Supreme Court ruling, which made possible the establishment of free-standing clinics outside the scrutiny of accreditation groups, contributes to the loss of statistical data for these purposes. The Department of Health, Education and Welfare, however, released an 'interim report' in 1978, indicating that women who have had an abortion face an 85 per cent higher 'spontaneous fetal death ratio' (miscarriage) in subsequent pregnancies.

The National Health Service in Britain keeps excellent records and has been in the abortion-on-demand business for several years longer than the United States. These records have revealed, accompanying an increase in abortion, an increase in illegitimacy, venereal disease, prostitution, and pelvic inflammatory disease from gonorrhoea, as well as sterility of previously aborted mothers and subsequent spontaneous abortions or miscarriages. Ectopic pregnancies—where the egg is implanted not in the uterus but in the fallopian tube, requiring an emergency abdominal operation—have doubled since abortion has been liberalised. Prematurity in British women who have had a previous abortion is 40 per cent higher than in those who have not.

In May 1976, the *British Medical Journal* reported a paper by Richardson and Dickson entitled 'The Effect of Legal Termination on Subsequent Pregnancy' (29 May, 1976, pp. 1303–04). This study from Bristol indicated again the higher risk of miscarriages in subsequent pregnancies for those who had had abortions; also that nearly half of their sample were pregnant again within a year of a previous abortion. Perhaps the most telling evidence, however, is that while many Western countries are 'liberalising' their abortion laws, Eastern bloc countries who have had abortion for much longer are tightening up their laws. For example, in 1968 Rumania, and in 1975 Bulgaria, Czechoslovakia and Hungary all imposed restrictions. This was partly for demographic reasons, but also in recognition of the real dangers caused by abortion.

This sort of evidence which points to the dangers of abortion to women probably won't, however, convince those whose opinion of the 1967 Act is founded on the belief that it has ended 'backstreet abortion'. In Britain this has been made the major issue and those defending the 1967 Act do so with the slogan of 'no return to the backstreets'. It's an emotional cry which makes rational discussion difficult. Obviously getting accurate information on this matter is fraught with problems but it does seem clear that those arguing for the 1967 Act, massively exaggerated the incidence of backstreet abortion before 1967. Moreover, when they point to the declining deaths since the Act, they forget that this started before 1967 and is mostly due to the effective use of antibiotics. Others have even argued that alongside the Act there has been an increase in illegal abortion. Whatever the true position, the discussion, even taking into account the desperate and tragic cases, too easily forgets the undisputed facts of aborted babies, well over a 100,000 a year in Britain. Also as is made clear in chapter 3 there can be alternatives to abortion, 'backstreet' or otherwise.

43. Harold O. J. Brown has this to say about the separation of church and state in the USA: 'No American historian would seriously contend that the phrase "regarding an establishment of religion" in the First Amendment means anything other than what it says: it forbids the establishment of a national religion or church. It certainly did not mean, in its conception, that nothing in public law or policy may reflect the convictions or insights of any church or of the Christian religion (*see* Harold O. J. Brown, 'The Passivity of American Christians', *Christianity Today*, 16 January, 1976.) Even in Britain where there is an established church, is there any reason why the law should not reflect Christian and human values without becoming involved in a distracting church–state debate?

44. More and more feminists are disgusted with the realities of the abortion situation. One such group in the United States is known as Women Exploited. Their leader, Sandra Haun, testified before the Pennsylvania legislature as follows: 'The members of our organisation have all had abortions and have come to realise, too late, that our decision was wrong. We were encouraged and pushed into a hasty decision that now we find impossible to live with. We were lied to and deliberately misinformed.' Another group, formed in Britain, are called 'Women for Life', based in London. In a statement their spokesperson, Debby Sanders, said, 'Those arguing for abortion are encouraging women to treat themselves, their bodies and their babies as objects.'

45. The number of countries 'liberalising' their abortion laws continues to grow, for example; India 1971; Singapore, France, Austria all in 1974, Hong Kong 1976 and Italy 1979 which is discouraging. New Zealand's restrictive Act 1977 is however some comfort.

Chapter 2   46. We are using the term infanticide in this chapter in its general sense and we are not referring to the narrow meaning in English law where infanticide involves the specific offence of a mother killing her baby.

47. From the same Children's Hospital in Sheffield where Robert Zachary works, paediatrician John Lorber, discouraged with the results of surgery on spina bifida (cleft spine) and its complications, has in visits to this country been urging his American counterparts to consider not operating on at least the 20 per cent of victims who are severely affected. Lorber claims that among 323 children treated vigorously from 1959 to 1963 only 7 per cent were normal.

This view has been countered particularly by Dr John M. Freeman at Johns Hopkins University School of Medicine. Freeman quoted a series of 171 patients with spina bifida treated at the University of Pennsylvania between 1963 and 1968. Of the children with thoracolumbar lesions, 42 per cent had IQs of 80 or better and were able to get around 'albeit often with braces and crutches', said Dr Freeman, 'so the outlook does not have to be as bad as Dr Lorber would have us believe'.

Patients with spina bifida have been frequently reported to die quickly if unattended. This is not so. About 60 per cent of untreated patients are alive at a month, 45 per cent at two months, 19 per cent at one year, and 16 per cent at two years. Though these untreated children do not die quickly, they die slowly, over months and years and sometimes don't die at all.

48. The terms *cost containment* or *cost benefit* are the magic phrases in medical economics today. For example in Britain the General Practitioner, 1 October, 1976 reported a Department of Health and Social Security cost benefit analysis as saying, 'The cost of caring for severely handicapped spina bifida children, may well make this type of selection (i.e. pre-natal diagnosis and abortion) economically worthwhile.' One is considered an intolerable reactionary if he compares the cost of medical care with that of unnecessary luxuries such as alcohol or tobacco. Nevertheless, the figures invite comparison.

In his Milroy Lecture, John Lorber argues for a policy of selective treatment of newborns with severe spina bifida, leaving many to die. He justifies this on the grounds that it spares the patient and their families the hard burdens of great physical and mental handicap. This is his main concern but he also points to the great costs involved including over £50,000 for the medical care and special education for those who are treated and survive with a severe handicap to 16 years old. *Journal of the Royal College of Physicians* Vol. 10:1975. This factor one feels will become ever more convincing to many, though the figure of £50,000 needs to be examined critically, since the costs for caring and educating a normal child are also very substantial.

One is amazed that in the debates concerning the cost of intensive care for premature babies (or youngsters born with congenital defects requiring surgery) so little mention is made of the good news concerning newborn intensive care. The kind of intensive care we are talking about has cut the neonatal death rate in half in less than a generation, and the cost of saving most babies referred to newborn intensive-care units is far less than the figures usually cited for extreme cases. At the Children's Hospital of Philadelphia (where one of us works in neonatal surgery), it would be absolutely impossible to achieve the results that we do in presenting perfectly normal, healthy youngsters to their parents were it not for our absolute dependence upon the technology of intensive care, coupled with the dedication and skill of physicians, nurses, and paramedical personnel.

Jeffrey J. Pomerantz, MD, of the Cedars-Sinai Medical Centre in Los Angeles, studied 75 infants weighing less than 1000 grams during the period from 1973 through 1975. He found that 30 infants (40 per cent) lived, and 70 per cent of these were judged to be neurologically and developmentally normal (1 to 3 years later). Thus the intact survival rate was 28 per cent.

Pomerantz calculated the average daily cost for each survivor to be $450. By dividing the total cost of all the babies by the 21 intact survivors, he found an average cost per 'normal' survivor of $88,058. Even with inflation adjustment, Pomerantz concluded, 'It is our belief, that the outcome justifies this expense' (*Paediatrics*, June 1978, as reported in *American Medical News*).

49. A study was done in 1977 on the impact of an abnormal child upon the parents. In summary, thirty families with a newborn mongoloid baby were matched with thirty families with a normal baby. Both groups were followed for eighteen months to two years and interviewed six times. Few differences could be found in the mental or physical health of the parents in the two groups.

Interestingly enough, a low rate of broken homes was found among the families of mongoloid children living at home. There was an increased incidence of divorce and separation in families of similar children in institutions.

Author Ann Gath reports, 'Despite their grief, the parents of almost half the mongol children in the study felt drawn closer together and their marriage rather strengthened than weakened by their shared tragedy, a view similar to that expressed by parents of older mongol children in a survey of school age siblings of mongol children [done earlier]' (*British Journal of Psychiatry*, 1977, 130:405–10).

A study by Burton in 1975 revealed that 64 per cent of mothers and 53 per cent of fathers of children with fibrocystic disease also believed that their problems and distress had brought them closer to their spouses. (*See* L. Burton, *The Family Life of Sick Children*, London: Routledge and Kegan, 1975).

50. One of the most remarkable medical achievements in the world today is to be found centred in the Parisian suburb of Garches. Here, after acute care at the Raymond Poincare Hospital, a private paramedical corporation is over-

seeing the care of 450 patients on respirators in their own homes. Some of these patients are on total respiratory support, others only on demand. Many have completed their higher education and some are employed in responsible consultant positions. It is a marvellous example of hospital personnel, paramedical technicians, the government's assisting private enterprise, and the will of individuals to succeed in spite of handicaps. The man whose vision this was is a paraplegic.

51. Another factor that must always be considered in such cases, although one does not plan them that way, is that what is learned in one individual spectacular success eventually has benefit to untold thousands of subsequent patients.

About a decade ago we had a newborn patient whose entire small bowel was gangrenous, and in desperation one of our surgeons put the bowel together after removing the gangrenous portion in the only possible way—but one which was incompatible with eventual survival. It was on this diminutive patient that the first total parenteral (other than intestinal) nutritional programme ever tried on an infant was carried out. Although that youngster tragically succumbed to sepsis well over a year after her initial operation, the knowledge gained in that instance has benefitted literally thousands upon thousands of children the world over, to say nothing of the adults who have benefitted as well. Total parenteral nutrition as worked out on this youngster is perhaps one of the four or five outstanding medical achievements of the past decade.

52. A questionnaire mailed to members of the surgical section of the American Academy of Paediatrics in 1975 sought to explore the beliefs and practices of the surgical Fellows concerning ethical issues in the care of the newborn with a life-threatening defect which was correctable by a surgical procedure.

While acknowledging the difficulties inherent in interpreting a questionnaire, it was clear that a substantial number of this group of elite surgeons would acquiesce to parents' wishes in not treating a newborn, but rather allowing him or her to die with intestinal atresia (obstruction with excellent prognosis after operation) alone (7.9 per cent) or accompanied by mongolism (76.8 per cent).

53. In response to the publication of 'Moral and Ethical Dilemmas in the Special-Care Nursery' in the *New England Journal of Medicine* (USA) by Duff and Campbell in October of 1973, there appeared among other letters to the editor in the same journal (28 February, 1974) one by Joan L. Venes, MD, and Peter R. Huttenlocher, MD, of the Yale University School of Medicine. They described themselves as some of the 'specialists based in the medical centre' referred to by Duff and Campbell. This is the final paragraph of that letter:

'As consultants to the Newborn Special Care Unit, we wish to dissociate ourselves from the opinions expressed by the authors. The "growing tendency to seek early death as a management option" that the authors referred to has been repeatedly called to the attention of those involved and has caused us deep concern. It is troubling to us to hear young paediatric interns ask first, "Should we treat?" rather than "How do we treat?": we are fearful that this feeling of nihilism may not remain restricted to the Newborn Special Care Unit. To suggest that the financial and psychological stresses imposed upon a family with the birth of a handicapped child constitutes sufficient justification for such a therapy of nihilism is untenable and allows us to escape what perhaps after all are the real issues—i.e., the obligation of an affluent society to provide financial support and the opportunity for a gainful life to its less fortunate citizens.'

54. Here is a quotation from a paediatric surgeon, appended to a questionnaire on his attitude toward patients with Down's syndrome: 'I have a 53-year-old cousin with Down's syndrome. His father is a 93-year-old arteriosclerotic, incontinent at night of urine and stool. He refuses to go to a nursing home. They live alone and the son with Down's syndrome provides most of the care.'

55. Anthony Shaw, 'Dilemmas of Informed Consent in Children', *New England Journal of Medicine*, 25 October, 1973, pp. 885–890.

56. *New England Journal of Medicine*, 6 September, 1979, pp. 550–553.

57. *The Hastings Centre Report* (USA), Vol. 2, no. 5 (November 1972).

58. 'Euthanasia and Children: The Injury of Continued Existence', *Journal of Paediatrics*, 83 (1973), pp. 170–171.

59. Jonathan Glover, 'Causing Death and Saving Lives,' (London: Penguin, 1977). Glover shows himself to be acutely aware of the dangers of his approach yet does not see that his version of utilitarianism, however sophisticated, can only create straw defences against his basic assumptions.

60. J. Philip Wogaman in *The Washington Post*, 16 August, 1977.

61. *The New York Times,* 28 July, 1977.

62. *Commentary* 53:8 (May 1972).

63. The prestigious Spastics Society is an example of such a charity. According to the Nursing Mirror, 17 June, 1976, the Society helps to fund the Paediatric Research Unit at Guys Hospital Medical School in London which offers genetic counselling and pre-natal screening for abortion where necessary. The Society handbooks make clear its approval of such procedure. This seems ironic when to support all its other good work the Society is promoting the Save a Baby Campaign.

64. Martha Willing, *Beyond Conception: Our Children's Children* (Ipswich, Massachusetts: Gambit, 1971), p. 174.

65. *Medical Tribune* (USA), 20 July, 1977, pp. 23, 29.

Chapter 3   66. In the USA the influence of the abortion on euthanasia is most clear because the Supreme Court decision on abortion stated, 'That only viable human beings who have the capability for meaningful life may, but need not be, protected by the state.' Soon this could be a death warrant for many.

67. This book was probably the beginning of the German rationale for what began as euthanasia programmes and ended up as attempted genocide of specific groups.

68. Since the Karen Quinlan case, medical and other literature has been filled with 'guidelines' for the physician in difficult situations. But see how easily guidelines for stopping life-prolonging treatments for dying or comatose patients (which is commonly practiced by reputable physicians all over the world) can readily be turned into directives for euthanasia. A perfect example is when the Swiss Academy of Medical Sciences issued such guidelines. As reported in *The New York Times* with a dateline of Basel, Switzerland: 'A doctor said if the "directives concerning euthanasia were applied in the United States, doctors would be permitted to end intravenous feedings of Karen Quinlan, the comatose New Jersey woman whose case set off an international debate".' There are a number of misconceptions in this Swiss doctor's statement. First of all, the directives given by the Swiss Academy of Medical Sciences were not euthanasia guidelines, but he saw fit immediately to use that term as being synonymous with the Academy's statement. Second, Karen Quinlan is not being fed by intravenous feedings, but by feedings introduced via a nasogastric tube. We call attention to this difference because improper reporting in this instance could legitimately raise the question of whether feedings by tube were as 'extraordinary' as intravenous feedings in the care of Karen Quinlan.

69. In the United States the 'living will' is a document (now enacted as law in several states) which directs physicians concerning the patient's terminal illness and extraordinary care. In Britain such a document is usually referred to as a 'Declaration'. It is not yet legal.

70. Hugh Trowell, *Euthanasia: the unfinished debate* (London: SCM Press, 1973).

71. *Medical Tribune,* 10 October, 1973.

72. Joseph Fletcher, 'Ethics and Euthanasia', *American Journal of Nursing* 73:670 (1973).

73. Medically, Fletcher's example is not a good one. It is possible to have brain metastases revealed by a brain scan and not be in either pain or extremis.

74. *Philadelphia Evening Bulletin,* 13 August, 1977.

75. *Time* magazine, 5 September, 1977.

76. *Philadelphia Evening Bulletin,* 13 August, 1977.

77. *Newsweek,* 4 July, 1977.

78. Richard L. Rubenstein, *The Cunning of History: Mass Death and the American Future* (New York: Harper & Row, 1975).

79. Frederic Wertham in *A Sign for Cain: An Exploration of Human Violence* (London, Hale, 1968) makes it quite clear that people of various classes in Germany surrendered their own individual will and conscience to that of the state. The dehumanisation and depersonalisation which followed in Germany—and this is the lesson for us—was not that the German people and the Nazis in particular were ideologically fanatical with hatred for their victims, but rather they were totally indifferent to their fate.

Those who carried out the killings in the euthanasia programmes were academic physicians, many times professors in outstanding universities. They were not 'mad' in the sense that we talk about mad scientists; they had fallen under the spell of utilitarianism and were more concerned about the cost of caring for a patient as opposed to killing him.

80. Leo Alexander, 'Medical Science Under Dictatorship', *New England Journal of Medicine* 241:39–47, 14 July, 1949. (This was also covered in *Newsweek,* 9 July, 1973.)

81. Ibid.

82. Ibid.

83. We believe that the 'living will' or 'declaration' will be one of the actual instruments which act as the *thin edge of the wedge* in opening up our society to the euthanasia movement.

The first major stumbling block in any such document centres around the use of the word *terminal* when it refers to the patient's illness. The living will gives to the physician certain rights which might not be the intent of the patient, who may not know that his illness is terminal and/or whose death might not be imminent.

It is very difficult to say when death is imminent. The first patient for whom one of us [C. E. Koop] would have ever been able to sign an affidavit in reference to the imminence of death had what was thought to be a *terminal* neuroblastoma. The patient has graduated from law school and is alive more than thirty years later. This experience has been repeated time after time. In the language of the California Act, it is the physician's decision which makes death 'imminent'.

In the Arkansas legislation, Section 1 includes the terms *artificial, extra-ordinary, extreme or radical,* and *medical or surgical means or procedures* in the case of a patient unable to discuss this matter with his physician. Even a layman could see that this opens Pandora's box.

84. Dr Richard M. Hunt, 'No Fault Guilt-Free History', *The New York Times,* 16 February, 1976.

85. Donald P. Warwich, 'The Moral Message of Bucharest', *The Hastings Centre Report* (USA), 19 December, 1974.

86. One can say things accurately but obscurely, so that the true meaning is

present but hidden. A fertilised egg is a zygote. Who would suspect that a postcoital antizygotic pill would prevent the implantation of the fertilised egg?

87. This is not to suggest that those working in the State system do not need our support, rather the opposite, especially in Britain with its National Health Service. The pressures when dealing with unwanted pregnancies, handicapped newborns, or dependent old people, either in terms of the system's different values, or just plain shortages of staff and money, are enormous. Frustration and discouragement in such circumstances can only too easily lead to the path of least resistance.

Chapter 4   88. 'When Scientists Play the Role of God', *The Times,* 16 November, 1978.

89. H. J. Blackham et al., *Objections to Humanism* (London: Penguin, 1965).

90. We would like to include a word about rationalism. The Enlightenment was a revolution in thought which took place in the eighteenth century in Europe. One of its main ideas was that man is autonomous; that is, man starts out from himself and measures all things by himself. Thus, there was no place for revelation. The philosophers felt that *reason* (man's) should be supreme, rather than any communication from God.

Looked at from this viewpoint, this movement is called rationalism. This word means that its proponents assumed that man (though finite and limited) can begin from himself and gather all the information needed to explain all things. Rationalism rejects knowledge outside of man himself, especially any knowledge from God. Rationalism led naturally to the present predominant world view we have described at the beginning of this chapter: that is, *materialism* (only matter exists) or *naturalism* (no supernatural exists).

Having this as their world view, the rationalists had increasingly no place for things which were said to be 'supernatural', such as miracles, the raising of the dead, and Christ's Transfiguration. These things were, therefore, first said to be beyond knowledge and thus of little or no value. Later they were arbitrarily said to be impossible. This view did not come because of scientific facts, but was rooted in the rationalist world view which they accepted.

91. Francis Bacon, *The New Organon and Related Writings* (London: Collected Works; Spedding, 1857–1874).

92. René Descartes, *Meditations on First Philosophy* (London: Everyman Library, Dent).

93. H. J. Blackham et al., *Objections to Humanism* (London: Penguin, 1965).

94. Ibid.

95. David Hume, *A Treatise of Human Nature* (London: Fontana Bk. 1, 1962; Bk. 2, 1972).

96. Steven Weinberg, *The First Three Minutes: A Modern View of the Origin of the Universe* (London: André Deutsch).

97. Aldous Huxley, *Brave New World* (London: Panther, 1977).

98. Robert M. Pirsig, *Zen and the Art of Motorcycle Maintenance: An Inquiry Into Values* (London: Corgi, 1976).

99. Pierre Teilhard de Chardin (1881–1955) is an example of this. He was a member of the Jesuit order and a French palaeontologist and philosopher. His approach to evolution was an attempt to solve these problems through the use of mystical language, which did justice to neither clear Christian teaching nor scientific thought.

100. Paul Hazard, *European Thought in the Eighteenth Century: From Montesquieu to Lessing* (Magnolia, Massachusetts: Peter Smith).

101. Albert Camus, *The Myth of Sisyphus and Other Essays* (London: Penguin, 1975).

102. William Barrett, *Irrational Man: A Study in Existential Philosophy* (Connecticut: Greenwood Press, 1977).

Appendix 1

A Comment on Darwin

It is worth noting almost in passing that two important arguments for Charles Darwin (1809–1882) and those he convinced have now been almost totally abandoned by evolutionists. The first involves vestigial organs, which (it was supposed) had served useful functions in an earlier stage of man's evolutionary development, but which later became literally useless by the changes brought about through natural selection. Vestigial organs are like crutches one uses after being injured in an accident. They serve a purpose for a time, but when the leg is better the crutches are no longer needed. Certain organs were said to be 'vestiges', that is, leftovers from a previous stage in evolution. The simple problem with the argument is that as medical science has developed, most of these organs have been found to serve useful functions in the body.

A second important argument for Darwin and those he convinced is the dictum that 'ontogeny recapitulates phylogeny'. This idea is that the human embryo goes through the stages of evolution inside the mother's womb, re-sembling at one stage the fish and so on. The better we understand the embryo, however, the more dubious this argument is seen to be.

Yet, even if these two arguments have been largely given up, many still place their faith in the theory of an unbroken line from the molecule to man by chance. However, they are faced in modern discussions with at least two problems. First, the more fossil evidence we find, the more apparent it becomes that there have always been distinct breaks in the fossil record. Darwin admitted that the palaeontological evidence in his day was slender, but, he said, as more is discovered the new evidence will support the hypothesis. This just has not happened.

The evidence of pre-man is sketchy, and recent discoveries in Africa and elsewhere have generated some difficult new problems in this area. But it is not just the so-called missing links between man and pre-man that constitute the problem, but *all* the missing links, right down the whole line. Not only are links missing; the chains themselves are missing. If one removes the speculative guesses, rather than links of different chains leading from simple to more complex organisms, one finds virtual explosions of mature life forms at different periods in geological time and many simple forms of life that remain unchanged for several millions of years up to their extinction or even to today.

The second major difficulty for today's evolutionist is that there is no sufficient mechanism to explain how lower life forms can be transformed into higher ones, no matter how much time is allowed. Natural selection cannot bear this weight. Current genetic theories seem even to point to natural selection as working *against* the direction of evolution. Despite the unlikely possibility of mutations that are advantageous, natural selection seems to simplify the genetic endowment of any group rather than lead it to higher orders of complexity.

Appendix 2

The Reliability of the Biblical Texts

Most of the Old Testament was originally written in Hebrew, and the New Testament in Greek. Many people have been troubled by the length of time that has elapsed between the original writing of the documents and the present translations. How could the originals be copied from generation to generation and not be grossly distorted in the process? There is, however, much to reassure confidence in the texts we have.

In the case of the New Testament, there are codes of the whole New Testament (that is, manuscripts in book form, like the Codex Sinaiticus and Codex Alexandrinus, dated around the fourth and fifth centuries respectively) and also thousands of fragments, some of them dating back to the second century. The earliest known so far is kept in the John Rylands Library in Manchester, England. It is only a small fragment, containing on one side John 18:31–33 and on the reverse, verses 37 and 38. It is important, however, both for its early date (about AD 125) and for the place where it was discovered, namely Egypt. This shows that John's Gospel was known and read in Egypt at that early time. There are thousands of such New Testament texts in Greek from the early centuries after Christ's death and Resurrection.

In the case of the Old Testament, however, there was once a problem. There were no copies of the Hebrew Old Testament in existence which dated from before the ninth century after Christ. This did not mean that there was no way to check the Old Testament, for there were other translations in existence, such as the Syriac and the Septuagint (a translation into Greek from several centuries before Christ). However, there was no *Hebrew* version of the Old Testament from earlier than the ninth century after Christ—because to the Jews the Scripture was so holy it was the common practice to destroy the copies of the Old Testament when they wore out, so that they would not fall into any disrespectful use.

Then, in 1947, a Bedouin Arab made the great discovery of what are called the Dead Sea Scrolls not far from Qumran, which changed everything. While looking for sheep, he came across a cave in which he discovered some earthenware jars containing these scrolls. (These jars are now in the Israeli Shrine of the Book in Jerusalem.) Since that time at least ten other caves in the same vicinity have yielded up other scrolls and fragments. Copies of all the Old

Testament books except Esther have been discovered (in part or complete) among these remains. One of the most dramatic single pieces was a copy of the Book of Isaiah dated approximately a hundred years before Christ. What was particularly striking about this is the great closeness of the discovered text to the Hebrew text, which we previously had, a text written about a thousand years later!

On this issue of text, the Bible is unique as ancient documents go. No other book from that long ago exists in even a small percentage of the copies we have of the Greek and Hebrew texts which make up the Bible. We can be satisfied that we have a copy in our hands which closely approximates the original. Of course, there have been some mistakes in copying, and all translations lose something of the original language. That is inevitable. But the fact that most of us use translations into French, German, Chinese, English, and so on does not mean that we have an inadequate idea of what was written originally. We lose some of the nuances of the language, even when the translation is good, but we do not lose the essential content and communication. On the reliability of the texts then, we can be confident.

Appendix 3

Archaeological Confirmation in the Old Testament

Here we shall show how archaeological discoveries have confirmed much of the history contained in the Old Testament. This confirmation is not merely limited to the Old Testament and we shall not try to give all the evidence; rather we will concentrate on some of the most striking examples. We will work our way back into the past so as to appreciate something of the scope of the time involved starting roughly 600 years before the birth of Christ.

For our first illustration let us take the 'ration tablets' discovered in the ruins of Babylon. The background to this story starts in the time when only the southern kingdom of Judah survived and it was under threat. In fact in 605 BC the Babylonian general Nebuchadnezzar—then crown prince—came west and completely defeated Necho II King of Egypt at the battle of Carchemish. As a result of this victory, King Jehoiakim of Judah was forced to pay tribute to the Babylonians. The Bible tells us, however, that Jehoiakim rebelled three years later. Now an explanation for this can be found by looking at the political background which we can discover in the Babylonian Chronicles (British Museum, Ref. 21946, records events from 597 BC down to 594). These were a compressed chronological summary of the principal events from the Babylonian court. There had been a crucial battle in 601 BC between the Egyptians and the Babylonians. This had left both sides weakened, and Jehoiakim took this opportunity to declare his independence of the Babylonian king. His independence, or rather Judah's independence, did not last long. For Jehoiakim died in 598 BC, leaving his throne and the crisis to his son, Jehoiachin, who Second Kings tells us was taken prisoner after a punitive siege by Nebuchadnezzar.

The story of Jehoiachin does not end there, however. The royal family were kept at the court of Nebuchadnezzar, and the Bible says that they, like other royal captives, were provided for by the king with rations of grain and oil:

> In the thirty-seventh year of the exile of Jehoiachin king of Judah, in the year Evil-Merodach [Nebuchadnezzar's successor] became king of Babylon, he released Jehoiachin from prison on the twenty-seventh day of the twelfth month. He spoke kindly to him and gave him a seat of honour higher than those of the other kings who were with him in Babylon. So Jehoiachin put aside his prison clothes and for the rest of his life ate regularly at the king's table. Day by day the king gave Jehoiachin a regular allowance as long as he lived.
> 2 Kings 25:27–30

The records of these allowances referred to in the Bible were unearthed in excavations in Babylon in basement storerooms of the royal palace (in Staat-Liches Museum, East Berlin, Vorderas Abteilung; Babylon 28122 and 28126). These are known as the 'ration tablets' and they record who received such 'rations'. In these, Jehoiachin is mentioned by name, so in our first example we see how the Bible's history is independently supported at this point in history.

We also have confirmation of the Babylonian advance towards Judah in Nebuchadnezzar's first campaign. Among the ruins of Lachish were discovered a number of ostraca. Ostraca are broken pieces of earthenware called potsherds, which were used for writing on in ink. (The Lachish ostraca are in the Palestinian Archaeological Museum, Jerusalem.) These brief letters reveal the increasing tensions within the growing state of Judah and tie in well with the picture given in the Bible by the Book of Jeremiah the Prophet. In Ostracon VI, the princes are accused of 'weakening our hands' (that is, discouraging the writers), which is the very phraseology used in the Bible by the Judean princes against Jeremiah. Also, the use of fire beacons for signalling is found in both Ostracon IV and Jeremiah 6:1, each using the same terminology.

For a further example let us go back 100 years and see what archaeology has told us about the city of Lachish in the time of Hezekiah. The site of the biblical city called Lachish is about thirty miles southwest of Jerusalem. This city is referred to on a number of occasions in the Old Testament. Imagine a busy city with high walls surrounding it, and a gate in front that is the only entrance to the city. We know so much about Lachish from archaeological studies that a reconstruction of the whole city has been made in detail. This can be seen at the British Museum in the Lachish Room in the Assyrian section.

There is also a picture made by artists in the eighth century before Christ, the Lachish Relief, which was discovered in the city of Nineveh in ancient Assyria. In this picture we can see the Jewish inhabitants of Lachish surrendering to Sennacherib, the king of Assyria. The details in the picture and the Assyrian writing on it give the Assyrian side of what the Bible tells us in Second Kings:

> In the fourteenth year of King Hezekiah's reign, Sennacherib king of Assyria attacked all the fortified cities of Judah and captured them. So Hezekiah king of Judah sent this message to the king of Assyria at Lachish: 'I have done wrong. Withdraw from me, and I will pay whatever you demand of me.' The king of Assyria exacted from Hezekiah king of Judah three hundred talents of silver and thirty talents of gold. So Hezekiah gave him all the silver that was found in the temple of the LORD and in the treasuries of the royal palace.
>
> At this time Hezekiah king of Judah stripped off the gold with which he had covered the doors and doorposts of the temple of the LORD, and gave it to the king of Assyria.
>
> 2 Kings 18:13–16

We should notice two things about this. First, this is a real-life situation—a real siege of a real city with real people on both sides of the war—and it happened at a particular date in history, near the turn of the eighth century BC. Second, the two accounts of this incident in 701 BC (the account from the Bible and the Assyrian account from Nineveh) do not contradict, but rather confirm each other. The history of Lachish itself is not so important for us, but it does illustrate how the Bible can be, and is, confirmed historically even in some of its smaller historical details.

Apart from what we know about Lachish, other material confirming the Bible has emerged from the time of Hezekiah.

Perhaps you remember the story of how Jesus healed a blind man and told him to go and wash in the Pool of Siloam. It is the same place known by King Hezekiah, approximately 700 years earlier. One of the remarkable things about the flow of the Bible is that historical events separated by hundreds of years took place in the same geographic spots, and, standing in these places today, we can feel that flow of history about us. The crucial archaeological discovery which relates to the Pool of Siloam is the tunnel which lies behind it.

One day in 1880 a small Arab boy was playing with his friend and fell into the pool. When he clambered out, he found a small opening about two feet wide and five feet high. On examination, it turned out to be a tunnel reaching back into the rock. But that was not all. On the side of the tunnel an inscribed stone (now kept in the museum in Istanbul) was discovered, which told how the tunnel had been built originally. The inscription in classical Hebrew reads as follows:

> The boring through is completed. And this is the story of the boring: while yet they plied the pick, each toward his fellow, and while there were yet three cubits [4 feet] to be bored through, there was heard the voice of one calling to the other that there was a hole in the rock on the right hand and on the left hand. And on the day of the boring through the workers on the tunnel struck each to meet his fellow, pick upon pick. Then the water poured from the source to the Pool 1,200 cubits [about 600 yards] and a 100 cubits was the height of the rock above the heads of the workers in the tunnel.

We know this as Hezekiah's Tunnel. The Bible tells us how Hezekiah made provision for a better water supply to the city: 'As for the other events of Hezekiah's reign, all his achievements and how he made the pool and the tunnel by which he brought water into the city, are they not written in the book of the annals of the kings of Judah?' (2 Kings 20:20). We know here three things: the biblical account, the tunnel itself of which the Bible speaks, and the original stone with its inscription in classical Hebrew.

From the Assyrian side, there is additional confirmation of the incidents mentioned in the Bible. There is a clay prism in the British Museum called the Taylor Prism (British Museum, Ref. 91032). It is only fifteen inches high and was discovered in the Assyrian palace at Nineveh. This particular prism dates from about 691 BC and tells about Sennacherib's exploits. A section from the prism reads, 'As for Hezekiah, the Jew, who did not submit to my yoke, 46 of his strong walled cities, as well as small cities in their neighbourhood I have besieged and took . . . himself like a caged bird, I shut up in Jerusalem, his royal city. Earthworks I threw up against him.' Thus, there is a three-way confirmation concerning Hezekiah's tunnel from the Hebrew side and this amazing confirmation from the Assyrian side.

There is also a confirmation of what the Bible says concerning the Egyptian King Tirhakah who came up to oppose the Assyrians. Confirmation of his reality is typified by a sphinx-ram in the British Museum (British Museum, Ref. B.B. 1779). The small figure between the legs of the ram is a representation of King Tirhakah. The Bible says that when Sennacherib heard that Tirhakah, king of Egypt, was coming to fight against him, he sent messengers to tell Hezekiah that help from Egypt would be of no use to him (*see* 2 Kings 19:9, 10 and Isaiah 37:9, 10).

The date of Sennacherib's campaign in Palestine is 701 BC, and something which has often puzzled historians is the role of Tirhakah, who was not king of Egypt and Ethiopia until 690 BC. But the solution to this problem is simple. In 701 BC Tirhakah was only a prince at the side of his military brother, the new Pharaoh Shebitku, who sent Tirhakah with an army to help Hezekiah fend off the Assyrian advance. But the story in Kings and Isaiah does not end in 701 BC. It carries right through to the death of Sennacherib in 681 BC, which is nine years after Tirhakah had become king of Egypt and Ethiopia. In other words, the biblical narrative, from the standpoint of 681 BC, mentions Tirhakah by the title he bore at that time (that is, 681 BC) not as he was in 701 BC. This is still done today, using a man's title as he is known at the time of writing even if one is speaking of a previous time in his personal history.

Unaware of the importance of these facts, and falling into wrong interpretations of some of Tirhakah's inscriptions, some Old Testament scholars have stumbled over each other in their eagerness to diagnose historical errors in the Books of Kings and Isaiah. But as the archaeological confirmation shows, they were quite mistaken. What is striking about these archaeological finds is the way they often converge; there is often not just one line of evidence but several in which the biblical account is confirmed. We do not have confirmation of every single detail in the biblical account, by any means. Nor do we need such total confirmation in view of the amount of evidence there is. To insist on confirmation at every point would be to treat the Bible in a prejudiced way, simply because it is the Bible. The fact that it is a religious book does not mean that it cannot also be true when it deals with history.

We now take a jump back in time to the middle of the ninth century before Christ, that is, about 850 BC. Most people have heard of Jezebel. She was the wife of Ahab, the king of the northern kingdom of Israel. Her wickedness has become so proverbial that we talk about someone as a 'Jezebel'. She urged her husband to have Naboth killed, simply because Ahab had expressed his liking for a piece of land owned by Naboth, who would not sell it. The Bible tells us also that she introduced into Israel the worship of her homeland, the Baal worship of Tyre. This led to the opposition of Elijah the Prophet and to the famous conflict on Mount Carmel between Elijah and the priests of Baal. Here again one finds archaeological confirmations of what the Bible says. Take for example: 'As for the other events of Ahab's reign, including all he did, the palace he built and inlaid with ivory, and the cities he fortified, are they not written in the book of the annals of the kings of Israel?' (1 Kings 22:39).

This is a very brief reference in the Bible to events which must have taken a long time: building projects which probably spanned decades. Archaeological excavations at the site of Samaria, the capital, reveal something of the former splendour of the royal citadel. Remnants of the 'ivory house' were found and attracted special attention (Palestinian Archaeological Museum, Jerusalem). This appears to have been a treasure pavilion in which the walls and furnishings had been adorned with coloured ivory work set with inlays giving a brilliant decorative effect. Numerous fragments of these were found. This ties in well, too, with the denunciations revealed by the prophet Amos:

> 'I will tear down the winter house
>   along with the summer house;
> the houses adorned with ivory will be destroyed
>   and the mansions will be demolished,'
>   declares the LORD.   Amos 3:15

Other archaeological confirmation exists for the time of Ahab. Excavations at Hazor and Megiddo have given evidence of the extent of fortifications carried out by Ahab. At Megiddo, in particular, Ahab's works were very extensive, including a large series of stables formerly assigned to Solomon's time.

On the political front, Ahab had to contend with danger from the Aramaeans just to the north (present-day Syria). Ben-hadad is named in 1 Kings 20:1 as the king of Syria who besieged Samaria, Ahab's capital. Ben-hadad's existence is attested by a stela (a column with writing on it) which has been discovered with his name written on it (Melquart Stela, Aleppo Museum, Syria). Again, a detail of history given in the Bible is shown to be correct.

Consider, too, the threat in the entire Middle East from the power of Assyria. In 853 BC King Shalmaneser III of Assyria came west from the region of the Euphrates River, only to be successfully repulsed by a determined alliance of all the states in that area at the Battle of Qarqar. Shalmaneser's record gives details of the alliance. In these he includes Ahab, who he tells us put 2,000 chariots and 10,000 infantry into the battle. However, after Ahab's death, Samaria was no longer strong enough to retain control, and Moab under King Mesha declared its independence, as 2 Kings 3:4, 5 makes clear: 'Now Mesha king of Moab raised sheep, and he had to supply the king of Israel with a hundred thousand lambs and with the wool of a hundred thousand rams. But after Ahab died, the king of Moab rebelled against the king of Israel.' The famous Moabite (Mesha) Stone, now in the Louvre, bears an inscription which testifies to Mesha's reality and of his success in throwing off the yoke of Israel. This is an inscribed black basalt stela, about four feet high, two feet wide, and several inches thick.

Ahab's line did not last long and was brutally overthrown by a man called Jehu. As one walks toward the Assyrian section in the British Museum, one of the first exhibits to be seen is the famous Black Obelisk. This stands about six feet high and was discovered at Nimrud (Calah) near the Assyrian capital at Nineveh. It describes how King Shalmeneser III compelled Jehu to submit to his authority and to pay him tribute. Here one can see a representation of the kneeling figure of either Jehu or his envoy before the Assyrian king. The inscription tells of Jehu's submission: 'The tribute of Jehu, son of Omri: I received from him silver, gold, a golden bowl, a golden vase with pointed bottom, golden tumblers, golden buckets, tin, a staff for a king and purukhti fruits.'

Jehu is referred to by the Assyrian records as son of Omri, not because he was literally his son, but because he was on the throne which had been occupied previously by the house of Omri. This event took place about 841 BC.

Putting them all together, these archaeological records show not only the existence historically of the people and events recorded in the Bible but the great accuracy of the details involved.

If we take another hundred-year step backwards in time, we come to King Solomon, son of David. On his death the Jewish kingdom was divided into two sections as a result of a civil revolt: Israel to the north with Jeroboam as king and Judah (as it was called subsequently) to the south under Rehoboam, Solomon's son. In both the Books of Kings and Chronicles in the Bible we read how during Rehoboam's reign: 'Shishak king of Egypt attacked Jerusalem' (1 Kings 14:25; 2 Chronicles 12:2), and how Shishak stripped Rehoboam of the wealth accumulated by his able father, Solomon. The reality of this event is confirmed by archaeology to a remarkable degree.

Shishak subdued not only Rehoboam but Jeroboam as well. The proof of this comes first from a fragment in a victory monument erected by Shishak and discovered at Megiddo, a city in the land of Israel. So the Egyptian king's force swept northwards, subdued the two Jewish kings, and then erected a victory monument to that effect. Traces of the destruction have also been discovered in such cities as Hazor, Gezer, and Megiddo. These confirm what was written in Second Chronicles:

> . . . he [Shishak] captured the fortified cities of Judah and came as far as Jerusalem.
>
> Then the prophet Shemaiah came to Rehoboam and to the leaders of Judah who had assembled in Jerusalem for fear of Shishak, and he said to them, 'This is what the LORD says, "You have abandoned me; therefore, I now abandon you to Shishak." '
>
> The leaders of Israel and the king humbled themselves and said, 'The LORD is just.'
>
> When the LORD saw that they humbled themselves, this word of the LORD came to Shemaiah: 'Since they have humbled themselves, I will not destroy them but will soon give them deliverance. My wrath will not be poured out on Jerusalem through Shishak. They will, however, become subject to him, so that they may learn the difference between serving me and serving the kings of other lands.'

> When Shishak king of Egypt attacked Jerusalem, he carried off the treasures of the temple of the LORD and the treasures of the royal palace. He took everything, including the gold shields Solomon had made.
>
> 2 Chronicles 12:4–9

Further confirmation comes from the huge victory scene engraved on Shishak's order at the Temple of Karnak in Egypt. The figure of the king is somewhat obscured, but he is clearly named and he is seen smiting Hebrew captives before the god Amon, and there are symbolic rows of names of conquered towns of Israel and Judah.

Solomon is remembered also for his great wealth. The Bible tells us:

> The weight of the gold that Solomon received yearly was 666 talents, not including the revenues from merchants and traders and from all the Arabian kings and the governors of the land.
>
> King Solomon made two hundred large shields of hammered gold; six hundred bekas of gold went into each shield. He also made three hundred small shields of hammered gold, with three minas of gold in each shield. The king put them in the Palace of the Forest of Lebanon.
>
> 1 Kings 10:14–17

This wealth that the Bible speaks of has been challenged. Surely, some have said, these figures are an exaggeration. Excavations, however, have confirmed enormous quantities of precious metals, owned and distributed by kings during this period. For example, Shishak's son Osorkon I (statuette of Osorkon I, Brooklyn Museum, New York), the one who stood to gain from the booty carried off from Rehoboam's capital, is reported to have made donations to his god Amon totalling 470 tons of precious metal, gold, and silver, during only the first 4 years of his reign. This, of course, is much more than Solomon's 666 talents which equals approximately 20 tons of gold per annum. We also have confirmation of the Bible's reference to Solomon's gold as coming from Ophir. The location of Ophir is still unknown, but an ostracon dated a little later than Solomon's time actually mentions that 30 shekels of gold had come from Ophir for Beth-horon.

So the story goes on. We have stopped at only a few incidents in the sweep back to the year 1000 BC. What we hope has emerged from this is a sense of the historical reliability of the Bible's text. When the Bible refers to historical incidents, it is speaking about the same sort of 'history' that historians examine elsewhere in other cultures and periods. This is borne out by the fact that some of the incidents, some of the individuals, and some of the places have been confirmed by archaeological discoveries. Of course, not all the incidents, individuals, and places have been confirmed, but the tide of archaeological discoveries in the past hundred years has swept away the possibility of a naïve scepticism about the Bible's history. And what is particularly striking is that the tide has built up concerning the time before the year 1000 BC. Our knowledge about the years 2500 BC to 1000 BC has been vastly increased through discoveries sometimes of whole libraries and even of hitherto unknown people and languages.

There was a time, for example, when the Hittite people, referred to in the early parts of the Bible, were treated as fictitious by critical scholars. Then came the discoveries after 1906 at Boghaz Koi (Boghazköy) which not only gave us the certainty of their existence but stacks of details from their own archives! Not that this is always the case.

When we come to the time of Moses we can acknowledge that the archaeological evidence is not of the same explicitness that we have found, say, in relation to the existence of Ahab or Jehu or Jehoiakim. We have no inscription from Egypt which refers to Moses being taken out of the bulrushes and removed from the waterproof basket his mother had made him. But this does not mean that the Book of Exodus is a legendary account, as some critics have suggested. Some say it is simply an idealised reading-back into history by the Jews under the later monarchy. But there is no reason why these 'books of Moses', as they are called, should not be treated as history, just as we have been forced to treat the Books of Kings and Chronicles dating 500 years later.

There is ample evidence about the building projects of the Egyptian kings, and the evidence we have fits well with Exodus. There are scenes of brick-making (for example, Theban Tomb 100 of Rekhmire). Contemporary parchments and papyri tell of production targets which had to be met. One speaks of a satisfied official's report of his men as 'making their quota of bricks daily' (Papyrus Anastasi III vso, p. 3, in the British Museum. Also Louvre Leather Roll in the Louvre, Paris, col ii, mentions quotas of bricks and 'taskmasters'). Actual bricks found show signs of straw which had to be mixed in with the clay, just as Exodus says. This matter of bricks and straw is further affirmed by the record that one despairing official complained, 'There are no men to make bricks nor straw in my area.'

We know from contemporary discoveries that Semites were found at all levels of Egypt's cosmopolitan society (Brooklyn Museum, New York, no. 35.1446. Papyrus Brooklyn). There is nothing strange therefore about Joseph's becoming so important in the pharaoh's court.

The store cities of Pithom and Raamses (Rameses) mentioned in Exodus 1:11 are well known in Egyptian inscriptions. Raamses was actually the east-Delta capital, Pi-Ramses (near Goshen), where the Israelites lived (to the east of the Nile Delta). It had fertile tracts, an area where the Israelites would have had ample experience of agriculture. Thus, the reference to agriculture found in the law of Moses would not have been strange to the Israelites even though they were in the desert at the time the law was given. Certainly there is no reason to say, as some critics do, that these sections on agriculture were an indication of a reading-back from a later period when the Jews were settled in Canaan.

Further evidence that the biblical account was not written at a later date than the Bible says it is, comes from the nature of the Mosaic covenant which could not have been written late. This is because the form of the covenant made at Sinai has remarkable parallels with the covenant forms of other people at that time. (On *covenants* and *parties to a treaty,* see C. F. A. Schaeffer, Ugaritica I 1 1 Louvre, Paris; the Code of Hammurabi in the Louvre; and Treaty Tablet from Boghaz Koi [i.e., Hittite] in Turkey, Museum of Archaeology in Istanbul.) The covenant form at Sinai resembles covenants from that period but *not* from later in the first millennium BC. Thus, just as the forms of letter writing of the first century after Christ (the types of introductions and greetings) are reflected in the letters of the apostles in the New Testament, it is not surprising to find the covenant form of the second millennium before Christ reflected in what occurred at Mount Sinai. God has always spoken to people within the culture of their time, which does not mean that God's communication is limited by that culture. It is God's communication but within the forms appropriate to the time.

The Pentateuch tells us that Moses led the Israelites up the east side of the Dead Sea after their long stay in the desert. There they encountered the hostile kingdom of Moab. We have firsthand evidence for the existence of this kingdom of Moab—contrary to what has been said by critical scholars who have denied the existence of Moab at this time. It can be found in a war scene from a temple at Luxor (Al Uqṣor). This commemorates a victory by Ramses II over the Moabite nation at Batora (Luxor Temple, Egypt).

Also, the definite presence of the Israelites in west Palestine (Canaan) no later than the end of the thirteenth century BC is attested by a victory stela of Pharaoh Merenptah (son and successor of Ramses II) to commemorate his victory over Libya (Israel Stela. Cairo Museum, no. 34025). In it he mentions his previous success in Canaan against Aschalon, Gize, Yenom, and *Israel;* hence there can be no doubt the nation of Israel was in existence at the *latest* by this time of approximately 1220 BC. This is not to say it could not have been earlier, but it cannot be later than this date.

We should take one last step back into the history of the Old Testament—approximately 500 years before Moses—to the time of Abraham. We are now back as far as Genesis 12, near the beginning of the Bible.

Do we find that the narrative fades away to a never-never land of myths and legends? By no means. For we have to remind ourselves that although Genesis 12 deals with events a long time ago from our moment of history (about 2000 BC or a bit later), the civilised world was already not just old but ancient when Abram/Abraham left 'Ur of the Chaldeans' (*see* Genesis 11:31).

Ur itself was excavated some fifty years ago. In the British Museum, for example, one can see the magnificent contents of a royal burial chamber from Ur. This includes a gold headdress still in position about the head of a queen who died in Ur about 2500 BC. It has also been possible to reconstruct from archaeological remains what the streets and buildings must have been like at the time.

Like Ur, the rest of the world of the patriarchs (that is, of Abraham, Isaac, and Jacob) was firm reality. Such places as Haran, where Abraham went first, have been discovered. So has Shechem from this time, with its Canaanite stone walls, which are still standing, and its temple.

> He [Abram] took his wife Sarai, his nephew Lot, all the possessions they had accumulated and the people they had acquired in Haran, and they set out for the land of Canaan, and they arrived there.
>
> Abram travelled through the land as far as the site of the great tree of Moreh at Shechem. The Canaanites were then in the land, but the LORD appeared to Abram and said, 'To your offspring I will give this land.' So he built an altar there to the LORD, who had appeared to him.
>
> From there he went on toward the hills east of Bethel and pitched his tent, with Bethel on the west and Ai on the east. There he built an altar to the LORD and called on the name of the LORD. Then Abram set out and continued toward the Negev.
>
> Genesis 12:5–9

Haran and Shechem may be unfamiliar names to us but the Negev (or Negeb) is a name we have all read frequently in the news accounts of our own day.

Now we should turn to one of the most spectacular of modern archaeological discoveries, Ebla. While digging on an extensive mound forty-four miles south of Aleppo in Syria in 1974/75, an Italian archaeological expedition came across another of the vast libraries to which we referred earlier. A small room within the palace suddenly yielded up a thousand tablets and fragments, while another not far away a further fourteen thousand. These lay row upon row, just where they had fallen from the burning wooden shelves when the palace was destroyed about 2250 BC.

What secrets did these tablets reveal? Without wishing to seem unnecessarily repetitive, we can say immediately that Ebla represents yet another discovery from the ancient past which does not make it harder for us to believe the Bible, but quite the opposite. And remember, these tablets date from well before the time of Abraham. The implications of this discovery will not be exhausted by even the turn of this century. The translation and publication of such a vast number of tablets will take years and years. It is important to understand that the information we now have from Ebla does not bear directly upon the Bible. As far as has been discovered, there is no certain reference to individuals mentioned in the Bible, though many names are similar, for example, Ishmael, Israel, and so forth. Biblical place names like Megiddo, Hazor, Lachish are also referred to. What *is* clear, however, is that certain individuals outside the Bible who previously had been considered fictitious by the critical scholars, simply because of the antiquity, are now quite definitely historic characters.

For example, the Assyrian's King Tudiya (approximately 2500 BC) had already been known from the Assyrian king list composed about 1000 BC. His name appeared at the head of the list, but his reality was dismissed by many scholars as 'free invention, or a corruption'. In fact, he was very much a real person and is known now from the Ebla records to have made a treaty with the king of Ebla. Thus, the genealogical tradition of the earlier parts of the Assyrian king list has been vindicated. It preserves faithfully, over a period of 1,500 years, the memory of real, early people who were Assyrian rulers. What we must learn from this is that when we find similar material in the Old Testament, such as the genealogical list in Genesis 7 or the patriarchal stories, we should be careful not to reject them out of hand, as the scholars have so often done. We must remember that these ancient cultures were just as capable of recording their histories as we are.

The most important aspect of the Ebla discoveries is undoubtedly their language. This has been found to be an ancient West-Semitic language to which such languages as Hebrew, Canaanite, Ugaritic, Aramaic, and Moabite are related. Thus we have now, for the first time, the whole 'tradition' of West-Semitic language stretching over 2,500 years—something which was previously true only of Egyptian and Akkadian, to which Babylonian and Assyrian belong.

Up until quite recently, therefore, this meant that scholars could argue that many words which appeared in the Hebrew Old Testament were what they called 'late'. What they meant by this was that these words indicated a much later authorship than the time stated by the text itself. It would be as if one of us pretended to write a sixteenth-century book using such modern words as *automobile* and *computer*. In the case of the Pentateuch, for example, this was one of the arguments which led some scholars to suggest that it was not Moses who wrote these books, as the Bible says, but anonymous scribes from approximately 1,000 years later. The discoveries at Ebla have shown that many of these words were not late, but very early. Here is yet another example of a claimed 'scientific' approach that merely reflects the philosophical prejudices of the scholars involved.

At this point we can remind ourselves of the history we have covered; from the disaster of the Late Monarchy, through to the activities of Ahab and Jezebel, back to Shishak's plunder of Solomon's wealth, then to the time of Moses and finally to the early period of Abraham. In this great sweep of time we have seen just some of the confirming evidence that the archaeological discoveries have made available.

This should have built up in our minds a vivid impression of the historic reliability of the biblical text, including even the seemingly obscure details such as the ration tablets in Babylon. We saw, in other words, not only that the Bible gives us a marvellous world view that ties in with the nature of reality and answers the basic problems which philosophers have asked down through the centuries, but also that the Bible is completely reliable, *even on the historical level.*

Appendix 4

*Religious
Liberalism and
Historical Truth
in the
New Testament*

The main barrier to understanding and appreciating the historical truth and reliability of the Bible has been 'religious liberalism'. Although its thinking affects the whole Bible we will especially consider some of its assumptions in relation to the New Testament. Religious liberalism has a rationalist view of the truth which has rejected any knowledge from outside man's reason. Liberal theologians made a division in the Bible between those things which fitted in with their rationalistic ideas and those which did not. Their attitude can be summed up simply: God cannot be known as One who acts in history. There-fore, they tried to divide the Bible roughly into natural and supernatural parts. They felt that the supernatural parts were unworthy to be accepted by 'modern man', that they belonged necessarily to the realm of primitive superstition, that there was nothing objectively true about them.

An example of one who took this approach is the German scholar David Friedrich Strauss who wrote *The Life of Jesus* in 1835. In it he said that most of the material in the Gospels is 'mythical'. Speaking of the transfiguration, he wrote, 'It is impossible to maintain this historical, supernatural interpretation which the New Testament sanctions.' So what he proposed was a thorough-going demythologising for the Gospel story. The real history, he said, had to be separated from this mythology.

Strauss was not the first scholar to state such opinions, but you can see from the date of *The Life of Jesus*— 1835—that the revolution took place a long time ago. The movement as a whole was called 'religious liberalism', because of its 'free' approach to the Bible. It grew in momentum during the nineteenth century, and its assumptions are still the assumptions of many scholars in the Protestant world today and of an increasing number of Roman Catholic theologians, too.

What is most disturbing about this approach to the Bible is not that it disagrees with past traditions, but rather that it claims to be 'scientific'. We must be clear that Christianity has nothing to fear from modern science. Indeed, Christianity was instrumental in the origin of science. Tradition and authority should not be just blindly accepted, but examined to see if the things previously believed are indeed true. What *is* dangerous is the misuse of the claim to be 'scientific'. We do not think it is too strong to speak of this as 'deception'.

By using the word *scientific,* the religious liberalists gave the impression of the same type of certainty and objectivity that had become accepted in regard to the physical sciences. Using this claim, they proposed their various theories of how the Bible had actually come into existence, and on the basis of these theories altered the teaching that Christians had previously accepted. They rejected the Bible's accounts of miracles, such as the feeding of the 5,000 or Jesus' walking on the water. But they went much further than that. For example, they rejected the idea of a coming judgment for mankind, of salvation through the substitutionary work of Christ, of the divinity of Christ, of the Resurrection, of the Virgin Birth, and so on. What was left was a religion of morality, called by some the 'Religion of the Sermon on the Mount' (though this itself was a serious misrepresentation, for the Sermon on the Mount, as well as teaching a very high moral code, also teaches quite explicitly such things as future judgment by Jesus Himself).

To ordinary people, these developments were bewildering. However, for many the radical conclusions of the scholars seemed to be irresistible, for they were presented as the result of careful and objective scientific scholarship. To disagree with the scholars was to be obscurantist. To maintain the traditional idea simply indicated a refusal to follow the truth wherever the truth led.

From where we stand today, it is easy to see how naïve these views really are. For what has happened since that time is, first, that the internal weaknesses of the so-called scientific theories have become apparent. Second, as we have seen, literally tons of archaeological materials have been unearthed from the periods and the geographic locations covered by the Bible. Archaeology as a science has made huge strides in the last hundred years.

The scholars fail at this point because they are not scientific enough! They have fallen into the same trap which they accuse those who preceded them of falling into—of bringing preconceived ideas about God's revelation to bear on the discipline of biblical criticism. Because of their world view they refuse to accept the possibility that God could have communicated to man in such a way that what is contained in the Bible is reliable. They caricature this idea with such terms as the 'dictation theory of inspiration'. By this they act as though the scholars through the centuries (who have held that God has given us truth through the Bible) have taught (and must teach) that God used the human writers of the Bible like typewriters, simply typing out what He wanted man to understand. But, while some may have taught the dictation theory of inspiration, it was not the generally held concept.

The generally held concept was that God used people in the writing of the Bible without destroying their individuality and their significance. What they finally wrote, however, was what God knew was necessary for people to have as a written authority. Each writer was 'himself', so to speak, but as each wrote— in a different style from others, in a different historical context, in different literary forms, and sometimes in different languages—he was led by God to write what God intended to be written. Thus, truth was given in all the areas the Bible touches upon.

The critics have continued the tradition received from the last century, which argued that God could not work into the world supernaturally. As Strauss said, 'It is *impossible* to maintain as historical the supernatural interpretations the New Testament sanctions.' Strauss was correct on one point here. What the New Testament (including the teaching of Christ) teaches about the supernatural happenings in observable history is exactly what Strauss and the other liberal theologians have denied.

It is this sort of thinking which still underlies so much liberal scholarship. Why is it impossible, for example, for God to have effected the Virgin Birth when Jesus was born? After all, since God designed the birth process in the first place, why can He not, in one case, interrupt the normal action of cause and effect that He created and initiate something different? In the same way, if God created everything at the beginning, why can He not also give life to the dead and raise up Jesus' body from the tomb? The only reason these things and others like them are so categorically denied is that the rationalist or naturalist world view has already been accepted.

When you hear people being critical about the Bible, remember that what seems to be scientific is not always so, and what are claimed to be the 'assured results of scholarship' are not always so assured.

Let us give a recent example relating to the dating of the New Testament documents. For over a hundred years the idea has circulated among many scholars that the documents of the New Testament (or most of them) could not have been written at, or soon after, the time of Jesus' ministry. These scholars suggested in some cases that the Gospels were written about 150 years later and were therefore quite unreliable. In the same way, it was common for scholars to suggest that letters supposedly written by Paul or Peter or John were not written by them but by unknown writers who used the apostles' names many years after they died to gain acceptance for what they had written.

A New Testament scholar, the ex-Bishop of Woolwich, John Robinson, now dean of Trinity College, Cambridge, has written a book called *Redating the New Testament* (1976). What is striking is that previously this author had taken a very 'liberal' position. At the outset of his book on the dating of the New Testament, he says he first began to question the late dates assigned to the New Testament writers when he realised how 'much more than is generally recognised, the chronology of the New Testament rests upon presuppositions rather than facts'. And he quotes the following from a letter from a famous New Testament scholar, C. H. Dodd: 'I should agree with you that much of this late dating is quite arbitrary, even wanton, the offspring not of any argument that can be presented.'

Apart from being sceptical about the 'assured results of scholarship' it is also worth being aware that a common assumption among liberal scholars is that because the Gospels are theologically motivated writings—which they are—they cannot also be historically accurate. In other words, because Luke, say (when he wrote the Book of Luke and the Book of Acts), was convinced of the deity of Christ, this influenced his work to the point where it ceased to be reliable as a historical account. The assumption that a writing cannot be both historical and theological is false.

The experience of the famous classical archaeologist Sir William Ramsay illustrates this well. When he began his pioneer work of exploration in Asia Minor, he accepted the view then current among the Tübingen scholars of his day that the Book of Acts was written long after the events in Paul's life and was therefore historically inaccurate. However, his travels and discoveries increasingly forced upon his mind a totally different picture, and he became convinced that Acts was minutely accurate in many details which could be checked.

What is even more interesting is the way 'liberal' modern scholars today deal with Ramsay's discoveries and others like them. In *The New Testament: The History of the Investigations of Its Problems,* the German scholar Werner G. Kümmel made no reference at all to Ramsay. This provoked a protest from British and American scholars, whereupon in a subsequent edition Kümmel responded. His response was revealing. He made it clear that it was his deliberate intention to leave Ramsay out of his work, since 'Ramsay's apologetic analysis of archaeology [in other words, relating it to the New Testament in a positive way] signified no methodologically essential advance for New Testament research.' This is a quite amazing assertion. Statements like these reveal the philosophic assumptions involved in much liberal scholarship.

A modern *classical* scholar, A. N. Sherwin-White says about the Book of Acts: 'For Acts the confirmation of historicity is overwhelming. . . . Any attempt to reject its basic historicity, even in matters of detail, must now appear absurd. Roman historians have long taken this for granted.' Acts is a fairly full account of Paul's journeys, starting in Pisidian Antioch and ending in Rome itself. The record is quite evidently that of an eyewitness of the events, in part at least. Throughout, however, it is the report of a meticulous historian. The narrative in the Book of Acts takes us back behind the missionary journeys to Paul's famous conversion on the Damascus Road, and back further through the Day of Pentecost to the time when Jesus finally left His disciples and ascended to be with the Father.

But we must understand that the story begins earlier still, for Acts is quite explicitly the second part of a continous narrative by the same author, Luke, which reaches back to the birth of Jesus:

> In those days Caesar Augustus issued a decree that a census should be taken of the entire Roman world. (This was the first census that took place while Quirinius was governor of Syria.) And everyone went to his own town to register.
> So Joseph also went up from the town of Nazareth in Galilee to Judea, to Bethlehem the town of David, because he belonged to the house and line of David.

He went there to register with Mary, who was pledged to be married to him and was expecting a child. While they were there, the time came for the baby to be born, and she gave birth to her firstborn, a son. She wrapped him in strips of cloth and placed him in a manger, because there was no room for them in the inn.

Luke 2:1–7

In the opening sentences of his Gospel, Luke states his reason for writing:

Many have undertaken to draw up an account of the things that have been fulfilled among us, just as they were handed down to us by those who from the first were eyewitnesses and servants of the word. Therefore, since I myself have carefully investigated everything from the beginning, it seemed good also to me to write an orderly account for you, most excellent Theophilus, so that you may know the certainty of the things you have been taught.

Luke 1:1–4

In Luke and Acts, therefore, we have something which purports to be an adequate history, something which Theophilus (or anyone) can rely on as its pages are read. This is not the language of 'myths and fables', and archaeological discoveries serve only to confirm this.

For example, it is now known that Luke's references to the titles of officials encountered along the way are uniformly accurate. This was no mean achievement in those days, for they varied from place to place and from time to time in the same place. They were *proconsuls* in Corinth and Cyprus, *asiarchs* at Ephesus, *politarchs* at Thessalonica, and *protos* or 'first man' in Malta. Back in Palestine, Luke was careful to give Herod Antipas the correct title of tetrarch of Galilee. And so on. The details are precise.

The mention of Pontius Pilate as Roman governor of Judea has been confirmed recently by an inscription discovered at Caesarea, which was the Roman capital of that part of the Roman Empire. Although Pilate's existence has been well known for the past 2,000 years by those who have read the Bible, now his governorship has been clearly attested outside the Bible.

When we next look at the pages of the New Testament we should remember what we are looking at. The New Testament writers themselves make abundantly clear that they are giving an account of objectively true events. The liberal view which denies their claim is neither reasonable, historical, nor objective.

Index

Abnormality
    Christian concept of   126, 127
    result of man's rebellion against God   126,
        127
Abortion. *See also* Fetus
    advice   32, 33, 34, 170 n.41
    Akron (Ohio) ordinance   32, 169 n.39
    alternatives to   90–95
    as form of birth control   48
    availability affects family breakdown   33
    back-street   171 n.42
    charities and   66, 175 n.63
    church and   61–64, 90, 91
    consumer attitude to   55
    costs   80, 172 n.48
    for demographic concerns   67, 80, 170 n.42
    for 'health' reasons   165 n.16
    for sex choice reasons   56
    funding by Planned Parenthood (USA)   166
        n.20
    increase of child abuse   16–19, 21, 52
    Jesse Jackson compares to slavery   164
        n.14
    law.   *See* Abortion Act
    legality   28, 168 n.32
    'liberalising' of laws (by other
        countries)   171 n.46
    live births and   27–31, 167 n.25, 167 n.27,
        168 n.32
    not a feminist issue   37, 92, 171 n.44
    not a religious issue   34–37, 171 n.43
    nurses revulsion to   29, 30, 168 n.34
    on-demand 20, 24, 32, 55, 56, 164 n.12, 166
        n.19
    physical dangers of   33, 169 n.40, 170 n.41
    pre-natal screening for   172 n.48, 175 n.63
    psychological consequences of   33, 34, 169
        n.40, 170 n.41
    ruling.   *See* United States Supreme Court
    semantics used to disguise   86, 87
    statistics   21, 167 n.21
    study of legal abortion patients   169 n.40
    techniques   25–28
    until birth   168 n.35
Abortion Act 1967
    arbitrariness of   19
    back-street abortion and   171 n.42
    background to 166 n.19
    BMA and   4, 163 n.3
    Christian leaders and   64
    conscience clause   29, 168 n.34, 169 n.35
    criteria for abortion   166 n.19

differences from USA   20, 165 n.16
    Infant Life Preservation Act   166 n.19
    Lane Report and   166 n.19
    lobbying and   12
    loose drafting   165 n.19
    on-demand and   20, 166 n.19
Abortion Amendment Bill
    Corrie, John MP, and   31, 33
    counselling and   33
    late abortions and   31
Abortion Law Reform Association
    Abortion Act and lobbying   12
    David Steele's speech to   163 n.5
    Infant Life Preservation Act and   168 n.35
Abraham (Abram)
    faithfulness of   138–141
    his life an historic event   138, 192–193
        App.3
Acts, Book of, its historical accuracy   142,
    143, 198–199 App.4
Adam and Eve. *See* Fall, the
Addison, Dr Philip H., report on dying
    patients' requests for euthanasia   77
Adoptions
    and unwanted children   90
    fewer children available   32
Aged. *See* Elderly
Ahab and Jezebel, confirmed by archaeological
    findings   187–188 App.3
Akron (Ohio) ordinance on abortion   32, 189
    n.39
Alexander, Dr Leo, 'Medical Service Under
    Dictatorship'   81–85
Allen, Woody, comedian, philosophy of   97,
    101, 109, 117
American Ethical Union, pro-abortion   61
American Jewish Congress, pro-abortion   61
'Ancient Attitudes' on abortion,
    infanticide   37
Anti-abortion feelings and medical, nursing
    staffs   29, 30
Anti-Catholic thinking as pro-abortion
    weapon   64
Anti-family climate   19, 33, 68, 164 n.12
Antonioni, Michelangelo, film *Blow-up,* state-
    ment of today's philosophy   105, 106
Apathy of population toward value of human
    life   80, 94, 156, 177 n.79
Arbitrary law. *See* Sociological law
Archaeology. *See also* chapter 5
    supports Bible validity   184–194 App.3, 196
        App.4

Assyria, early threat to Middle East, verified by archaeological findings 188 App. 3

Bacon, Francis, early modern scientist and Bible view 105, 106
Barrett, Professor William, New York University, on existentialism 119
Battered-child syndrome 16
Becker, Professor Ernest, 'no invisible world' 101
Beckett, Samuel, humanist playwright 111
Behaviour standards
  changes in 3, 4
  humanistic 3, 19
  'thinkable' and 'unthinkable' 3, 4
Bhagavad-Gita, Eastern religious writings 115
Blackham, H. J., *Objections to Humanism* 98
Bible. *See also* Gospels; 'Image of God'; New Testament; Personal God and orderly universe 128, 149
  accepted by early modern scientists 104, 105
  alternatives. *See* Eastern philosophy; Humanism
  as viewed by rationalists 195 App.4
  authority of 195 App.4
  Creation account 125, 127, 129, 130
  Dead Sea Scrolls 182–183 App.2
  Fall, the 126, 127
  Genesis, importance of 129, 131
  inspiration of 196 App.4
  provides freedom 128
  revelation from God 124
  rules for living 127, 128, 150
  'scientific' approach to 196 App. 4
  supported by archaeology, modern sciences 196 App.4
  verified by historical facts. *See* Chapter 5 and App.2, 3, 5
  view of truth 134, 135
  world view of 100, 127, 128, 134, 135
  writers of 124, 125, 196 App.4
Bickel, Alexander M., of Yale, on Supreme Court 12
Binding, Karl, and Hoche, Alfred, originators of 'death with dignity' 69, 176 n.67
Biologist view of conception 24, 67
Birth control
  abortion as form of 48
Birth defects. *See* Congenital defects
Blackmun, Justice Harry (USA), opinion on abortion 37
Bourne Case 1938 166 n.19
Brewer, Dr Colin, on the starvation of *spina bifida* newborns 41
British Medical Association, *Handbook on Medical Ethics* position on abortion 4
Bronowski, Jacob, humanist, *The Identity of Man* 98

Broward General Hospital (Fort Lauderdale, Florida) attitude toward abortions 29, 30
Brown, Harold O. J.
  on child abuse 21, 167 n.22, 167 n.23
  on separation of church and state 171 n.43
'Built-in obsolescence' 55
Bulfin, Dr Matthew, and study of patients having legal abortions 169 n.40

Caesarean section abortion. *See* Hysterotomy
Campbell, Dr A. G. M., infanticide advocate 54, 55, 59, 60, 174 n.53
Camus, Albert, humanist writer 98, 117
Child abuse 16, 17, 164 n.9, 164 n.13
  as cause of death 17
  case histories 16
  forms of 16, 17
  Giarretto, Dr Harry 17
  Hedlener, Dr Irwin 17
  Kempe, Dr C. Henry 16
  incest 17
  increase despite abortions 19, 21, 52
Children's Hospital of Philadelphia 51
  neonatal surgery at 173 n.48
Children's Hospital, Sheffield, 40, 110–113, 126
Choice of good or evil up to man 3, 110–113, 126, 127
  of life and death 52. *See also* Living will
Christian consensus 9, 39. *See also* World view
  view of normal and abnormal contrasted with humanists 125, 126
Christianity. *See also* Bible
  acceptance of as truth 149
  alternatives to, Eastern philosophy 103, 112, 115. *See also* Humanism
  leading others to 153
  not autonomous, like humanism 125
  personal God of 118, 127, 129, 130
  provides order yet freedom 128
  rooted in history. *See* chapter 5 and App.3, App.4
  science indebted to 128
  'utilitarian' use of by unbelievers 149
Christians For a Free Choice, pro abortion 64
Christians, role of in opposing abortions, infanticide, euthanasia 88–94. *See also* chapter 6
Chromosomes. *See* DNA; Genetic knowledge
Church
  and abortion 61–66
  and the Holocaust 81
  can help prevent abortion 90, 91
Cities, ancient, in Old Testament verified by archaeological findings 192–193 App. 3
Citizens for Informed Consent (USA), anti-abortionists 168 n.39
Claudius, Roman emperor, and expulsion of Jews 142

Cohen, Lord of Birkenhead, National Health
    Service   41
Communication
    and behavioural changes   4
    by God to man through Bible   124, 125, 196
        App.4
Communist countries, dominance of humanism
    16
Congenital defects. *See also* Handicapped and
    Spina bifida
    correcting   50, 52, 172 n.47
    types of   50, 52, 172 n.47
Conscience clause   29, 30, 169 n.35
Copernican revolution   104
Cornelsen, Dr Ronald, witness in Waddill case
    167 n.27
Corrie, John, MP. *See* Abortion Amendment
    Bill
Cost containment and cost benefit in medical
    economics   172 n.48
Counterculture. *See* Sixties; Mysticism,
    modern
Covenant on Mount Sinai
    Moses reminds his people of   133, 135
    parallel to forms of the time   192 App.3
Cox, Archibald, *The Role of the Supreme Court*
    20
Creation. *See also* Bible, Genesis, Book of
    and 'chance' concept   8, 9, 13, 125
    biblical account   125, 126, 128, 129, 130
    rejection of by humanists   12–14, 97
Crick, Francis, Nobel Prize winner, on infanti-
    cide   53
Criminal Law Revision Committee   76
Cruelty, personal, result of humanism   9–13.
    See also Child abuse
Cultures, judgment of   2

D&C, abortion technique   26
DNA (whole genetic code)   24
Darwin, Charles, evolution theories
    failure of basic arguments   180 App.1
    seen by humanists as progress   113, 114
Dead Sea Scrolls   182 App.2
Death, 'brain death' and definition of death
    73
Death pill for aged   78, 79
Death selection   70, 78, 79, 84, 85, 176 n.68
'Death with dignity'   69, 70, 78, 176 n.67. *See
    also* Euthanasia
Declaration   77, 176 n.69, 177 n.83
Declaration of Geneva
    adopted by World Medical
        Organisation   4
    use of in medical schools   4
Defects, birth. *See* Congenital defects
Democracy
    incompatible with genetic engineering   14
    in the USA   12
    violated by Warren Court   14
Department of Health and Social Security
    (DHSS)   74, 172 n.48

Descartes, René, philosopher, first raised
    questions of God's authority, epistem-
    ology   105
Development of fetus   22–25
Diamond, Sondra, handicapped   60
Didache, early Christian document, opposed
    abortion   65
Divorce as anti-family force   164
Dodd, C. H., Bible scholar   197 App.4
Doe v. *Bolton*, US Supreme Court decision
    19, 20
Down's syndrome. *See also* Congenital defects
    effect of mongoloids on marriages   173 n.49
    permitted to die   38
    useful life of mongoloid   175 n.54
Dred Scott decision and rights of blacks   61
Drug culture. *See also* Sixties
    Timothy Leary's experiments   121
Duff, Dr Raymond S., and infanticide   54, 55,
    59, 60, 174 n.53
Dunphy, J. Engelburt, traditional medical view
    of infanticide   39, 40
Dying patients and requests for
    euthanasia   77

Eastern philosophy
    acts of charity   115
    and the counterculture   119, 120
    as alternative to Christianity   102, 112–117
    Bhagavad-Gita writings   115
    compared to materialistic humanism   112
    endless cycles   115
    impersonal God   112
    impersonal system   112
    introduction of personal gods   114, 115
    maya, illusion   113
    no right or wrong   123
Ebla, modern archaeological discovery, dates
    back before Abraham   193–194 App.3
Economic burden of handicapped on society
    50, 52, 82, 172 n.48, 174 n.53
Edelin, Dr Kenneth, abortionist   166 n.25
Elderly
    death pill for   78–80
    economic burden   68, 73, 74, 79, 80
    hospice care for   92, 93
    prime candidates for euthanasia   68, 69
    'right to choose death'   74
Embryo
    'created' in labs   31, 168 n.37
    refutes Darwin's evolution theory   180
        App.1
    separate, unique individual   24
Emotional distress for women who had
    abortions   26–27, 32, 33, 34, 169 n.41
Engelhart, Professor H. Tristam, Jr,
    on 'wrongful life'   58
Enlightenment humanists   99, 101, 178 n.90
    and optimism   109, 116
    countered by modern mysticism   119
    'Reason Is King'   116

Environmental protection by US Supreme
    Court 165 n.18
Epistemology (the theory of knowledge) 105
Ethics
    'biologised' 15
    BMA's *Handbook of Medical Ethics* 4
    Christian 8, 88, 94
    disposal of lab embryos 31, 32
    of medical profession 33, 87, 152. *See also*
        Hippocratic Oath
    situational 78
    US Supreme Court abortion decision 167
        n.22
Euthanasia. *See also* Mercy killing
    advocacy of 58, 74, 176 n.67
    alternatives to 90–94
    candidates for 68, 70, 73, 84
    death pill 78, 79
    'death with dignity' concept 69, 70, 78, 176
        n.67
    declarations and 77, 176 n.69, 177 n.83
    definition of death 73
    economical answer to prolonged care 68,
        73, 74, 82
    legalisation of, weakened by modern medical
        technology 77
    legislative proposals 77
    living will 40, 96, 176 n.69, 177 n.83
    Nazis and 81, 92, 177 n.79
    'passive', deliberate starvation 41, 46, 69
    practice of 76, 79
    punishment of 77
    'right to choose' 74
Evil
    responsibility for is man's 126, 127
    result of the Fall 126, 127
Evolution
    as seen in sociobiology 14
    concept of higher and lower plants, animals
        113, 114
    failure of Darwin's arguments 180 App.1
    meaninglessness derived from 114
    mystical view of Teilhard de Chardin, Pierre
        179 n.99
    seen by humanists as progress 113, 114
Existentialism
    as counter-Enlightenment 119
    as irrationalism 116, 117, 118
    contrary to biblical view of truth 135
    difference between secular and
        religious 121
    explanation of 116–118, 121
    no right or wrong 123
    philosophical approach of 119
Extermination of Jews by Nazis. *See*
    Holocaust, the

Fall, the, in Genesis 3 126–128
Feminists, abortion not feminist issue 37, 92,
    171 n.44

Fetus. *See also* Abortion
    as non-person 20
    compared to slaves 20, 164 n.14
    defined by US Supreme Court 165 n.16
    denied law protection 164 n.14
    destruction of 22, 24, 25
    determining sex of 55, 56
    growth of 22–24
    living, after abortion attempt 26–31
    states' rights in the USA 165 n.16
    uniqueness of 24
First International Conference on
    Abortion 167 n.24
Fletcher, John, ethicist, on abortion for sex
    choice 56
Fletcher, Joseph, theologian
    on abortion and euthanasia as inseparable
        67, 78
    on death with dignity 78, 176 n.73
    on 'meaningful' humanhood 58
Freedom
    and order go together 128
    under Christian consensus 12, 128
    under humanism 12, 13, 87
Freeman, Dr John M., Johns Hopkins
    University, and *spina bifida* 172 n.47

Gallio, Roman governor in Acts 143
Gandhi, Mahatma, Indian spiritual leader
    115
Garrow, Dr John and starvation of *spina bifida*
    baby 46
Gauguin, Paul, artist 99
Gay liberation movement as anti-family force
    164 n.12
Genesis, Book of
    historical role 129, 192–193 App.3
    importance of 129–131
    significance of chapter 3 126
    'spiritualising' first chapters of 129
Genetic knowledge
    abuse of 13–16, 66, 67
    application of tests to determine right to
        live 53, 66
    of fetus 22
    works against Darwin's theories 180–181
        App.1
Geneva Oath. *See* Declaration of Geneva
Genocide 3, 70, 84, 176 n.67. *See also* Holo-
    caust, Nazi
Germany under Hitler 14, 61, 163 n.1. *See
    also* Holocaust, Nazi
Giarretto, Dr Harry, on incest 17
Glover, Jonathan, philosopher, on infanticide
    and euthanasia 58, 175 n.59
Gospels. *See also* Bible; New Testament
    historically accurate 146, 147, 198–199
        App.4
Goundry, Dr John, and death pill 78–80
Griffith, Mrs Joanne, nurse, witness in Waddill
    case 167 n.27

Handicapped. *See also* Congenital defects and
      spina bifida
   as economic burdens   50, 52, 82, 172 n.48,
      174 n.53
   children, effect on marriage   59, 173 n.49
   church's help for   91, 92
   correcting defects   22, 59, 172 n.48
   Diamond, Sondra   60
   facilities for   21
   interviews with   47, 48
   potential of   33, 39, 47, 48
   pre-natal screening for abortion and   172
      n.48, 175 n.63
   society's view   21, 22
   traditional medical view on the care of
      39–41, 45
Happiness not based on physical, mental
      faculties   39, 47, 48
Harvard Divinity School, abortion conference
      sponsor   167 n.24
Health, Education and Welfare (US), Depart-
      ment of
   report on abortion and fetal death
      ratio   170 n.42
   report on living-will laws   73, 74
   report on Medicaid abortion cost and un-
      wanted children   80
Hebrew view of truth. *See* Truth
Hedlener, Dr Irwin, Jackson Memorial
      Hospital (Miami), on child abuse   17
Hegel, philosophy of Georg Wilhelm, and
      influence on the Holocaust   81
Hezekiah's Tunnel, verified by archaeological
      findings   186 App.3
Himmler, Heinrich, Nazi SS chief and exter-
      mination of Jews   163 n.1
Hindell, Keith, and Simms, Madeleine, on
      Abortion Act   165 n.19
Hippocratic Oath   4, 79, 163 n.2
History. *See also* chapter 5
   different concept for Christians, materialists
      127
   pre-secular, gives meaning to present   129
   proves early existence of Israel   192 App.3
   studies and Bible accuracy   132, 146, 147,
      190–191 App.3
Hitler, Adolf   84, 85. *See also* Holocaust, Nazi
      instituted euthanasia
Hittites of early Old Testament verified by
      archaeological findings   191
Hobman, David, director, Help for the Aged,
      and death pill   79
Holland opposition to Nazi persecution of
      Jews   89, 90
Hollywood Memorial Hospital (Florida), staff
      rebellion at abortions   29
Holmes, Justice Oliver Wendell, on law   11
Holocaust, Nazi   3, 61, 70, 80–87, 163 n.1, 176
      n.67, 177 n.79
   Harvard students' views of   85, 86
Homes for unmarried mothers   90, 91

Hospices, care for elderly and terminally
      ill   92, 93
Hospice Home Care Team of New Haven
      (Connecticut)   93
Human life. *See also* 'Image of God'; Medical
      profession
   apathy toward   80, 156
   as machinery   8
   as viewed by handicapped   47, 48
   biologist view   38–43
   creation of   125, 126
   dehumanisation of   9, 17
   destruction by abortion   25–33
   destruction by euthanasia   81–87
   destruction by infanticide   41, 42, 45, 46
   creativity of   100
   devaluation of   85, 101
   growth of   22–25
   in 20th century, as viewed by history   2, 154,
      156
   quality of, as opposed to sanctity of   55
   uniqueness of individual   24, 100, 126, 130,
      153
   value of   9, 15, 55, 58, 65, 88, 153, 154, 164
      n.14, 165 n.18
   verbal ability of   100, 124
   'viability'   24, 165 n.16, 168 n.32
Humanism. *See also* Rationalism; World view
   and abortion   20, 65
   and liberal theologians   65
   and personal cruelty   9, 12
   and today's student view of Holocaust   85,
      86
   concept of man   5, 13
   endless cycles of   115
   Enlightenment era   99, 101, 178 n.90
   ethics of   12, 15, 17, 19, 67
   evolution and   113, 114, 125, 126, 180–181
      App.1
   'fact' answers   101
   man as a machine   8, 9
   manipulation of natural processes   13, 14
   materialistic. *See* World view
   meaninglessness of all things   109, 112–114
   no basis for values   110–113
   pessimistic view of   97–98, 109, 110, 148,
      149
   replaces Christianity   5–8
   same final position as Eastern
      philosophy   112, 115
   spiritually ill   157
   view of Christianity   97, 99, 101
   view of normal, abnormal   126, 127
   world view   96–100, 103–113, 125, 126,
      148–149
Hume, David, humanist philosopher   106,
      107, 111
Hunt, Richard M., Harvard University, and
      'no-fault history'   85, 86
Huntingford, Professor Peter, on 'live
      births'   28

Hutchison, Joan, on child abuse   164 n.9
Huxley, Aldous, humanist novelist   110
Huxley, Sir Julian, atheist   113
Hyperosmoler urea, abortion ingredient   28
Hysterotomy, abortion method   25, 26, 167
   n.25
   possibility of live birth   26

I Accuse, film favouring euthanasia   84
Ibsen, Henrik, playwright   113
'Image of God'   9, 13, 15, 65, 67, 79, 88, 89
   as scriptural concept   125–131, 148, 153,
      154
   as viewed by Nazis   61
Incarnation of Christ   148
Incest   17
Individuals. *See also* Human life
   dignity of   2, 3
   exploitation of   2, 3
   treatment of   2, 3, 154
   uniqueness of   24, 100, 125, 126, 130, 131,
      153
Infant. *See also* Embryo; Fetus; Infanticide
   sacrifice of, in Old Testament   89
   self-sustaining   41, 42, 45, 46
Infant Life Preservation Act 1929   166 n.19,
   168 n.32
Infanticide. *See also Spina bifida*
   advocates   51, 53, 55, 58, 174 n.53
   alternatives to   90–94
   and the church   61–66
   genetic tests   54, 55, 56
   Johns Hopkins University effort to inform
      medical profession   38
   law in Britain   172 n.46
   medical view   39–45, 54–55, 174 n.53
   parent-physician decision   46, 54, 55, 174
      n.53
   practice of   38, 41, 42, 45, 46, 69
   semantics used to disguise   86, 87
Inhumanity, stemming the tide toward
   149–157
   acceptance of Christ as Saviour   149, 150
   acknowledging Christianity as the truth   149
International Correspondence Society of
   Obstetrics and Gynaecologists, on
   abortions   26
Irrationalism. *See* Existentialism
Isaac, son of Abraham   138, 140, 141
   'almost sacrifice' foretold sacrifice of
      Jesus   138
   his remarkable birth   140

Jackson, Rev Jesse, on abortion and slavery
   164 n.14
Jehoiachin, biblical ruler. *See* Nebuchadnezzar
Jehu. *See* Assyria, early threat to Middle East
Jeremiah the Prophet, confirmed by archaeological findings   185 App.3
Jesus Christ
   acceptance as Saviour   149–153, 157
   acceptance means salvation   150

belief in, essential to stem inhumanity   148,
   149
belief in, not blind leap of faith   146, 147
can cure spiritual ill of humanism   157
Lordship in all areas of life   150–153
Jews, extermination of. *See* Holocaust, Nazi
Johns Hopkins University
   abortion technique   28
   infanticide documentary   38
Joint Committee on Accreditation of
   Hospitals, in the USA, and abortion   165
   n.16
Joshua and historic emphasis on God's role in
   history   136
Judaeo-Christian World View. *See* World view,
   based on Bible

Kant, Immanuel, philosopher   107, 108, 116
Kass, Dr Leon, biologist, disposal of
   embryos   31, 32
Kempe, Dr C. Henry, paediatrician, 'battered-
   child syndrome'   16
Kennedy, Joseph P., Jr, Foundation, sponsor
   of abortion conference   167 n.24
Knowledge. *See also* Epistemology
   relativity of   116
   source of   107–109
Kümmel, Werner G., liberal scholar and New
   Testament studies   198 App.4

L'Abri, Christian community
   care of elderly   93
   help for unmarried mothers   91
Lachish, biblical city, verified by archaeological
   findings   185 App.3
Lane Report 1974 on the Abortion Act   166
   n.19
Laufe, Dr Leonard, abortionist   31
Leach, Dr Edmund R., Cambridge University,
   humanist view   8, 97
Leary, Dr Timothy and drug 'mind-expanding'
   121
Lee, Dr Wing K., report on Mount Sinai
   (Hartford, Connecticut), live births   28
Lewis, C. S., Christian philosopher,
   writer   103
Live births after abortion attempts. *See*
   Abortion, unsuccessful
Living will   40, 74, 176 n.69, 177 n.83
Locke, John, philosopher, denied concept of
   innate ideas of right and wrong   106
Lorber, Dr John, paediatrician, Sheffield   172
   n.47, 172 n.48
Lordship of Jesus Christ   150, 153
Luke the apostle, historical accuracy of his
   writings   198–199 App.4

Malpractice climate in USA and Quinlan
   case   72
'Mannishness of man'
   aspect of reality   100, 111, 125
   Bible is key to   129

Markle v. *Abele,* live births after
    abortion   26
Marx, Karl, communist founder   111
Materialism. *See* Humanism; World view
Mauthausen, Austria, concentration camp   61
Maya, illusion, in Eastern philosophy   112,
    113
McShane, Yolande, urged mother to take
    overdose   79
Meaninglessness
    from a humanist base   109, 111, 114
    if individual is not made in the image of
        God   149
Medicaid expenditures
    for abortions   80
Medical profession
    advocates of infanticide   53–55, 58–61, 174
        n.53
    and the Holocaust   80–87, 89, 90, 177 n.79
    attitude toward infanticide   39–47, 174 n.52
    Dutch opposed to persecution of Jews   89
    opponents of abortion   88
    opponents of infanticide   173 n.48, 174 n.53
    'playing God'   60
    refusal to abort   152
    stewardship   52, 69
    withholding 'extraordinary' care   69, 70, 73,
        74, 79, 176 n.68
Medical schools
    and Hippocratic Oath   4
    ethical guidelines   4
    Johns Hopkins and infanticide   38
    Yale professors and infanticide   54, 55, 58–
        61, 174 n.53
Mercy killing. *See also* Euthanasia
Messiah, promised in Bible   149
Middle East of the Old Testament verified by
        archaeological findings. *See* chapter 5
    App.2, App.3
Minors
    and abortion-on-demand   20
    and the age of consent   17
    Akron (Ohio) ordinance on abortion   32
Mizrachi, Nan, abortion 'killing'
    acceptable   67
Moab, kingdom of, verified by archaeological
    findings   192 App.3
Moore, Mrs Jean, nurse supervisor, on
    abortions   30
Morals, relativity of   110–113, 116
Moses
    books of, treated as history   191–192 App.3
    recalled historical events to show what God
        had done   135, 138
    reminded people of God's Covenant   133,
        134
Mount Sinai Hospital (Hartford, Connecticut)
    live births after abortions   27, 28
Mudano, Sal, hospital administrator, on
    abortions   29
Muggeridge, Malcolm, writer, on the Lane
    Report   166 n.19

Mysticism, modern   120–123
    as counter-Enlightenment   119
    as opposed to Christian mysticism   118
    differences between religious and
        secular   121
    spread of TM, yoga, cults in West   120

National Abortion Campaign, proposals   168
    n.35
National Health Service
    abortion report   170 n.42
    pressure for euthanasia   74
    problems of   178 n.87
Naturalism. *See* Humanism; World view
Nature
    as remaining criterion   13
    manipulation of   13
Nazi Holocaust. *See* Holocaust, Nazi
Nebuchadnezzar reign verified by archaeo-
        logical findings   184–185 App. 3
Neglect, physical, by deliberate starvation of
        newborn   69
    of children   16, 164 n.9
New Testament. *See also* Gospels; Bible
    dates written   197 App. 4
    historical accuracy of Luke   198–199 App. 4
    verified by Dead Sea Scrolls   182–183
        App.2
New Zealand's restrictive abortion laws   172
    n.45
Nietzsche, Friedrich, nihilist philosopher   118
Noonan, Professor John T., Jr, on US Supreme
        Court abortion decision   19
Norcross, Keith, FRCS, on abortion and
        population control   67
Nott, Kathleen, modern humanist, on David
        Hume   106, 107
Nurses Concerned for Life, Inc, USA   30
Nurses, revulsion to live births   29, 30, 168
    n.34

Offences Against the Person Act 1861   166
    n.19
Old Testament verified by Dead Sea Scrolls,
        other archaeological findings   App.2,
    App.3. *See also* Bible; Genesis, Book of

Paedophile Information Exchange and the age
        of consent   17
Pantin, Professor C. F. A., Cambridge
        University   102
Parental decisions on infanticide   54–56
Parliament
    Corrie's Bill   31
    makes law   12
    report of, 'Violence in the Family'   17
Patient-physician-family relationship   73
Paul the apostle
    in Corinth   142, 143
    his writings verified by events of
        history   142, 198

Personal God   118, 127, 129, 130, 135
    gave Covenant on Mount Sinai   133
    role of, in history   135, 146
    speaks to people within own culture   192
        App.4
    spoke to Abraham   138–141
Personal response to counteract loss of
    humanness of our age   87–94. *See also*
    chapter 6
Pessimism and humanists   97–99, 109, 148
Pirsig, Robert N., novelist, and Eastern
    philosophy   112
Pittsburgh, University of, School of Medicine,
    and oath   4
Planned Parenthood (USA), funding of   166
    n.20
Podhoretz, Norman, report of population
    control conference   66
Pool of Siloam, biblical site, verified by
    archaeological findings   186 App.3
Pomerantz, Dr Jeffrey J., study of premature
    babies   173 n.48
Pontius Pilate, verified by secular writings as
    Roman governor   199 App.4
Pornography, child   16, 17
Poverty solution   55
Powell, Justice Lewis (USA), opinion on
    abortions   80
Premature infants. *See also* Infanticide
    cost of saving   173 n.48
    saving lives of   22
Principles, necessity of, to reverse devaluation
    of human life   99, 100
Prostaglandin
    abortion inducer   27
    possibility of live births   27, 28, 30, 31
Prostin E., abortion inducer, manufactured by
    Upjohn   28, 30

Quinlan, Karen, case of   72, 73, 176 n.68
Qumran findings. *See* Dead Sea Scrolls

Radhakrishnan, Sarvepalli, Hindu philosopher
    123
Raglan, Lord, and euthanasia proposals   77
Ramsay, Sir William, archaeologist, convinced
    of accuracy of New Testament   198
    App.4
Rationalism   101, 178 n.90, 195 App.4
    and supernatural   178 n.90
    rejects divinity of Christ, Virgin Birth,
        Resurrection   196 App.4
Reason, Age of. *See* Enlightenment humanists
Rebellion of man against God   126–128
Religion of the Sermon on the Mount, as
    religion of morality   196 App.4
Religious Coalition for Abortion Rights,
    membership of   64
Religious liberalism. *See* Theology, liberal
Responsibility for ill, elderly, handicapped
    not solely the state's   92–94

Resurrection of Jesus Christ
    historical accuracy of   145
    without it, there is no Christianity   144–147
Richardson and Dickson, Drs, British report
    on subsequent pregnancies after
    abortions   170 n.42
Rickham, Professor Peter Paul, traditional
    medical view of infanticide   39, 40, 42
Rifkin, Jeremy, of People's Business Commis-
    sion, opposed to genetic engineering   14
Right to life
    as viewed by ancients   37
    as viewed by Judaeo-Christian tradition
        153, 154
    compared to right to privacy   164 n.14
    not a feminist issue   37, 92, 171 n.44
    not a religious issue   36, 37, 64, 171 n.43
    viewed by US Supreme Court   19, 20, 165
        n.16
Right to privacy
    and abortion   29
    and slavery   164 n.14
Robertson, Dr John A., University of
    Wisconsin, on infanticide   45
Robins, Dr Joel, report on live births after
    abortions   28
Robinson, Bishop John
    on dating of the New Testament   197 App.4
    pro-abortion views   65
Roe v. *Wade,* US Supreme Court decision on
    abortion   19, 167 n.22
Roman Catholic Church and abortion   36, 64
Roman culture
    and abortion   5, 37
    and infanticide   5, 37, 39
Rookmaaker, H. R., Dutch professor, on
    modern mysticism   118
Roszak, Theodore, of People's Business
    Commission (USA), opposed to genetic
    engineering   14
Royal College of Obstetricians and Gynae-
    cologists, attitude to 1967 Abortion
    Act   163 n.5
Rubenstein, Richard L., and Nazi Holocaust
    81
Russell, Professor O. Ruth, on 'right to choose
    death'   74
Ryan, Dr George M., Jr, Boston Hospital for
    Women, on infanticide   41, 45

St Joseph's Hospice, London   92, 93
Saline abortion   25
    live birth after   26
'Salting out.' *See* Saline abortion
Salvation as gift of God   150
Samaria, biblical city, verified by
    archaeological findings   188 App.3
Sanders, Debby, spokesperson for Women for
    Life   171 n.44
Sarah. *See* Abraham
Schizophrenic society symptoms   20, 21

Schmidt, Dr R. T. F., Cincinnati (Ohio), view
    of infanticide 45
Science
    assumptions of 102, 103
    early modern
        accepted Bible 104, 105
        rejected medieval findings 104
    Francis Bacon and Bible 104, 105
    hypothesis, finding the 101
    modern, indebted to Christian world
        view 128
    theories rejecting Bible 196 App.4
    world view 196 App.4
Scripture. *See also* Bible; Dead Sea Scrolls
    Genesis
        1:1 127
        12:1–3 139
        12:5–9 193
        13:14, 15 139
        15:4–6 139
        17:1–5 140
        18:1–3, 9–14 140
        22:1–14 141
    Deuteronomy
        4:9 134
        4:11, 12 133
        7:18, 19 134
        11:7 134
    1 Kings
        10:14–17 190 App.3
        14:25 189 App.3
        22:39 188 App.3
    2 Kings
        3:4, 5 188 App.3
        18:13–16 185 App.3
        20:20 186 App.3
        25:27–30 184 App.3
    2 Chronicles
        12:2 189 App.3
        12:4–9 190 App.3
    Joshua
        4:9 136
        4:20 138
    Isaiah
        53:6 149
    Amos
        3:15 188 App.3
    Luke
        1:1–4 199
        2:1–7 199
    John
        20:24–29 146
        21:1–14 147
    Acts
        17:23 124
        18:2–4, 11 142
    1 Corinthians
        2:9, 10 124
        15:1–24 143
    Colossians
        2:9 124
    Revelation
        4:11 130

Selection of newborn babies to survive 40
Semantics used to disguise abortion,
    infanticide, euthanasia 87, 178 n.86
Separation of church and state, abortion not a
    religious issue 36, 171 n.43
Sex, determining before birth 55, 56
Sexual permissiveness demands abortion 33
Shaw, Anthony, paediatric surgeon, view of
    infanticide 55
Sherwin-White, A. N., modern classical
    scholar, and historical accuracy of
    Acts 198 App.3
Single-parent family 164 n.12
Sixties
    counterculture of 119, 120
    failure of radical movements of 99
Social action to counteract the loss of
    humanness of our age. *See* chapter 6
'Social contract', basis of materialistic
    morality 110
Sociobiology
    concept of 14
    conflict as essence of life 14
    explanation of evolution 14
    Wilson, Edward W. and 15
Sociological law 9–13, 50, 80
    and Oliver Wendell Holmes 11
Solomon, son of David
    his successors, Jeroboam and Rehoboam,
        archaeological findings confirm Bible
        writings 189–190 App.3
    his temple looted by Shishak 189–190
        App.3
    wealth of confirmed by archaeological
        findings 190 App.3
Solzhenitsyn, Alexander, Russian novelist,
    philosopher, and relative morality 111
Sonoma (California) Conference, 'Ethics of
    Newborn Intensive Care' 41
Soper, Lord, and pro-abortion view 65
Sorenson, Dr James R., pro-abortionist 66
Spastics Society and prenatal screening for
    abortion 175 n.63
Spina bifida. See also Congenital defects
    evidence of starvation of severe *spina
        bifida* 41, 45–46
    happiness of *spina bifida* child 48
    newborns 41, 45, 46
    policy of selection 172 n.47, 172 n.48
States' rights and abortions in the USA 165
    n.16
Steele, David MP, and Abortion Act 12, 164
    n.5, 165 n.19
Steptoe and Edwards, Drs, fertilisation in the
    laboratory 31, 168 n.37
Sterilisation
    of those with mental illness 84
Stewardship of the surgeon 52, 70
Stirrat, Dr Gordon, on consumer attitude to
    pregnancy 55
Strauss, David Friedrich, *The Life of Jesus*,
    rationalist 195 App.4

Suction abortion 25
Suetonius, Roman biographer, and expulsion of Jews 142
Suicides, Swedish, 'how-to' clinics 79
Supernatural
    as viewed by rationalists 178 n.90
Supreme Court. *See* United States Supreme Court
Survival of the fittest
    in Hitler Germany 14
Swiss Academy of Medical Sciences and Quinlan decision 175 n.68

Tampon, vaginal, with Prostin E. for abortion 29
Tax disincentives to limit population 66
Techniques, abortion. *See* Abortion
Terminal illness
    difficulty of determining 73, 177 n.83
    hospice care 92, 93
Tertullian, AD 197 opposed abortion 65
Tests for newborn 53, 66
Theology, liberal
    and new mysticism 120
    humanistic view of man 5, 65
    opposed by Bible-based pastors 152
    validity of Bible denied 195–198 App.4
Thomas the doubter 146
Thorpe, Professor W. H., Cambridge University 102, 103
Thought control 40
Tirhakah, king of Egypt, biblical account verified by archaeological findings 187 App.3
Toss, Dr Ragnar, advocate of how-to suicide clinics for Swedish 79
Townsend, Cyril MP, and legislation against child pornography 17
Translations of the Bible 186–187 n.94
Trowell, Hugh, author 76
Truth
    as viewed by Bible 135
    contrary to existential concept 135
    individual must choose 125
    of Bible verified by archaeological findings. *See* chapter 5
    unveiling the 123–125
Tudiya, king of Assyria, verified by findings at Ebla 193 App.2

UFOology 120, 121
Union of American Hebrew Congregations, pro-abortion 64
Unitarian Universal Association, pro-abortion 64
United States Supreme Court
    and abortion issue 19, 20, 24, 80, 164 n.16, 165 n.18
    compared to West Germany's 167 n.22

decision on abortion, effect on euthanasia 176 n.66
Dred Scott decision 61
infanticide 45
nfluence of 12
Noonan, Professor John T., Jr, on abortion decision 19
prohibits state abortion ban 80
Roe v. *Wade* and *Doe* v. *Bolton* 19
rulings to protect environment 165 n.18
viewed by Archibald Cox 20
Universe, form of, aspect of reality 100, 111, 124, 125, 129
Bible key to understanding of 129, 149

Value of human life as opposed to quality of human life 55
Vaughn, Dr Victor, physician, on infanticide 45
Virgin Birth 196 App.4
Von Daniken, Erich, 'scientist', on ancient spacemen 120

Waddill, Dr William B., Jr, abortionist 26, 167 n.27
Wall, Christopher, *ectopia cordis* patient 52
Warren Court. *See* United States Supreme Court
Watson, James D., Nobel Prize winner, and infanticide 53
Weinberg, Steven, Harvard University, and materialistic view of universe 109
Weinberger, Marvin, formulated Akron (Ohio) abortion ordinance 168 n.39
West German Federal Constitutional Court, abortion decision 21, 167 n.22
Wilberforce, William, anti-slavery movement 66
Williams, Professor Glanville, on Abortion Act 165 n.19
Willing, Martha, on population control, sterilisation, tax disincentives 66, 67
Wilson, Edward W., Harvard zoologist: *Sociobiology: The New Synthesis* 15, 163 n.7
Winchester, Bishop of, and abortion prayer 64
Winter, Ralph, and Warren Court 12
Wittgenstein, Ludwig, linguistic philosophy 107
Wogaman, Dean J. Philip, Wesley Theological Seminary, pro-abortion 64
Wolfe, Tom, and Haight-Ashbury 119
Women in labour force 164 n.12
Women's Lib
    abortion not feminist issue 37, 92, 171 n.44
    extremists are anti-family 164 n.12
Women's rights movement. *See* Women's Lib
Wootton, Baroness, and euthanasia proposals 77

World view   94, 96–104. *See also* Humanism
    based on Bible   100, 128, 129
    based on Eastern philosophy   102, 112–115
    based on ultimate truth   96
    of our age, materialistic humanism   96–100,
        103, 111, 112, 114, 126
    of rationalists   178 n.90
    science   196 App.4
    search for adequate   100–104

Yun-Men, Zen master   123

Zachary, Professor Robert B., paediatric
        surgeon and the traditional medical view
        39, 40
    on the practice of infanticide   41, 42
    on a *spina bifida* patient   48

Index of
Photographs

The photographs in this book are taken from the film series, 'Whatever Happened to the Human Race'. They are intended to provide both a glimpse of that series and to illustrate the concerns of this book. Uncaptioned, they for the most part speak for themselves but it was considered helpful to give their context in the film, below. This does not apply to the photographs displayed at the beginning of each chapter nor to the Cage Sequence at the end of the book whose significance and place is clear.

Chapter 1   *6–7*   Dr Koop in the Infant Intensive Care Unit of the Children's Hospital of Philadelphia.

   10–11   Francis Schaeffer describing the ugliness and poverty of materialistic thinking in a scrap yard.

   18   Francis Schaeffer sitting on the steps of the U.S. Supreme Court which handed down the pro-abortion decision.

   22   A baby in the womb showing the growth of human life.

   34–35   Plastic dolls, representing the destruction of babies by abortion, scattered on the shoreline of the Dead Sea in Israel. This is where Sodom, the symbol of degradation, once stood.

Chapter 2   *42–43*   An assembly line of dolls representing the flow of human life into the world; some had their arms and legs removed and were thrown away as rejects, depicting the fate of handicapped newborns.

   48   Craig enjoying a walk by the sea.

   50   Christopher Wall, a patient of Dr Koop.

   56–57   In the operating theatre of the Children's Hospital in Philadelphia.

   62–63   Actors costumed as slaves walking up the steps of the Lincoln Memorial.

Chapter 3   *70–71*   While shooting in a cemetery this old lady brought flowers to a grave.

   74–75   A banquet for young and old arranged for the film.

   82–83   An actual photo of a mother and her children going to the gas chamber at Auschwitz.

Chapter 4   *94*   A monument constructed for the film to demonstrate how the future will hold us responsible for what happens today.

Chapter 5   *136–137*   The Jordan Valley as depicted in the film, a place where history is still being made.

Chapter 6 150–151 Francis Schaeffer in his study, presenting Christ as the answer to halt the decadent tide in our society.

 154–155 Dr Koop at work where each patient must be treated as an individual.